Heraclitus

Northwestern University
Studies in Phenomenology and Existential Philosophy

HERACLITUS SEMINAR

MARTIN HEIDEGGER AND EUGEN FINK

Translated by
Charles H. Seibert

NORTHWESTERN UNIVERSITY PRESS
Evanston, Illinois

The translator gratefully acknowledges permission to quote from copyrighted works as follows: (1) from G. S. Kirk, *Heraclitus: The Cosmic Fragments*, edited with an Introduction and Commentary (Cambridge: Cambridge University Press, 1970); (2) from G. S. Kirk and J. E. Raven, *The Presocratic Philosophers: A Critical History with a Selection of Texts* (Cambridge: Cambridge University Press, 1957); (3) from *Friedrich Hölderlin: Poems & Fragments*, translated by Michael Hamburger (Ann Arbor: University of Michigan Press, 1966); and (4) from *Alcaic Poems* by Friedrich Hölderlin, translated by Elizabeth Henderson, copyright © 1962 by Elizabeth Henderson, published by Oswald Wolff (Publishers) Ltd., London.

Northwestern University Press
Evanston, Illinois 60208

Printed in the United States of America

ISBN 0-8101-1067-9

Library of Congress Cataloging-in-Publication Data

Heidegger, Martin, 1889-1976.
    [Heraklit. English]
    Heraclitus seminar, 1966/67 / Martin Heidegger and Eugen Fink ; translated by Charles H. Seibert.
        p. cm. — (Northwestern University studies in phenomenology & existential philosophy)
    Originally published: University, Ala. : University of Alabama Press, c1979.
    Papers from the seminar held at the Universität Freiburg im Breisgau, 1966/67.
    Includes bibliographical references.
    ISBN 0-8101-1067-9 (paper)
    1. Heraclitus, of Ephesus. 2. Heidegger, Martin, 1889-1976.
I. Fink, Eugen. II. Title. III. Series.
B223.H4313   1993
182'.4—dc20   92-39842
                                                      CIP

CONTENTS

TRANSLATOR'S FOREWORD

The fragments of Heraclitus have, from the beginning, attracted and influenced philosophical thinking. It is hoped that this translation will allow access by English-speaking readers to the continuing attempt at interpretation.

The two principal contributors to these conversations are Martin Heidegger and Eugen Fink. Of the two, Heidegger is certainly the better known to English-speaking readers. His readers will find a familiar voice here. His interpretation of Heraclitus continues to take its orientation from the fragments that deal with λόγος and with ἀλήθεια.[1] These themes have recurred in *Being and Time*, Section 44, *An Introduction to Metaphysics*, *What is Called Thinking?*, the "*Logos (Heraklit, Fragment 50)*" and "*Aletheia (Heraklit, Fragment 16)*" essays in *Vorträge und Aufsätze*, and *Nietzsche*, II, Section IX. In addition to continuing Heidegger's interpretation of Heraclitus, the present work is the occasion for interpretation of other thinkers and poets, notably Hegel and Hölderlin, as well as self-interpretation by Heidegger.

Eugen Fink, the other principal contributor, is less familiar in the English-speaking philosophical world. This book is the first translation of Fink's work into English. His role in these conversations is to provide a preliminary interpretation of the fragments that will give the discussion a "basis and a starting place for a critical surpassing or even destruction, and [will enable] us to establish a certain common ground appropriate to inquiring discourse." Throughout the book, the conversations take their sustenance from Fink's lead.

The pervading theme of interpretation is the relatedness of ἕν [the one] and τὰ πάντα [the many]. This relatedness is exemplified in many different instances in the conversations of this book. Moreover, the conversations as a whole might well be understood as one more instance of this fundamental theme in Heraclitus' thinking. For, while there is a tension between the multiple interpretations of Heidegger, Fink, and the seminar participants, the interpretation is nonetheless unified at important points of agreement. While it is not a translator's place to rehearse the details of a text, it may be helpful to alert the reader to passages in which the conversants speak for themselves about their agreements and differences.

Regarding the multiplicity of interpretations, it may be worth noting that the present book records conversations, and is not the finished work of a single author. Not only does the conversational origin of the book set it apart from other recent interpretive attempts, it also accounts, at least in part, for the imaginative and experimental character of the interpretations. In conversations, we can rarely anticipate the responses of those with whom we talk. And if an interlocutor disagrees with us, we are often forced to take an imaginative, experimental step into areas about which we have not previously thought. What results in the present case is a mixture of premeditated consideration of the text and imaginative, extemporaneous response. Of course, not all the experiments work, as Fink himself predicts in the opening remarks and affirms at times throughout the text.

Regarding more specific points of disagreement, it may not be accidental that Heidegger cites Fragment 1, with its concern for the λόγος, soon after Fink begins his interpretation with a reference to Fragment 64, which deals with κεραυνός [lightning] and τὰ πάντα. But perhaps the clearest summary of the differences of interpretation of Heidegger and Fink is elicited by Heidegger from one of the participants in the beginning of the seventh seminar session. In contrast to Fink's "surprising" and "unusual" beginning, Heidegger makes clear his different beginning from the λόγος and from ἀλήθεια. While the participants record diversity of opinion at many points, perhaps the most general expression of difference is the remark that, "More is said in the interpretation of the Fragments than stands in them."[2] Regarding this difference of opinion, more is said below.

The unity that binds the multiplicity of the Heraclitus interpretations is indicated by Heidegger toward the end of the sixth seminar session. He says, "Both of us are in agreement that if we speak with a thinker, we must heed what is unsaid in what is said. The question is only which way leads to this, and of what kind is the foundation of the interpretive step."[3] This observation marks not only a unifying theme in these conversations, but also a unifying theme in Heidegger's own method of thinking about the tradition. As early as *Kant and the Problem of Metaphysics* (1929), Heidegger says:

> Nevertheless, an interpretation limited to a recapitulation of what Kant explicitly said can never be a real explication, if the business of the latter is to bring to light what Kant, over and above his express formulation, uncovered in the course of his laying of the foundation. To be sure, Kant himself is no longer able to say anything concerning this, but what is essential in all philosophical discourse is not found in the specific propositions of which it is composed but in that which, although unstated as such, is made evident through these propositions.[4]

The same position is maintained in Heidegger's closing remarks in seminar session thirteen in the present book. There, as in Section 44 of *Being and Time* (1927), it is ἀλήθεια that lies unsaid at the base of what is said by the Greeks.

In similar fashion, though not in the same words, Fink's "speculative" interpretation is consonant with Heidegger's method of interpretation. This is perhaps most explicitly shown in the opening considerations of seminar session five. There Fink indicates that the method of interpretation consists in the attempt to pass from the concrete state of affairs presented in the fragments over to an unsensuous, though not transcendent, domain.[5] Again, Fink speaks of the attempt to comprehend macrocosmic relations from the microcosmic relations which are directly presented in the fragments.[6] And finally:

> When I speak of thoughtful transposition into another dimension, that is only a first attempt to circumscribe the manner of our procedure, because we still do not know what it means to go over into another dimension. If we wish to speak of an analogy in this connection, then we must think it in a specific way. In this analogy, only one side is given to us, namely the phenomenal one. As we hold selectively to specific phenomenal structures, we translate them into large scale in an adventurous attempt.[7]

Readers who are familiar with recent English-language scholarship and interpretation of Heraclitus may find the speculative method of these conversations injudicious or lacking in caution. Some may object with one of the participants that, "More is said in the interpretation of the fragments than stands in them." Or the reader may, with Heidegger, regard the speculative treatment as "venturesome" or even "hazardous."[8] The more fragmentary the evidence, it might be argued, the more cautious we should be, and the more we must eschew speculative flights of imagination.

But before dismissing this interpretation just because it is speculative, we ourselves must be a bit more cautious. Professor Fink goes to some lengths to explain how and why he departs speculatively from the specific content of a given fragment. And it may also be argued that, given the very nature of these fragments, no interpretation, cautious or uncautious, can remain only with what is immediately given in the fragments. It is precisely the fragmentary character of the fragments that not only allows but even demands a speculative approach in interpretation. This fragmentary character demands that we seek what is unsaid in what is said, since it is clear that Heraclitus was concerned with much more than the fragments of experience to which we are, for the most part, limited and that are often recorded in the existing fragments. If Heraclitus meant no more than is said in the fragments, many would be trivial and useful only as exercises for learning the ancient Greek language. Even though a particular fragment may, for example, explicitly mention only the continually flowing waters of a river (Fragments 91, 12), Heraclitus himself in other fragments sets these concrete images into the context of the dynamic relatedness of all things to the one, and of the one to all things. The fragmentary character of the fragments is an invitation to see beyond them.

Within the context of recent interpretive and critical scholarship on Heraclitus, one of Fink's particular interpretive strategies is noteworthy. This strategy may be most easily indicated by reference to some remarks in the preface to G. S. Kirk's *Heraclitus: The Cosmological Fragments*. On page xii of the preface, Kirk writes:

> In the present study only about half the total number of extant fragments receive detailed consideration. "The cosmic fragments" are those whose subject-matter is the world as a whole, as opposed to men; they include those which deal with the Logos and the opposites, and those which describe the large-scale physical changes in which fire plays a primary part. They do *not* include those which deal with religion, with god in relation to men, with the nature of the soul, with epistemology, ethics or politics; nor do they include Heraclitus' attack upon particular individuals or upon men in general, although the ground of these attacks is very often an impercipience of the Logos or its equivalents. These fragments, which might be termed "the anthropocentric fragments," could be made the subject of a later study.

Defending this procedure, Kirk writes further:

> . . . the fragments fall not unnaturally into the two classes which I have indicated, which can be separately treated—provided full cross-reference is carried out—without distortion either of individual fragments or of the subject as a whole. This justification only applies, or course, to a work which, like this one, consists essentially of a series of commentaries on individual fragments. It remains true that Heraclitus took a synoptic view of the problems he was facing, and that his answer to any one of them cannot be entirely dissociated from his answers to all the others; in particular, his views on the constitution of the soul and its means of contact with the outside world bear upon the nature of the Logos, and vice versa. The author has had the anthropocentric fragments in mind when considering the cosmic ones; and since most of his readers are likely to be familiar with all the extant fragments, the dangers of misunderstanding are slight.

Against the background of these remarks, two passages in Fink's interpretation stand out. In seminar session 7, while attempting to understand the words πυρὸς τροπαί [transformations of fire], Fink says:

> We do not understand the turning over of fire into what is not fire in the sense of a chemical change or in the sense of an original substance which changes (ἀλλοίωσις) or in the sense of an original element which masks itself through its emanations. Rather we will view the entire range which binds fire, sea, earth, and breath of fire in connection with life and death. Apparently, we revert to anthropological fragments in opposition to cosmological fragments. In truth, however, it is not a question of a restriction to human phenomena; rather, what pertains to being human, such as life

and death, becomes in a distinctive sense the clue for understanding of the entirety of the opposing relatedness of ἕν and πάντα.[9]

Again at the end of seminar session eight, Fink summarizes the interpretive struggle with τροπή [turning] in the following words.

We came to no result, and perhaps we will come to no final result at all. But the all too familiar explication of τροπή has wandered into the foreignness and darkness of the formula, "to live the death of something." We could perhaps think the relationship of fire to earth, to air, and to water rather in reference to life and death, so that, with reference to the difficult relationship of tension of life and death, we could come to a certain anthropological key for the non-anthropological foundational relatedness of ἕν and πάντα.[10]

Fink has used precisely the human phenomena of life and death, as well as the relationship between mortals and immortals, in his interpretive attempt to understand the relatedness of ἕν and τὰ πάντα. The present work is a complement to Kirk's book, and partially fulfills, in its main outline, the task left undone by Kirk.

The strategy of using the anthropological fragments as a clue for interpreting the cosmological fragments is important in another respect, namely with regard to the previously expressed doubt that, "More is said in the interpretation of the fragments than stands in them." I allude here to Kirk's observation concerning the "synoptic" character of Heraclitus' thinking. Fink's method of employing one set of fragments to interpret another would seem to strengthen the interpretation. Despite many implicit and explicit references to other, later thinkers, Fink's interpretive strategy may allow some assurance that in the long run Heraclitus' thought is interpreted as an integral whole, and is not interpreted by means of reference to a foreign scheme of thought.

This translation is not the product of one person working alone. My aim has been to hear the book with two sets of ears, one English and one German, hoping thereby to lose or distort as little as possible of the original. The help of Professor Manfred S. Frings, editor of the German edition of the *Collected Works of Max Scheler*, has been crucial in pursing this aim. Because his native tongue is German, he has frequently been the needed supplement that allowed retrieval of nuances that would otherwise have been lost. I remain indebted to him, and thankful for his sentence-by-sentence reading of the text.

Other people have been consulted regarding various portions of the manuscript. John Cody of the Classics department of Northwestern University has read the manuscript with a concern for correcting my gloss of Greek words and translation of Greek phrases. The book has surely benefitted from his checking of my Greek "homework." F. Joseph

Smith was consulted on points of particular difficulty, and he has read some of the chapters in their entirety. The advice and encouragement of these men are greatly appreciated. Ultimately, however, I am alone responsible for this translation and for any defects it may contain.

All footnotes of the original book are retained in the present translation. Footnotes of the translator are followed by "(Tr.)." To facilitate access to the text, the first occurrence of each Greek work is accompanied by an English gloss within square brackets, provided none is given by the authors. A glossary of Greek terms is at the back of the book. A page guide correlating the page numbers of this translation and those of the German edition is also provided.

Winnetka, Illinois   CHARLES H. SEIBERT

PREFACE TO THE GERMAN EDITION

In the Winter Semester of 1966/67, a Heraclitus seminar was held at the University of Freiburg i. Br., organized mutually by Martin Heidegger and Eugen Fink. The summary text of the seminar is herewith submitted. It was planned to continue the interpretation over a series of semesters, but this plan cannot be realized. The present publication is a torso, a fragment concerning fragments.

Freiburg im Breisgau
April 1970

EUGEN FINK

HERACLITUS

1

Mode of Procedure.—Beginning with Fragment 64
(Correlated Fragments: 41, 1, 50, 47).

FINK: I open the seminar with hearty thanks to Professor Heidegger for his readiness to assume spiritual leadership in our common attempt to advance into the area of the great and historically important thinker Heraclitus. Heraclitus' voice, like that of Python, reaches us over a thousand years. Although this thinker lived at the origin of the West, and to that extent is longest past, we have not overtaken him even now. From Martin Heidegger's dialogue with the Greeks, in many of his writings, we can learn how the furthest becomes near and the most familiar becomes strange, and how we remain restless and are unable to rely on a sure interpretation of the Greeks. For us, the Greeks signify an enormous challenge.

Our seminar should be an exercise in thinking, that is, in reflection on the thoughts anticipated by Heraclitus. Confronted with his texts, left to us only as fragments, we are not so much concerned with the philological problematic, as important as it might be,[1] as with advancing into the matter itself, that is, toward the matter that must have stood before Heraclitus' spiritual view. This matter is not simply on hand like a result or like some spoken tradition; rather, it can be opened up or blocked from view precisely through the spoken tradition. It is not correct to view the matter of philosophy, particularly the matter of thinking as Martin Heidegger has formulated it, as a product lying before us. The matter of thinking does not lie somewhere before us like a land of truth into which one can advance; it is not a thing that we can discover and uncover. The reality of, and the appropriate manner of access to, the matter of thinking is still dark for us. We are still seeking the matter of thinking of the thinker Heraclitus, and we are therefore a little like the poor man who has forgotten where the road leads. Our seminar is not concerned with a spectacular business. It is concerned, however, with serious-minded work. Our common attempt at reflection will not be free from certain disappointments and defeats. Nevertheless, reading the text of the ancient thinker, we make the attempt to come into the spiritual movement that releases us to the matter that merits being named the matter of thinking.

Professor Heidegger is in agreement that I should first advance a preliminary interpretation of the sayings of Heraclitus. This interpretation will give our discussion a basis and a starting place for a critical surpassing or even destruction, and it will enable us to establish a certain common ground appropriate to inquiring discourse. Perhaps a preview of the particular language of Heraclitus' sayings is premature before we have read and interpreted them individually. The language of Heraclitus has an inner ambiguity and multidimensionality, so that we cannot give it any unambiguous reference. It moves from gnomic, sentential, and ambiguous-sounding expression to an extreme flight of thought.

As assigned text in our seminar, we will work with *Fragmente der Vorsokratiker* by Hermann Diels.[2] For our part, we choose another arrangement. This should cast light on an inner coherence of the fragments' meaning, but without pretending to reconstruct the original form of Heraclitus' lost writing, Περὶ φύσεως [*On Nature*]. We shall attempt to trace a thread throughout the multiplicity of his sayings in the hope that a certain track can thereby show itself. Whether our arrangement of the fragments is better than that adopted by Diels is a question that should remain unsettled.

Without further preliminary considerations, we shall proceed directly to the midst of the matter, beginning our interpretation with Fr. 64: τὰ δὲ πάντα οἰακίζει κεραυνός. This sentence is clearly intelligible to everyone in what it appears to mean. Whether it is also intelligible in what this meaning concerns, however, is another question. But first, we ask what this sentence means. As soon as we reflect on it somewhat more, we immediately depart from the easy intelligibility and apparent familiarity of the sentence. Diels' translation reads: "Lightning steers the universe." But is "universe" the fitting translation of τὰ πάντα? After due deliberation, one can indeed come to equate τὰ πάντα and "universe." But first of all, τὰ πάντα names "everything" and signifies: all things, all of what is. Heraclitus speaks of τὰ πάντα vis-à-vis Κεραυνός [lightning]. In so doing, he enunciates a connection between many things and the one of lightning. In the lightning bolt the many, in the sense of "everything," flash up, whereby "everything" is a plural. If we first ask naïvely about τὰ πάντα, we are dealing with a quintessential relatedness. If we translate τὰ πάντα as "all things," we must first ask, what kinds of things there are. At the outset, we choose the way of a certain tactical naïveté. On the one hand, we take the concept of thing in a wider sense, and then we mean all that is. On the other hand, we also use it in a narrower sense. If we mean things in the narrower sense, then we can distinguish between such things as are from nature (φύσει ὄντα) and such as are the product of human technics (τέχνη ὄντα). With all the things of nature—with the inanimate, like stone, and with the living, like plant, beast, and human (in so far as we may speak of a human as a thing)—we mean only such things as are individuated and have determinate outlines. We have in view the determinate, individual thing that, to be sure, also has a particular, common character in itself, as being of a certain kind. We make the tacit assumption that τὰ πάντα, in the sense of the many in entirety, forms the entirety of finite bounded things. The stone, for example, is part of a mountain. We can also speak of the mountain as of a thing. Or is it only a linguistic convention to call what has a determinate outline a thing? The stone is found as rubble on the mountain; the mountain belongs in the mountain range; the latter on the earth's crust; and the earth itself as a great thing that belongs, as a gravitational center, in our solar system.

HEIDEGGER: To begin, wouldn't it perhaps be appropriate to ask whether Heraclitus also speaks of τὰ πάντα in other fragments, in order to have a specific clue from him about what he understands by τὰ πάντα? In this way we get closer to Heraclitus. That is one question. The second question I would like to put under discussion is what lightning has to do with τὰ πάντα. We must ask concretely what it can mean when Heraclitus says that lightning steers τὰ πάντα. Can lightning steer the universe at all?

PARTICIPANT: If we begin by taking lightning only as a phenomenon, then we must wonder that it should steer the universe, since lightning as a phenomenal entity, as a sensuously perceptible, luminous appearance, still belongs together with all other entities in the universe.

HEIDEGGER: We must bring lightning into connection with the phenomenon of nature, if we wish to understand it "in Greek."

FINK: Lightning, regarded as a phenomenon of nature, means the outbreak of the shining lightning-flash in the dark of night. Just as lightning in the night momentarily flashes up and, in the brightness of the gleam, shows things in their articulated outline, so lightning in a deeper sense brings to light the multiple things in their articulated gathering.

HEIDEGGER: I remember an afternoon during my journey in Aegina. Suddenly I saw a single bolt of lightning, after which no more followed. My thought was: Zeus.

Our task now consists in looking with Heraclitus for what τὰ πάντα means. It is an open question how far a distinction was already possible with him between "everything" in the sense of the sum of individuals and "everything" in the meaning of the embracing allness. The other task, which is first posed for us by Fr. 64, is the connection between τὰ πάντα and lightning. We must also bring Heraclitus' lightning into connection with fire (πῦρ). It is also essential to observe who has handed Fr. 64 down to us. It is the Church Father Hippolytus who died roughtly A.D. 236/37. From Heraclitus' time approximately eight hundred years pass before our fragment is cited by Hippolytus. In the context, πῦρ and χόσμος [cosmos] are also mentioned. But we do not wish to enter here into the philological problematic that emerges in view of the connection of the fragment and the context of Hippolytus. In a conversation that I held with Carl Reinhardt in 1941, when he stayed here in Freiburg, I spoke to him about the middle ground between pure philology, which intends to find the real Heraclitus with its philological tools, and the kind of philosophizing that consists in thinking without discipline and thereby assuming too much. Between these two extremes there is a middle ground concerned with the role of the transmission of understanding, of sense as well as interpretation.

With Hippolytus we find not only πῦρ but also ἐκπύρωσις [conflagration], which for him has the meaning of the end of the world. If we now ask what τὰ πάντα, lightning, and also steering mean in Fr. 64, we must at the same time attempt to transfer ourselves into the Greek world with the clarification of these words. So that we can understand Fr. 64 in a genuine manner, I would propose that Fr. 41 be added to it: εἶναι γὰρ ἕν τὸ σοφόν, ἐπίστασθαι γνώμην, ὁτέη ἐκυβέρνησε πάντα διὰ πάντων. Diels translates: "The wise is one thing only, to understand the thoughts that steer everything through everything." Literally translated, πάντα διὰ πάντων means: everything throughout everything. The importance of this saying lies, on the one hand, in ἕν τὸ σοφόν [the wise is one thing only] and, on the other, in πάντα διὰ πάντων. Here above all we must take into view the connection of the beginning and the end of the sentence.

FINK: There is a similar connection, on the one hand between the oneness of the lightning-flash, in the brightness of which the many show themselves in their outline and their articulations, and τὰ πάντα, and, on the other, between the oneness of σοφόν [the wise] and πάντα διὰ πάντων. As Κεραυνός relates to τὰ πάντα, ἕν τὸ σοφόν relates analogously to πάντα διὰ πάντων.

HEIDEGGER: I certainly grant that lightning and ἕν τὸ σοφόν stand in a relation to one another. But there is still more to notice in Fr. 41. In Fr. 64 Heraclitus speaks of τὰ πάντα, in Fr. 41 of πάντα διὰ πάντων. In Parmenides 1/32 we also find a similar phrase: διὰ πάντος πάντα περῶντα. In the phrase πάντα διὰ πάντυν, the meaning of διὰ is above all to be questioned. To begin, it means "throughout." But how should we understand "throughout:" topographically, spatially, causally, or how else?

FINK: In Fr. 64 τὰ πάντα does not mean a calm, static multiplicity, but rather a dynamic multiplicity of entities. In τὰ πάντα a kind of movement is thought precisely in the reference back to lightning. In the brightness, specifically the clearing which the lightning bolt tears open, τὰ πάντα flash up and step into appearance. The being moved of τὰ πάντα is also thought in the lighting up of entities in the clearing of lightning.

HEIDEGGER: At first, let us leave aside words like "clearing" and "brightness."

FINK: If I have spoken of movement, we must distinguish, on the one hand between the movement that lies in the lighting of lightning, in the outbreak of brightness, and on the other hand, the movement in τὰ πάντα, in things. The movement of brightness of lightning corresponds to the movement that goes out from ἕν τὸ σοφόν and continues on in the many things in entirety. Things are not blocks at rest; rather, they are diversified in movement.

HEIDEGGER: τὰ πάντα are thus not a whole, present in front of us, but entities in movement. On the other hand, movement does not occur as κίνησις [motion] in Heraclitus.

FINK: If movement does not also belong among the fundamental words in Heraclitus, it still always stands in the horizon of problems of his thinking.

HEIDEGGER: To Frs. 64 and 41, we now add Fr. 1: τοῦ δὲ λόγου τοῦδ᾽ ἐόντος ἀεὶ ἀξύνετοι γίνονται ἄνθρωποι καὶ πρόσθεν ἢ ἀκοῦσαι καὶ ἀκούσαντες τὸ πρῶτον. γινομένων γὰρ πάντων κατὰ τὸν λόγον τόνδε ἀπείροισιν ἐοίκασι, πειρώμενοι καὶ ἐπέων καὶ ἔργων τοιούτων, ὁκοίων ἐγὼ διηγεῦμαι κατὰ φύσιν διαιρέων ἕκαστον καὶ φράζων ὅκως ἔχει. τοὺς δὲ ἄλλους ἀνθρώπους λανθάνει ὁκόσα ἐγερθέντες ποιοῦσιν, ὅκωσπερ ὁκόσα εὕδοντες ἐπιλανθάνονται.[3] At first, only γινομένων γὰρ πάντων κατὰ τὸν λόγον τόνδε interests us. We translate, "For although everything happens according to this λόγος [reason, speech, word]." If Heraclitus speaks here of γινομένων [coming into being], he is, nevertheless, talking of movement.

FINK: In γινομένων γὰρ πάντων [coming into being of everything], we are dealing with things being moved within the cosmos, and not with the movement that issues from λόγος.

HEIDEGGER: γινομένων belongs to γένεσις [genesis]. When the Bible speaks of γένεσις, it means by this the Creation, in which things are brought into existence. But what does γένεσις signify in Greek?

PARTICIPANT: γένεσις is also no concept in Heraclitus.

HEIDEGGER: Since when do we have concepts at all?

PARTICIPANT: Only since Plato and Aristotle. We even have the first philosophical dictionary with Aristotle.

HEIDEGGER: While Plato manages to deal with concepts only with difficulty, we see that Aristotle deals with them more easily. The word γινομένων stands in a fundamental place in Fr. 1.

FINK: Perhaps we can add a comment to our discussion. We find γένεσις in an easily understood sense with living beings, phenomenally seen. Plants spring up from seeds, beasts from the pairing of parents, and humans from sexual union between man and woman. γένεσις is also native to the phenomenal region of the vegetative-animal. Coming into existence (γίγνεσθαι) in this region is at the same time coupled with passing away (φθείρεσθαι). If we now refer γένεσις also to the region of lifeless things, we operate with an expanded, more general, sense of this word. For if we refer γένεσις to τὰ πάντα, we expand the sense of γένεσις beyond the phenomenal region in which the genesis-phenomenon is otherwise at home.

HEIDEGGER: What you understand by the phenomenal sense of the word γένεσις we can also label as ontic.

FINK: We also meet the widening of the original, phenomenal meaning of γένεσις in common language, for example, when we speak of the world's coming into existence. We use specific images and domains of ideas in our representations. With γινομένων, in Fr. 1, we are concerned with the more general sense of γένεσις. For τὰ πάντα does not come into existence like that entity which comes into existence in accordance with γένεσις in the narrower sense, and also not like living beings. It is another matter when, in the coming-into-existence of things, manufacture and production (τέχνη and ποίησις) are also meant. The ποίησις of phenomena is, however, something other than the γένεσις. The jug does not come into existence by means of the potter's hand like the man is begotten by parents.

HEIDEGGER: Let us once again clarify for oursevles what our task is. We ask: what does τὰ πάντα mean in Fr. 64; and πάντα διὰ πάντων in Fr. 41; and γινομένων γὰρ πάντων in Fr. 1? κατὰ τὸν λόγον [according to the Logos] in Fr. 1 corresponds with ἕν τὸ σοφόν in Fr. 41 and κεραυνός in Fr. 64.

FINK: In γινομένων the sense of γένεσις is used in widened manner.

HEIDEGGER: But can one actually speak of a widening here? I mean that we should try to understand "steering," "everything throughout everything," and now the movement that is thought in γινομένων, in a genuine Greek sense. I agree that we may not take the meaning of γένεσις in γινομένων narrowly; rather, it is here a matter of a general expression. Fr. 1 is considered to be the beginning of Heraclitus' writing. Something fundamental is said in it. But may we now refer γινομένων, thought in γένεσις in a wide sense, to coming-forth [Hervorkommen]? In anticipation, we can say that we must keep in view the fundamental trait of what the Greeks called being. Although I do not like to use this word any more, we now take it up nevertheless. When Heraclitus thinks γένεσις in γινομένων, he does not mean "becoming" in the modern sense; that is, he does not mean a process. But thought in Greek, γένεσις means "to come into being," to come forth in presence. We now have three different concerns, drawn out of Frs. 64, 41, and 1, to which we must hold ourselves, if we wish to come into the clear concerning τὰ πάντα. Let us also draw on Fr. 50: οὐκ ἐμοῦ, ἀλλὰ τοῦ λόγου ἀκούσαντας ὁμολογεῖν σοφόν ἐστιν ἕν πάντα εἶναι. Diels' translation runs, "Listening not to me but to the Logos (λόγος), it is wise to say that everything is one." Before all else, this saying centers on ἕν, πάντα, and ὁμολογεῖν.

FINK: If we now start out from coming-forth, coming-forth-to-appearance [*Zum-Vorschein-Kommen*], wherein you see the Greek meaning of γινομένων as thought in γένεσις, then we also have a reference to the brightness and gleam of lightning in which the individual thing stands and flashes up. Then we would have the following analogical correlation: as lightning on a dark night lets us see everything individual in its specific outline all at once, so this would be in a short time span the same as that which happens perpetually in πῦρ ἀείζωον [ever-living fire] in Fr. 30. The entry of entities in their determinateness is thought in the moment of brightness. Out of Fr. 64 comes τὰ πάντα; out of Fr. 41 comes πάντα διὰ πάντων; and out of Fr. 1, γινομένων πάντων κατὰ τὸν λόγον. Earlier we tried to discern the movement of lighting in the lightning bolt. Now we can say that it is the movement of bringing-forth-to-appearance. But bringing-forth-to-appearance, which lightning accomplishes in entities, is also a steering intervention in the moving of things themselves. Things are moved in the manner of advancing and receding, waxing and waning, of local movement and alteration. The movement of lightning corresponds to the moving of ἓν τὸ σοφόν. The steering movement is not thought with respect to the lightning, or with respect to ἓν τὸ σοφόν, but with respect to the efficacy of the lightning and of ἓν τὸ σοφόν, which effects bringing-forth-to-appearance and continues to effect things. The movement of steering intervention in the moving of things happens in accord with the λόγος. The movement of things that stand in the brightness of lightning has a wisdomlike nature that must, however, be distinguished from the movement that issues itself from σοφόν. Fr. 41 does not concern itself only with the relatedness of the one and the many that appear in the one, but also with the efficacy of the one in reference to τὰ πάντα, which comes to expression in πάντα διὰ πάντων. It could be that λόγος in Fr. 1 is another word for σοφόν in Fr. 41, for Κεραυνός in Fr. 64, as well as for πῦρ [fire] and πόλεμος [war]. πόλεμος is the πάντων Βασιλεύς [king of everything], the war that determines the antithetical movement of things that stand in the sphere of appearance.

HEIDEGGER: Do you wish to say that what is meant by γένεσις in γινομένων γὰρ πάντων serves to determine more closely the διὰ of Fr. 41? Do you then understand διὰ causally?

FINK: In no way. I would only like to say that lightning, which tears open the dark of night and, in its gleam, lights up and lets all individual things be seen, at the same time is also the mobile power of γένεσις in the manner of διὰ; and that this movement passes into the movements of things. Like the lightning, the λόγος of Fr. 1 also relates to τὰ πάντα. The movement of λόγος, which brings-forth and establishes, steers and determines everything, corresponds to the lightning movement that brings-forth.

PARTICIPANT: The relationship of the lightning movement and the movement of entities is no relationship of effect. When it was said that the lightning movement that brings-forth-to-appearance passes into the movement of things, no causal relationship is intended between the movement that brings-forth and the movement of what is brought-forth. Rather, that which stands here in the problem-horizon is the difference between movement in being and movement in entities, specifically between movement in unconcealing and movement in what is unconcealed.

FINK: We distinguish the lightning outbreak of light, as movement of bringing-forth, and the coming-forth in it of every specific entity in its movement. The instantaneousness of lightning is an indication of an impermanence. We must understand lightning as the briefest time, precisely as the instantaneousness that is a symbol for the movement of bringing-forth, not itself in time but allowing time.

HEIDEGGER: Isn't lightning eternal, and not merely momentary?

FINK: The problem of the movement that brings-forth, in its relationship to the movement of what is brought-forth, we must think in the nexus of lightning, sun, fire, and also the seasons, in which time is thought. The fiery with Heraclitus must be thought in more aspects, for example, the fire in the sun and the transformations of fire (πυρὸς τροπαί). Fire, which underlies everything, is the bringing-forth that withdraws itself in its transformations as that which is brought-forth. I would like to bring πάντα διὰ πάντων in Fr. 41 into connection with πυρὸς τροπαί. Lightning is the sudden burst of light in the dark of night. If now the lightning is perpetual, it is a symbol for the movement of bringing-forth.

HEIDEGGER: Are you opposed to an identification of lightning, fire, and also war?

FINK: No, but the identification here is one of identity and nonidentity.

HEIDEGGER: We must then understand identity as belonging-together.

FINK: Lightning, fire, sun, war, λόγος, and σοφόν are different lines of thinking on one and the same ground. In πυρὸς τροπαὶ the ground of everything is thought, which, changing itself over, shifts into water and earth.

HEIDEGGER: Thus, you mean the transformations of things with respect to one ground.

FINK: The ground meant here is not some substance or the absolute, but light and time.

HEIDEGGER: If we now stay with our source material and especially with the question concerning διὰ in Fr. 41, can't we then determine διὰ from steering (οἰακίζειν)? What does steering mean?

FINK: One can also subsume steering under movement. But with Heraclitus, the steering of lightning is that which stands face to face with all movement in entities like the lightning stands face to face with that which shows itself in its light. Thus, steering does not have the character of being moved like entities, but rather the character of bringing movement forth in entities. Add to this that steering, which concerns τὰ πάντα, is no steering of individual things, but of the quintessential whole of entities. The phenomenon of steering a ship is only a jumping off place for the thought which thinks the bringing-forth of the whole of entities in the articulate jointed-whole. As the captain, in the movement of the sea and winds to which the ship is exposed, brings a course to the movement of the ship, so the steering bringing-forth-to-appearance of lightning gives to all entities not only their outline but also their thrust. The steering bringing-forth-to-appearance is the more original movement that brings to light the whole of entities in their manifold being moved and at the same time withdraws into it.

HEIDEGGER: Can one bring the steering of Fr. 64 (οἰακίζει) and of Fr. 41 (ἐκυβέρνησε) into association with διά? If so, what then results as the meaning of διά?

FINK: In διά a transitive moment is thought.

HEIDEGGER: What meaning does "everything throughout everything" now have?

FINK: I would like to bring πάντα διὰ πάντων into association with πυρὸς τροπαί. The transformations of fire then imply that everything goes over into everything; so that nothing retains the definiteness of its character but, following an indiscernable wisdom, moves itself throughout by opposites.

HEIDEGGER: But why does Heraclitus then speak of steering?

FINK: The transformations of fire are in some measure a circular movement that gets steered by lightning, specifically by σοφόν. The movement, in which everything moves throughout everything through opposites, gets guided.

HEIDEGGER: But may we here speak of opposites or of dialectic at all? Heraclitus knows neither something of opposites nor of dialectic.

FINK: True, opposites are not thematic with Heraclitus. But on the other hand, it cannot be contested that from the phenomenon he points to opposites. The movement in which everything is transformed throughout everything is a steered movement. For Plato, the helm is the analogy for exhibiting the power of rationality in the world.

HEIDEGGER: You wish to illustrate what steering means by naming that which steers, the λόγος. But what is steering as a phenomenon?

FINK: Steering as a phenomenon is the movement of a human who, for example, brings a ship into a desired course. It is the directing of movement which a rational human pursues.

HEIDEGGER: In the experiment which we undertake, there is no question of wanting to conjure up Heraclitus himself. Rather, he speaks with us and we speak with him. At present, we reflect on the phenomenon of steering. This phenomenon has today, in the age of cybernetics, become so fundamental that it occupies and determines the whole of natural science and the behavior of humans so that it is necessary for us to gain more clarity about it. You said first that steering means "bringing something into a desired course." Let us attempt a still more precise description of the phenomenon.

FINK: Steering is the bringing-into-control [*In-die Gewalt-Bringen*] of a movement. A ship without rudder and helmsman is a plaything of the waves and winds. It is forcibly brought into the desired course only through steering. Steering is an intervening, transfiguring movement that compels the ship along a specific course. It has the character of violence in itself. Aristotle distinguishes the movement that is native to things and the movement that is forcibly conveyed to things.

HEIDEGGER: Isn't there also a nonviolent steering? Does the character of violence belong intrinsically to the phenomenon of steering? The phenomenon of steering is ever and again unclarified in reference to Heraclitus and to our present-day distress. That natural science and our life today become ruled by cybernetics in increasing measure is not accidental; rather, it is foreshadowed in the historical origin of modern knowledge and technology.

FINK: The human phenomenon of steering is characterized by the moment of coercive and precalculated regulation. It is associated with calculative knowledge and coercive intervention. The steering of Zeus is something else. When he steers he does not calculate, but he rules effortlessly. There tends to be noncoercive steering in the region of the gods, but not in the human region.

HEIDEGGER: Is there really an essential connection between steering and coercion?

FINK: The helmsman of a ship is a man of skill. He knows his way about in the tides and winds. He must make use of the driving wind and tide in correct manner. Through his steering he removes the ship coercively from the play of wind and waves. To this extent one must thus see and also posit the moment of coercive acts in the phenomenon of steering.

HEIDEGGER: Isn't present day cybernetics itself also steered?

FINK: If one would think of εἱμαρμένη [destiny] in this, or even fate.

HEIDEGGER: Isn't this steering noncoercive? We must look at various phenomena of steering. Steering can be, on the one hand, a coercive holding in line, on the other hand, the noncoercive steering of the gods. The gods of the Greeks, however, have nothing to do with religion.

The Greeks did not have faith in their gods. There is—to recall Wilamowitz—no faith of the Hellenes.

FINK: However, the Greeks had myth.

HEIDEGGER: Nevertheless, myth is something other than faith.— But to come back to noncoercive steering, we could ask how things stand with genetics. Would you also speak of a coercive steering there?

FINK: Here one must distinguish between the natural behavior of genes, which can be interpreted cybernetically, on the one hand, and the manipulation of factors of inheritance, on the other.

HEIDEGGER: Would you speak of coercion here?

FINK: Even if coercion is not felt by the one overpowered, it is still coercion. Because one can today coercively intervene and alter the behavior of genes, it is possible that one day the world will be ruled by druggists.

HEIDEGGER: Regarding genes, the geneticist speaks of an alphabet, of a store of information, which stores up in itself a definite quantity of information. Does one think of coercion in this information theory?

FINK: The genes that we discover are a biological finding. However, as soon as one comes to the thought of wanting to improve the human race through an altering steering of genes, it is thereby not a question of compulsion which brings pain, but indeed a question of coercion.

HEIDEGGER: Thus, we must make a two-fold distinction: on the one hand, the information-theoretical interpretation of the biological; and on the other, the attempt, grounded on the former, to actively steer. What is in question is whether the concept of coercive steering is in place in cybernetic biology.

FINK: Taken strictly, one cannot speak here of steering.

HEIDEGGER: At issue is whether an ambiguity presents itself in the concept of information.

FINK: Genes exhibit a determinate stamping and have, thereby, the character of a lasting stock [*Langspeichern*]. A human lives his life, which he apparently spends as a free being, through genetic conditioning. Everyone is determined by his ancestors. One also speaks of the learning ability of genes, which can learn like a computer.

HEIDEGGER: But how do things stand with the concept of information?

FINK: By the concept of information one understands, on one hand, *informare*, the stamping, impressing of form; and on the other, a technique of communication.

HEIDEGGER: If genes determine human behavior, do they develop the information that is innate to them?

FINK: In some measure. As to information, we are not dealing here with the kind of information that one picks up. What is meant here is that he behaves as if he were to get a command from the genetic stock. From this point of view, freedom is planned freedom.

HEIDEGGER: Information thus implies, on the one hand, the stamping and, on the other, information-giving, upon which the informed being reacts. The human mode of behavior becomes formalized through cybernetic biology, and the entire causal structure becomes converted. We need no philosophy of nature; it suffices, rather, if we clarify for ourselves where cybernetics comes from and where it leads to. The general charge, that philosophy understands nothing of natural science and always limps along behind it, we can take without being perturbed. It is important for us to say to natural scientists what they are, in effect, doing.

We now have seen a multitude of aspects in the phenomenon of steering. Κεραυνός, ἕν, σοφόν, λόγος, πῦρ, Ἥλιος, and πόλεμος are not one and the same, and we may not simply equate them; rather, certain relations hold sway between them which we wish to see, if we want to become clear to ourselves about the phenomena. Heraclitus has described no phenomena; rather, he has simply seen them. In closing, let me recall Fr. 47: μὴ εἰκῆ περὶ τῶν μεγίστων συμβαλλώμεθα. Translated, it says: concerning the highest things, let us not collect our words out of the blue, that is, rashly. This could be a motto for our seminar.

2

Hermeneutical Circle.—Relatedness of ἕν and πάντα (Correlated Fragments: 1, 7, 80, 10, 29, 30, 41, 53, 90, 100, 102, 108, 114).

FINK: As a result of Fr. 64, we are driven to the difficulty of elucidating the expression τὰ πάντα. I intentionally do not speak of the concept of τὰ πάντα in order to avoid the idea of a Heraclitean technical vocabulary. The expression τὰ πάντα has shown itself to us in Fr. 64 as that on which lightning comes to bear in a steering way. Lightning, as the opening light, as instantaneous fire, brings τὰ πάντα to light, outlines each thing in its form, and guides the movement, change, and passage of all which belongs in τὰ πάντα. In order to focus more sharply the question of what or who τὰ πάντα are, whether individual things or elements or counterreferences, we began with a preliminary look at other fragments that also name τὰ πάντα. If we disregard what we have already brought into relation to Fr. 64, fifteen text citations follow in which we wish to examine how far, that is, in what respects τὰ πάντα are addressed. In Fr. 64 it has been indicated that lightning is the steerer. It is not a question of an immanent self-regulation of πάντα. We must distinguish lightning as the one from the quintessential many of πάντα.

PARTICIPANT: If the steering principle does not lie within the whole, must it be found outside or above the whole? But how can it be outside the whole?

FINK: If we press it, the concept of the whole means a quintessence that allows nothing outside itself; thus, it apparently does not allow what you call the steering principle. But with Heraclitus, it is a question of a counterreference, at present still not discernible by us, between the ἕν of lightning and τὰ πάντα, which are torn open, steered, and guided by lightning. As a formal logical quintessence τὰ πάντα signifies a concept of "everything," which allows nothing outside itself. It is, nevertheless, questionable whether the steering is something external to τὰ πάντα at all. Here a very peculiar relatedness lies before us, which cannot be expressed at all with current relationship-categories. The relatedness in question, between the lightning that guides τὰ πάντα and τὰ πάντα itself, is the relatedness of one to many. It is not, however, the relationship of the singular to the plural, but the relatedness of a still unclarified one to the many in the one, whereby the many are meant in the sense of quintessence.

HEIDEGGER: Why do you reject Diels' translation of τὰ πάντα as universe?

FINK: If, in Fr. 64, τὸ πᾶν [the whole] were to stand in place of τὰ
πάντα, it would be justifiable to translate with "universe." τὰ πάντα do
not form the universe; rather, they form the quintessence of things
found in the world. The universe is not τὰ πάντα; rather, lightning itself
is world-forming. In the gleam of lightning, the many things in entirety
come into differentiated appearance. τὰ πάντα is the realm of differences. Lightning as ἕν, however, is not contrasted with τὰ πάντα as
one neighborhood against another or as cold against warm.

HEIDEGGER: On your interpretation, are lightning and universe
thus the same?

FINK: I would like to formulate it otherwise. Lightning is not the
universe, but it is as the world-forming. It is only as world-form. What is
to be understood here by world-form must be elucidated more precisely.

HEIDEGGER: I myself would like to add a supplement to what I
explained during the last session concerning cybernetics. I don't want to
allow a misunderstanding to arise from my allusion to modern cybernetics in the course of the discussion about what steering is. Misunderstanding would arise if we restricted ourselves to what is said about
steering in Frs. 64 and 41, and if we constructed a connection between
Heraclitus and cybernetics. This connection between Heraclitus and
cybernetics lies much deeper hidden and is not so easy to grasp. It goes
in another direction that we could not discuss in the context of our
present awareness of Heraclitus. Nevertheless, the meaning of cybernetics lies in the origin of that which prepares itself here with Heraclitus in
the relatedness of ἕν and τὰ πάντα.

FINK: If we now make the attempt to look at how τὰ πάντα is mentioned in other fragments, we still intend no explication of the separate
fragments.

HEIDEGGER: If I have postponed a question put by one of the participants, it has happened under the constraint of a fundamental difficulty in which we now find ourselves. Wherein lies this difficulty?

PARTICIPANT: The questions thus far touched on can only be an-
swered when we have won a deeper understanding of what our considerations have referred to up to now. But above all: we are supposed to
know at the very beginning, as well as after consideration of a fragment,
what τὰ πάντα means. However, we can understand the meaning of τὰ
πάντα only in the context of all the fragments in which τὰ πάντα is
mentioned. On the other hand, we can work out the contextual whole
only through a step-by-step procedure through individual fragments,
which already presupposes a prior understanding of what is meant by τὰ
πάντα. The basic difficulty before which we stand is, therefore, the hermeneutical circle.

HEIDEGER: Can we get out of this circle?

FINK: Mustn't we rather enter into this circle.

HEIDEGGER: Wittgenstein says the following. The difficulty in which thinking stands compares with a man in a room, from which he wants to get out. At first, he attempts to get out through the window, but it is too high for him. Then he attempts to get out through the chimney, which is too narrow for him. If he simply turned around, he would see that the door was open all along.

We ourselves are permanently set in motion and caught in the hermeneutical circle. Our difficulty now consists in the fact that we search for a clue about the meaning of τὰ πάντα in central Heraclitean fragments without having already involved ourselves in a detailed interpretation. For this reason our search for the meaning of Heraclitus' τὰ πάντα must also remain provisional.

PARTICIPANT: If we attempt to make clear to ourselves the meaning of τὰ πάντα starting from a fragment, can't we revert to Fr. 50 in which it is said, "Everything is one?"

HEIDEGGER: But everything we have of Heraclitus' fragments is not the whole, is not the whole Heraclitus.

FINK: I don't imagine that one can jump at Heraclitus' obscure saying as a maxim for interpretation. Likewise, we cannot appeal to Fr. 60, which says that the way up and the way down are one and the same, for an understanding of what a way is, for instance, a way in philosophy or a way through the fragments of Heraclitus. Here Heraclitus does not express the customary understanding of way. It also pertains to the hermeneutical difficulty mentioned by us that each fragment remains fragmentary in its explication, and in connection with all other fragments, it does not yield the whole of Heraclitus' thought.

HEIDEGGER: In the course of our seminar we must make the attempt to come through interpretation into the dimension required by Heraclitus. Indeed, the question emerges how far we implicitly or explicitly interpret, that is, how far we can make the dimensions of Heraclitus visible from out of our thought. Philosophy can only speak and say, but it cannot paint pictures.

FINK: Perhaps also it can never even point out.

HEIDEGGER: There is an old Chinese proverb that runs, "Once pointed out is better than a hundred times said." To the contrary, philosophy is obligated to point out precisely through saying.

FINK: We begin with the passages in which πάντα are mentioned in order to look at how πάντα are spoken of. We begin with Fr. 1, which has already concerned us. The phrase which alone now interests us runs: γινομένων γὰρ πάντων κατὰ τὸν λόγον. We ask in what respect πάντα are mentioned. πάντα are designated as γινόμενα. But what does that mean? If we conceive γίγνεσθαι narrowly, it means the coming-forth, the burgeoning of a living being from another. But in order to understand the extent to which πάντα are γινόμενα in Fr. 1, we must bear in mind the κατὰ τὸν λόγον. πάντα are moved in accord with λόγος. γινόμενα πάντα at the same time stand in a relationship to humans who become uncomprehending (ἀξύνετοι γίνονται ἄνθρωποι), who do not understand the λόγος in accord with which πάντα happen and are moved.

HEIDEGGER: Let us also include among κατὰ τὸν λόγον the τόνδε.

FINK: The demonstrative τόνδε means: in accord with this λόγος, which then is discussed in what follows.

PARTICIPANT: Isn't it more appropriate to translate ἀξύνετοι γίνονται not with "becoming uncomprehending," but with "prove to be uncomprehending"?

FINK: When I translate γίνονται with "become," and put it in a relationship to γινομένων γὰρ πάντων, I understand by it only a colorless becoming.

HEIDEGGER: The beginning of our consideration was Fr. 64, in which we view the relatedness of steering lightning to τὰ πάντα, that is, the relatedness of ἕν and πάντα. Further fragments should now show us in what manner and in what respects this relatedness is mentioned.

FINK: In Fr. 1, in which πάντα are spoken of as moved, their movement is related to λόγος. In the same fragment, the relationship of humans to λόγος is also mentioned in so far as humans do not understand the λόγος in its moving relatedness to the moved πάντα. From Fr. 1, I would like to move to Fr. 7: εἰ πάντα τὰ ὄντα καπνὸς γένοιτο, ῥῖνες ἂν διαγνοῖεν.⁴ In what manner are πάντα spoken of here? Do ὄντα [things that actually exist] elucidate πάντα or is πάντα meant as an indeterminate number of a quintessential kind, so that we must translate: every ὄντα? I believe that πάντα are understood here as distinction.

HEIDEGGER: That they are distinct emerges from διαγνοῖεν [would discriminate].

FINK: In Fr. 7, a familiar phenomenon is mentioned, a phenomenon which disguises differences, namely, smoke. In smoke, to be sure, distinctions become ellusive, but it does not eliminate those distinctions which become evident in διαγνοῖεν. Above all, the moment of being distinct is to be noticed in the word combination πάντα τὰ ὄντα.

HEIDEGGER: How is πάντα thus to be comprehended?

FINK: πάντα τὰ ὄντα does not mean an enumeration of ὄντα and does not signify "all which is," but the πάντα which are, are set off from one another, are distinguished. πάντα, collectively as ὄντα, are the correlate of a διάγνωσις [diagnosis]. The diagnostic character of a distinguishing is sharpened in regard to smoke as a distinction-obscuring phenomenon. Thus, πάντα in Fr. 7 are viewed as distinct.

HEIDEGGER: What information concerning πάντα does Fr. 7 give us vis-à-vis Fr. 1?

FINK: In Fr. 7, the emphasis lies on the distinctness, on the individuality of πάντα that, in Fr. 1, are spoken of as moved, and moved, that is, in accord with the λόγος.

HEIDEGGER: Following the overall sense of Fr. 7, πάντα are thus related to γνῶσις [inquiry], to grasping humans.

FINK: γνῶσις with respect to πάντα is possible, however, only in so far as πάντα are distinct in themselves. πάντα are moved in accord with λόγος. In their movement, in their change and passage, which lightning steers, they are at the same time distinct by themselves. The movement of the outbreaking lightning gleam lets πάντα come forth as distinct by themselves.

HEIDEGGER: Yet with the preliminary orientation, concerning the way τὰ πάντα are addressed by Heraclitus, you have already landed us in an entire philosophy.

FINK: But I still want to stick to the point that the essential thing in Fr. 7 is the reference of πάντα back to γνῶσις and διάγνωσις.

HEIDEGGER: While πάντα in Fr. 1 are seen in their reference to λόγος, which is not of human character, they are mentioned in Fr. 7 in their reference to human cognizance. Subsequently, διανοεῖσθαι [think through] and διαλέγεσθαι [dialogue] then develop themselves out of διαγιγνώσκειν [distinguish]. διαγνοῖεν is an indication that πάντα are characterized as what is distinguishable, but not what is already distinguished.

PARTICIPANT: If λόγος is discussed in Fr. 1, and διάγνωσις is discussed in Fr. 7, can't one then refer the γνῶσις of πάντα to λόγος?

HEIDEGGER: You assume too much thereby. You pursue the connection between human γνῶσις and λόγος. But we want first to get acquainted with the different ways in which Heraclitus speaks of τὰ πάντα.

PARTICIPANT: But isn't the ontic being [Seiendsein] of πάντα, which comes to speech in ὄντα, a quality of πάντα which is a necessary presupposition for διάγνωσις?

FINK: I concede that the ontic being of πάντα is a necessary presupposition for the discerning human cognizance. But ὄντα is no quality of πάντα. We must, however, keep in mind that ὄντα is added to the content of πάντα in Fr. 7 as hitherto treated.

HEIDEGGER: But do we then know what τὰ ὄντα means? We would only come closer to the matter, if we would be concerned with the nose, the eyes, and with hearing.

FINK: In our context, the phrase καὶ γινόμενα πάντα κατ᾽ ἔριν καὶ χρεών in Fr. 80 now interests us.[5] Here also πάντα γινόμενα are named; now, however, not κατὰ τὸν λόγον τόνδε as in Fr. 1, but κατ᾽ ἔριν [according to strife]. At first, we leave out of account the phrase καὶ χρεών [according to obligation]. Now πάντα and their manner of movement are referred not to λόγος, but to strife. In Fr. 80, πάντα enter into a context of meaning with strife. It is reminiscent of πόλεμος—Fr. 53, to which we will yet turn.—From Fr. 10, we single out the phrase: ἐκ πάντων ἒν καὶ ἐξ ἑνὸς πάντα.[6] Here also we meet with a becoming, but not with what is meant by the movement of individual entities; rather, we meet with the becoming of a whole.

HEIDEGGER: If we view it naïvely, how could ἐκ πάντων ἒν be understood?

PARTICIPANT: Read naïvely it would mean that a whole gets put together out of all the parts.

HEIDEGGER: But the second phrase, ἐξ ἑνὸς πάντα, already indicates to us that it is not a question of a relationship of a part and a whole which is composed of parts.

FINK: In Frs. 1 and 80, πάντα γιγνόμενα are mentioned. Their being moved was referred on one hand to λόγος and on the other hand to strife. In accord with λόγος and strife means: in accord with the movement of λόγος and strife. We have distinguished this movement from the being moved of πάντα. It is not the same kind of movement as the movement of πάντα. In Fr. 10, movement is brought up, but in the sense of how one comes out of everything and everything comes out of one.

HEIDEGGER: Which movement do you mean here?

FINK: The world-movement. With this, nevertheless, too much has been said. We have noticed that one can understand ἐκ πάντων ἒν naïvely as a relationship of part and whole. That one comes out of many is a familiar phenomenon. However, the same thing does not allow expression in reverse manner. Many does not come out of one, unless we mean only bounded allness in the sense of a multiplicity and a set. τὰ πάντα is, however, no concept of bounded allness, no concept of set, but a quintessence. We must distinguish the concept of allness, in the sense of quintessence as it is given in τὰ πάντα, from the numerical or generic allness, that is, from a concept of relative allness.

HEIDEGGER: Do all the books that are arranged here in this room constitute a library?

PARTICIPANT: The concept of a library is ambiguous. On one hand, it can mean the entire set of books lying here before us; but on the other hand, it can also mean the equipment other than the books, that is, the room, the shelves, etc. The library is not restricted to the books that belong to it. Also, when some books are taken out, it is still a library.

HEIDEGGER: If we take out one book after another, how long does it remain a library? But we see already that all the individual books together do not make up a library. "All," understood as summative, is quite different from allness in the sense of the unity of the peculiar sort that is not so easy to specify at first.

FINK: In Fr. 10, a relatedness is articulated between πάντα, in the sense of many in entirety, and the one, and a relatedness of the one to the many in entirety. Here, the one does not mean a part.

HEIDEGGER: Our German word *Eins* [one] is fatal for the Greek ἕν. To what extent?

FINK: In the relatedness of ἕν and πάντα, it is not only a matter of a counterreference, but also of a unification.

PARTICIPANT: I would like to understand ἕν as something complex in opposition to a numerical conception. The tension between ἕν and πάντα has the character of a complex.

FINK: ἕν is lightning and fire. If one wishes to speak here of a complex, one can do so only if one understands by it an encompassing unity that the many in entirety gather in themselves.

HEIDEGGER: We must think ἕν, the one [*das Eine*], as the unifying. To be sure, the one can have the meaning of the one and only, but here it has the character of unifying. If one translates the passage in question from Fr. 10, "out of everything, one; and out of one, everything," this is a thoughtless translation. ἕν is not by itself a one that would have nothing to do with πάντα; rather, it is unifying.

FINK: In order to make clear the unifying unity of ἕν, one can take as a comparison the unity of an element. However, this is not enough; rather, the unifying unity must be thought back to the one of lightning, which, in its gleam, gathers and unifies the many in entirety in their distinctness.

HEIDEGGER: ἕν runs throughout all philosophy till Kant's Transcendental Apperception. You said just now that one had to consider ἕν in its relatedness to πάντα, and πάντα in its relatedness to ἕν in Fr. 10, together with λόγος and strife in its reference to πάντα in Frs. 1 and 80. However, that is only possible when we understand λόγος as gathering and ἔρις [strife] as dismantling. Fr. 10 begins with the word συνάψιες [contact]. How should we translate this?

PARTICIPANT: I would propose: joining-together [*Zusammenfügen*].

HEIDEGGER: In this, we would be concerned with the word "together." Accordingly, ἕν is that which unifies.

FINK: Fr. 29 seems at first not to belong in the series of fragments in which πάντα are mentioned: αἱρεῦνται γὰρ ἓν ἀντὶ ἁπάντων οἱ ἄριστοι, κλέος ἀέναον θνητῶν.[7] For here πάντα are not mentioned directly in a specific respect; rather, a human phenomenon is mentioned, specifically, that the noble minded prefer one thing rather than all else, namely everlasting glory rather than transient things. The comportment of the noble minded is opposed to that of the πολλοί, the many, who lie there like well-fed cattle. And here, nevertheless, the reference in question of ἕν and πάντα is also to be seen. According to the prima facie meaning, ἕν is here the everlasting glory that occupies a special place vis-à-vis all else.

But the fragment expresses not only the comportment of the noble minded in reference to glory. Glory is standing in radiance. Radiance, however, reminds us of the light of lightning and fire. Glory relates itself to all other things as radiance to dullness. Fr. 90 also belongs here in so far as it speaks of the relationship of gold and goods. Gold also relates itself to goods as radiance to dullness.

HEIDEGGER: Fr. 29 also names the πολλοί next to the ἄριστοι [the best]. In Fr. 1, the πολλοί are compared with the ἀπείροισιν, with the untried, who are contrasted with ἐγώ, that is, with Heraclitus. But we may not understand this opposition, as Nietzsche did, as a separation of the prideful from the herd. Heraclitus also mentions one of the seven wise men, Bias, who was born in Priênê, and says of him that his reputation is greater than that of others (Fr. 39). Bias has also said: οἱ πλεῖστοι ἄνθρωποι κακοί, most men are bad. The many do not strive, like the noble minded, after the radiance of glory; they indulge in transitory things and therefore do not see the one.

FINK: In Fr. 29, we must think of glory in regard to radiance. The radiant is the fiery in opposition to that which the many and the bad prefer. The noble minded, who aspire above all else to glory, stand near the thinker, whose glance is oriented not only to πάντα, but to ἕν in its relatedness to πάντα.

HEIDEGGER: Pindar also connected gold, and thus the radiant, with fire and lightning. The preceding inspection of Fr. 29 has indicated to us that a specific human comportment is at first mentioned.

FINK: In this comportment of the noble minded, the fundamental relatedness of ἕν and πάντα is mirrored in a certain manner in everlasting glory. Also in Fr. 7, πάντα stepped into association with human comportment. There, however, it was discerning cognizance. In Fr. 29, πάντα are also seen in their reference back to a human comportment. But it is not a question of a knowledge relationship; rather, it is a question of a relationship of preference of one thing over another. Glory, however, is not distinguished by degrees from other possessions; rather, it has the character of distinction in opposition to all other things. It is not a question of preference for one over another, but of preference of the only important matter as against all others. As the noble minded prefer the only important matter, the radiance of glory rather than all other things, so the thinker thinks on the unifying one of lightning, in the light of which πάντα come to appearance, not only about πάντα. And just as the many prefer transient things to the radiance of glory, so humans, the many, do not understand the unifying ἕν (which includes πάντα in their distinction) but only the πάντα, the many things.

In Fr. 30, the focus of thought is oriented to the relationship of πάντα and κόσμος. The citation which alone is now interesting to us runs: κόσμον τόνδε, τὸν αὐτὸν ἁπάντων. Diels translates: "This world-order, the same for all beings." By beings, he evidently understands living beings. We wish, however, to translate ἀπάντων: for the entirety of πάντα.

HEIDEGGER: τὸν αὐτὸν ἀπάντων stands only in Clement of Alexandria, and is missing in Plutarch and Simplicius. Karl Reinhardt strikes it. I would like to mention him once again, because I would like to refer to his essay, "*Heraklits Lehre vom Feuer*" (first published in *Hermes* 77, 1942, pp. 1–27), which is especially important in methodological respects.[8] It was just thirty years ago, in the period during which I held the three lectures on the origin of the work of art, that I spoke at length with Karl Reinhardt, in his garret, about Heraclitus. At the time, he told me of his plan to write a commentary on Heraclitus with an orientation toward tradition and history. Had he realized his plan, we would be much aided today. Reinhardt had also shown in the aforementioned essay that πῦρ φρόνιμον [sagacious fire], standing in the context of Fr. 64, is genuine and on that account is to be looked at as a fragment of Heraclitus. What the discovery of new Heraclitus fragments implies, he indicated thus: "An unpleasant outcome results. It is not impossible that with Clement and the Church Fathers a few unknown words of Heraclitus flood about, as though in a great river, which we will never succeed in catching unless we were referred to them from another source. To recognize an important word as important is not always easy." Karl Reinhardt is still with us.

FINK: In Fr. 30, the reference of πάντα and κόσμος is thought. We leave open what κόσμος means with Heraclitus. Let us look once again at Fr. 41 which has already occupied us: ἓν τὸ σοφόν, ἐπίστασθαι γνώμην, ὀτέη ἐκυβέρνησε πάντα διὰ πάντων.[9] Here σοφόν is added to ἕν. We have already looked for the relatedness of ἕν and πάντα in the fragments. We must ask whether σοφόν is only a property of ἕν as unifying unity, or whether it is not precisely the essence of ἕν.

HEIDEGGER: Then we could put a colon between ἕν and σοφόν. ἕν: σοφόν.

FINK: σοφόν, as the essence of the unifying ἕν, grasps ἕν in its complete fullness of sense. If ἕν up till now appears to us to withdraw, we have in Fr. 41 the first more accurate characterization as a kind of ἕνωσις [unification], although this concept is laden with Neoplatonic meaning.

HEIDEGGER: ἕν runs through all of metaphysics; and dialectic is also not to be thought without ἕν.

FINK: In Fr. 53, to which we have already alluded in connection with Fr. 80, πάντα gets placed in relationship to πόλεμος. The fragment has the following word order: Πόλεμος πάντων μὲν πατήρ ἐστι, πάντων δὲ βασιλεύς, καὶ τοὺς μὲν θεοὺς ἔδειξε τοὺς δὲ ἀνθρώπους, τοὺς μὲν δούλους ἐποίησε τοὺς δὲ ἐλευθέρους. Diels translates: "War is the father and king of all things. He established some as gods and the others as humans; some he made slaves and the others free." The reference of πάντα to πόλεμος has already indicated itself to us in Fr. 80, where ἔρις is mentioned. Now war, that is, strife, is named father and king of all things. As the father is the source of children, so is strife, which we must think together with ἕν as lightning and fire, the source of πάντα. The connection of πόλεμος as father to πάντα repeats itself in a certain way in the relationship of πόλεμος as sovereign to πάντα. We must bring βασιλεύς [king] into association with the steering and directing of lightning. As lightning tears open the field of πάντα and works there as the driving and reigning, so war as ruler directs and reigns over πάντα.

HEIDEGGER: When he speaks of father and ruler, Heraclitus grasps in an almost poetic speech the sense of the ἀρχή [ultimate principle] of movement: πρῶτον ὅθεν ἡ ἀρχὴ τῆς κινήσεως. The origin of movement is also the origin of ruling and directing.

FINK: The phrases πόλεμος πάντων πατήρ and πάντων βασιλεύς are not only two new images; rather, a new moment in the relatedness of ἕν and πάντα comes to speech in them. The way that war is the father of πάντα is designated in ἔδειξε [established, brought to light]; the way that war is king of πάντα is said in ἐποίησε [made].

Fr. 90 mentions the reference between πάντα and the exchange of fire: πυρός τε ἀνταμοιβὴ τὰ πάντα καὶ πῦρ ἁπάντων.[10] Here ἕν is addressed by name as fire, as it was formerly designated as lightning. The relationship between fire and πάντα does not have the character here of bare γένεσις, of bring-about or bringing-forth (making), but rather the character of exchange.

HEIDEGGER: The talk of exchange as the way that fire as ἕν relates itself to πάντα has the appearance of a certain leveling.

FINK: This appearance is perhaps intended. Fr. 100 offers itself now for consideration. It runs: ὥρας αἳ πάντα φέρουσι "The seasons which bring πάντα." Till now we have heard of steering and directing, showing and making, and now Heraclitus speaks of a bringing. The hours, that is, the times, bring πάντα. Therewith, time comes into ἕν in an express manner. Time was already named in a covert manner in lightning, and is also thought in the seasonal times of fire and in the sun. πάντα are what is brought by the times.

HEIDEGGER: Do you lay more emphasis on time or on bringing?

FINK: I am concerned with the very connection between them. But we must still leave open how time and bringing are here to be thought.

HEIDEGGER: Bringing is an important moment which we must later heed in the question concerning dialectic in συμφερόμενον [something that is brought together] and διαφερόμενον [something that is brought apart].

FINK: In Fr. 102, πάντα is viewed in a two-fold manner. It runs: τῷ μὲν θεῷ καλὰ πάντα καὶ ἀγαθὰ καὶ δίκαια, ἄνθρωποι δὲ ἃ μὲν ἄδικα ὑπειλήφασιν ἃ δὲ δίκαια. Diels translates: "For god everything is beautiful, good, and just; but humans have assumed some to be unjust and others to be just." In Fr. 7, πάντα were related to human grasping. Now Heraclitus speaks not only from the human but also from the divine reference to πάντα. Everything is beautiful, good, and just for god. Only humans make a distinction between the just and the unjust. The genuine and true view on πάντα and ἕν is the divine; the human is ingenuine and deficient. In Fr. 29, we see a similar double relatedness of πάντα and ἕν. There it was the noble minded who preferred the radiance of glory rather than all else, whereas the many indulged themselves in transient things and did not aspire to everlasting glory. Here it is the divine and the human aspects that are placed in opposition.

Fr. 108 names σοφόν as that which is set apart from everything: σοφόν ἐστι πάντων κεχωρισμένον.[11] Here σοφόν is not only a determination of ἕν as in Fr. 41, but as ἕν it is that which is set apart from πάντα. σοφόν is that which holds itself separated from πάντα, while still encompassing them. Thus, πάντα are thought from the separation of ἕν.

HEIDEGGER: κεχωρισμένον [set apart] is the most difficult question with Heraclitus. Karl Jaspers says about this word of Heraclitus: "Here the thought of transcendence as absolutely other is reached, and indeed in full awareness of the uniqueness of this thought." (*Die grossen Philosophen, Bd.* I, S. 634).[12] This interpretation of κεχωρισμένον as transcendence entirely misses the point.

FINK: Again, Fr. 114 provides another reference to τὰ πάντα: ξὺν νόῳ λέγοντας ἰσχυρίζεσθαι χρὴ τῷ ευνῷ πάντων, ὅκωσπερ νόμῳ πόλις, καὶ πολὺ ἰσχυροτέρως. τρέφονται γὰρ πάντες οἱ ἀνθρώπειοι νόμοι ὑπὸ ἑνὸς τοῦ θείου. We can skip over the last sentence for our present consideration. Diels translates: "If one wants to talk with understanding, one must strengthen himself with what is common to all, like a city with the law, and even more strongly." Here also, πάντα are viewed from a specific human behavior. It cannot be decided at first glance whether only the χοινόν [public realm] of the city is meant by what is common to everything, or whether it does not also refer to πάντα. In the latter case, the fundamental relatedness of ἕν and πάντα would reflect itself in the human domain. As the one who wants to talk with understanding must make himself strong with what is common to everything, so must the judicious one make himself strong in a deeper sense with the ἕν, which is in company with πάντα.

HEIDEGGER: After ξυνόν [common] we must put a big question mark, just as we do after κεχωρισμένον. The question mark, however, means that we must set aside all familiar ideas and ask and reflect. ξυνόν ᾽ is a separate, complex problem, because here ξὺν νόῳ [with mind] comes into play.

FINK: Now we have examined in which respect τὰ πάντα are mentioned in a series of fragments. We have still given no interpretation, therewith. Nevertheless, in passing through the many citations what τὰ πάντα means has not become clearer to us. Rather, the expression τὰ πάντα has become more questionable in reference to the cases exhibited. It has become more questionable to us what πάντα are, what their coming to appearance is, and how the reference of πάντα and ἕν must be thought, and where this reference belongs. When we say "questionable" [*fragwürdig*], it means that the emerging questions [*Fragen*] are worthy [*würdig*] of being asked.

PARTICIPANT: Frs. 50 and 66 also belong in the series of enumerated fragments that treat of πάντα.

HEIDEGGER: Fr. 66 is disputed by Clement, whom Karl Reinhardt characterizes as the Greek Isaiah. For Clement sees Heraclitus eschatologically. Again, I emphasize that it would be of inestimable value if Karl Reinhardt's commentary, oriented toward tradition and history, had come down to us. True, Reinhardt was no professional philosopher, but he could think and see.

3

πάντα-ὅλον, πάντα-ὄντα—Different
Exposition of Fragment 7 (Correlated Fragment 67).
πᾶν ἑρπετόν (Fragment 11).
Maturation Character of the Seasons (Fragment 100).

HEIDEGGER: Let us look back to the theme of the last seminar.

PARTICIPANT: In passage through the fragments in which τὰ πάντα is mentioned, we attempted to view the respects in which the phrase τὰ πάντα is spoken by Heraclitus. These respects are the reference of πάντα to λόγος, to strife, to war as father and king of πάντα, to the unifying ἕν, to κόσμος, to the exchange of fire, to σοφόν, to κεχωρισμένον, to the seasons, moreover, to the human comportment of discerning cognizance, to the preference for one rather than all else, to strengthening oneself with what is common to all, and to the different divine and human relation to πάντα.

HEIDEGGER: Have we yet extracted what τὰ πάντα means from these manifold references?

PARTICIPANT: Provisionally, we have interpreted τὰ πάντα as the quintessence of what is individual.

HEIDEGGER: But where do you get the individual from?

PARTICIPANT: In all the fragments, the view is oriented toward the individual, which is taken together in the quintessence, τὰ πάντα.

HEIDEGGER: What does "individual" mean in Greek?

PARTICIPANT: ἕκαστον.

HEIDEGGER: In passage through a series of fragments, we have viewed the reference of τὰ πάντα to ἕν and that which belongs to ἕν. But in pursuit of the manifold references in which τὰ πάντα are mentioned, we are still not successful in characterizing more closely the phrase τὰ πάντα. τὰ πάντα are also spoken of as distinguished within themselves. How is that to be understood?

PARTICIPANT: The entirety of πάντα can be addressed as τὸ ὅλον. This entirety is the quintessence of self-distinguishing πάντα.

HEIDEGGER: But what is the quintessence? Doesn't it mean the whole?

PARTICIPANT: The quintessence is that which incloses.

HEIDEGGER: Is there something like an inclosing quintessence with Heraclitus? Obviously not. Quintessence, inclosing, grasping and comprehending is already by itself un-Greek. With Heraclitus, there is no concept. And also with Aristotle, there still are no concepts in the proper sense. When does the concept arise for the first time?

PARTICIPANT: When λόγος, specifically the stoic κατάληψις [direct apprehension], gets translated and understood as *conceptus* [concept].

HEIDEGGER: To talk of the concept is not Greek. It is not consonant with what we will treat in the next seminar. There we must also deal cautiously with the word "quintessence."

FINK: When I speak of quintessence, I would like to lay the emphasis on συνέχον [keep together]. When the participant said that I have explained τὰ πάντα as the quintessence of the individual, he has claimed more than I have said. I have precisely not decided whether τὰ πάντα means an entire constellation of what is individual, or whether this phrase does not rather refer to the elements and the counterreferences. At first, I understand τὰ πάντα only as the entire region to which nothing is lacking; to which region, nevertheless, something is opposed. That to which πάντα stands in opposition, however, is not alongside them; rather, it is something in which πάντα are. Thus seen, Κεραυνός is no longer a phenomenon of light among others in the entirety of τὰ πάντα. We do not deny that in the entirety of what there is, lightning too is included in a pre-eminent manner which points in the direction of a *summum ens* [supreme entity]. Perhaps Κεραυνός as thought by Heraclitus is, however, no *ens* [entity] which belongs with τὰ πάντα, also no distinct *ens*, but something which stands in a relationship, still unclear to us, to τὰ πάντα. We have first formulated this relationship in a simile. As lightning tears open light, and gives visibility to things in its gleam, so lightning in a deeper sense lets πάντα come forth to appearance in its clearing. πάντα, coming forth to appearance, are gathered in the brightness of lightning. Because the lightning is not a light phenomenon interior to the entirety of πάντα, but brings πάντα forth to appearance, the lightning is in a certain sense set apart from πάντα. Lightning is, therefore, the Κεραυνὸς πάντων κεχωρισμένος. But as thus set apart, lightning is in a certain manner also the joining and again the dismantling in reference to πάντα. τὰ πάντα means not only the entirety of individual things. Precisely when one thinks from out of πυρὸς τροπαί [transformations of fire], it is rather the transformations of fire throughout the great number of elements which makes up the entirety of individual things. Individual things are then μικτά, that is, mixed, out of the elements.

HEIDEGGER: In what would you see the distinction between entirety and wholeness?

FINK: We speak of wholeness in the whole structure of things which we can address as ὅλα, and of the entirety of things, of the ὅλον, in which everything distinguished is gathered and set apart in a specific ordering.

HEIDEGGER: Do you understand entirety as ὅλον or καθόλον [universal]?

FINK: But ὅλον, the entirety of πάντα, is derivative from ἕν, which is a wholeness of a completely different kind than the structural wholeness of things, or than the wholeness of a summative kind. ἕν is also not to be understood like the κόσμος in Τίμαιος [*Timaeus*], which Plato specifies as a living being with extremities turned inside.[13] The wholeness of ἕν means the totality which we must rather think as Σφαῖρος [sphere]. Thus we must discriminate the manifold of things and elements, the quintessential entirety of πάντα, and the totality thought in ἕν, which lets the entirety of πάντα come forth to appearance, and which surrounds it.

HEIDEGGER: What do you mean by entirety? Once one has arrived at entirety in thinking, the opinion may emerge that one is at the end of thinking. Is that the danger which you see?

FINK: At this point, I would like to speak of a double ray of thought. We must distinguish the thought of things in the whole and the thought that thinks the universe, the totality, or ἕν. I would like thereby to avoid τὰ πάντα, which are referred back to ἕν as lightning, becoming understood as a universe closed in itself.

HEIDEGGER: If we speak of wholeness in reference to τὰ πάντα, the danger then consists in ἕν becoming superfluous. Therefore, we must speak of entirety and not of wholeness with regard to τὰ πάντα. The word "entirety" means that πάντα are in entirety not as in a box, but in the manner of their thorough individuality. We choose the word "entirety" on two grounds: first, in order not to run the danger that the last word be spoken with "the whole"; and second, in order not to understand τὰ πάντα only in the sense of ἕκαστα.

FINK: In a certain manner τὰ πάντα are the many, but precisely not the many of an enumerated set; rather, of a quintessential entirety.

HEIDEGGER: The word "quintessence" is on the one hand too static, and on the other it is un-Greek in so far as it has to do with grasping. In Greek, we could speak of περιέχον [embrace]. But ἔχειν [to hold] does not mean grasping and grip. What comes into play here, we will see from the following fragments.

In order to return now to the fragments which we went through in the last seminar: we have seen that they speak of τὰ πάντα in different ways. For example, Fr. 7 is the only one in which Heraclitus speaks of πάντα as ὄντα, and in which ὄντα is used at all. Precisely translated, it runs: If everything which is were smoke, noses would discriminate. Here διαγιγνώσκειν is mentioned. We also speak of a diagnosis. Is a diagnosis also a distinguishing?

PARTICIPANT: A diagnosis distinguishes what is healthy and what is sick, what is conspicuous and what is not conspicuous in relation to sickness.

PARTICIPANT: To speak in the terminology of the physician: the physician seeks specific symptoms of sickness. The diagnosis is a passing through the body and a precise, distinguishing cognition of symptoms.

HEIDEGGER: The diagnosis rests on the original meaning of δία and means, first of all, a running through and a going through the entire body in order to come then to a distinguishing and a decision. From this we already observe that the διαγιγνώσκειν is not only a distinguishing. We must, therefore, say: If everything that is were smoke, noses would have the possibility to go through them.

PARTICIPANT: The distinguishing of entities would then happen by means of the sense of smell.

HEIDEGGER: But can the senses distinguish at all? This question will still occupy us later with Heraclitus. But how does Heraclitus come to smoke? The answer is not difficult to find. Where there is smoke, there is also fire.

FINK: If Heraclitus speaks of smoke in Fr. 7, then it means that the smoke makes ὄψις [sight] more difficult in reference to πάντα τὰ ὄντα, that, nevertheless, in passing through the concealing smoke a διαγιγνώσκειν is possible by way of ῥῖνες [the nostrils]. We must also observe that Heraclitus does not say something like: If everything that is becomes smoke. Rather, he says: If everything which is would become smoke.

HEIDEGGER: We must understand the γίνεσθαι [coming into existence] in γένοιτο [would become] as "coming-forth." If everything that is would come forth as smoke . . . In the fragment, the πάντα τὰ ὄντα are straight away allied with a διάγνωσις. In the background, however, they are spoken of in respect to a character that is connected with fire.

FINK: You bring smoke into connection with fire. Smoke stands in relation to the nose. That would mean that the nose also stands over the smoke in a relation to fire. However, is it not precisely the ὄψις which is the most fire-like in meaning? I would suppose that the sunlike nature of sight can receive the firey more than the nose. Additionally, smoke is something derivative from fire. Smoke is, so to speak, the shadow of fire. One must say: If everything which is would become smoke, as that which is derivative from fire, then noses could cognize what is by means of resistance. However, I would suppose that ὄψις, rather than the nose, is allied with fire.

HEIDEGGER: Nevertheless, I believe that something else is meant by the nose and smoke. Let us look at Fr. 67. There it says, among other things: ἀλλοιοῦται δὲ ὅκωσπερ (πῦρ), ὁπόταν συμμιγῇ θυώμασιν, ὀνομάζεται καθ᾽ ἡδονὴν ἑκάστου. "But he changes just like fire which, when it is mixed with incense, is named according to the fragrance of each one." In our context of meaning, the word we are concerned with is θύωμα, incense. Depending on the incense, which is mixed with fire, a fragrance is spread by which the fragrance is then named. It is important here that the smoke of fire can be variously fragrant. That means that the smoke itself has an inherent manifold of distinctions, so that it can be cognized with the nose as a specific this or that.

FINK: I understand smoke as a phenomenon that veils the distinctions of πάντα, without the distinctions disappearing entirely. For it is the nose that, in passing through the veil of πάντα, cognizes distinctions.

HEIDEGGER: Thus you take διά as "throughout the smoke." To the contrary, I understand διά as "along the smoke." διαγιγνώσκειν here means that the possible manifold, immanent to the smoke, can be gone through and cognized.

FINK: Whereas, on my preliminary interpretation, smoke veils a multiplicity, on your explication smoke is itself a dimension of multiplicity. The question about τὰ ὄντα depends on the way we understand smoke. διαγιγνώσκειν in the sense of distinction and decision presupposes the διά in the sense of "throughout" (minced).

PARTICIPANT: If all things would become smoke, then isn't everything one, without distinction?

HEIDEGGER: Then noses would have nothing more to do, and there would be no διά. Fr. 7 denies precisely that everything that is would become homogeneous smoke. If that were the statement of the fragment, then no διαγνοῖεν could follow. We have brought Fr. 67 into play precisely because it contains an allusion to the fact that smoke is filled with a manifold.

FINK: Our attempt at interpreting the fragments of Heraclitus began with Fr. 64. Although we have already discussed a number of other fragments, this was above all because we wanted to learn in what respects τὰ πάντα are mentioned. From Fr. 64, with which we began our sequence of fragments, we now turn to Fr. 11. It runs: πᾶν γὰρ ἑρπετὸν πληγῇ νέμεται, Deils translates: "Everything that crawls is tended by (god's) (whip)blow." What can be the reason for arranging this fragment, which declares that all crawling things are driven to pasture with a blow, behind the Κεραυνός-fragment? Approaching from another viewpoint, is it also declared here how lightning steers and how it guides πάντα; or is something entirely different aimed at in this fragment? Let us proceed in the explication of this fragment from the word πληγῇ [blow]. Diels translates: with god's whipblow. True, god is mentioned in the context, but not in the fragment itself. We attempt an explication of the saying without thereby putting it in the context.

HEIDEGGER: You wish not to include the god. But with Aeschylus and Sophocles we find πληγή in connection with the god (Agamemnon 367, Ajax 137).

FINK: In πληγή, I see another fundamental word for lightning. It means, then, the lightning bolt. On this ground, it is justified to turn from the Κεραυνός-fragment to Fr. 11. But let us first stay with the literal language of Heraclitus' saying: everything that crawls is tended and driven to pasture by the blow. The whip blow drives the herd forward and tends it while it is on the pasture. Apparently, in the literal language, a grazing herd is spoken of, which is driven forward and tended by means of the blow of the whip. But if we now refer the blow to the lightning bolt, then the blow is also thunder, which resounds through the wide spaces, the voice of lightning, which drives forward and guides all crawling things. νέμειν means on one hand to drive to pasture, tend and feed; on the other, however, to dispense and allot. We can then say: everything which crawls is alloted by the blow as the voice of lightning.

HEIDEGGER: νέμεται also refers to Νέμεσις [goddess of retribution].

FINK: Νέμεσις, however, does not have only the meaning of alloting and dispensing.

PARTICIPANT: νέμεται refers equally to νόμος [custom, law].

FINK: νόμος regulates for all the citizens of the city the dispensing of what is appropriate to them. The obvious image, which is, however, no allegory, means that everything which crawls is put to pasture with a blow being allotted to it. In νέμεται the coerciveness of what befalls one (being driven forward by a blow) connects with the tranquility of grazing. We must hear many things together in νέμεται: guiding, pursuing, and steering of the blow and being driven. To the latter there also belongs a tending and being steered. Allotment also belongs to the tranquil sense of grazing. Grazing as allotment is protection as well as getting steered in the sense of being forced.

HEIDEGGER: I would like to read a few verses from Hölderlin's poem, "Peace."

> Unyielding and unvanquished, you strike alike
> The lion-hearted, Nemesis, and the weak,
>   And from the blow your victims tremble
>   Down to the ultimate generation.
> You hold the secret power to goad and curb
> For thorn and reins are given into your hands,
> (Stuttgart edition, vol. 2, 1, p. 6, lines 13–18)[14]

FINK: A strophe from Hölderlin's poem, "Voice of the People" (first edition), also belongs here:

> And, as the eagle pushes his young and throws
> Them from the nest, to look in the fields for prey,
>   So, too, the sons of man are driven
>   Out and away by the God's own kindness
> (Stuttgart edition, vol. 2, 1, p. 50, lines 33–36)[14]

The kindness of the gods unites in itself the grace and the coercion which we must listen for in νέμεται in Fr. 11. Therewith we have a preliminary orientation concerning that which πληγῇ and νέμεται mean. But does the blow, which guides and allots, refer generally to τὰ πάντα? In the saying itself, τὰ πάντα are not mentioned. Instead of this, it mentions πᾶν ἑρπετόν. It would seem as though a specific field were carved out of τὰ πάντα. πᾶν ἑρπετόν means everything which crawls. Here it is not a question of the grammatical singular, but of a singular that means a plurality: everything that crawls. Is the sphere of land creatures that crawl outlined in opposition to creatures which live in the air and in the water? Is the manner of movement of land creatures characterized as crawling in contrast to the quicker flight of birds or the quicker swimming of water creatures? I would like to answer the question in the negative. My hunch is that with πᾶν ἑρπετόν we are not concerned with a bordered region, but rather with the entire region of τὰ πάντα; that is, from a specific aspect that specifies πάντα in entirety as crawling. πᾶν ἑρπετόν must then be read τὰ πάντα ὡς ἑρπετά [everything as crawling]. In that case, Fr. 11 speaks of πάντα in so far as they are crawling. To what extent? What crawls is a conspicuously slow movement, the slowness of which is measured by a quicker movement. Which quicker movement is meant here? If we bring πᾶν ἑρπετόν, or πάντα ὡς ἑρπετά into connection with πληγή, it is the unsurpassably quick movement of the lightning bolt by which the movement of πάντα as crawling must be measured.

HEIDEGGER: If we no longer understand the lightning bolt only phenomenally but in a deeper sense, then we can no longer say of its movement that it is quick or quicker than the movement of πάντα. For "quick" is a speed characteristic that only pertains to the movement of πάντα.

FINK: The talk about "quick" in relation to the lightning bolt is inappropriate. Measured by the quickness of lightning, everything that comes to appearance in the brightness of lightning, and has its passage and change, is crawling. Seen in this way, πᾶν ἑρπετόν is also a statement about τὰ πάντα. Now, howevever, τὰ πάντα are looked back at from lightning. The crawling of πάντα is a trait that we could not immediately attribute to them as a qualitative determination. The manifold movements that πάντα in entirety went through are a lame movement as compared to the movement of the lightning blow that tears open lighted space.

HEIDEGGER: In order to bring to mind again the course of the interpretation of Fr. 11, just now put forward, we ask ourselves how the fragment is, therefore, to be read.

PARTICIPANT: The explication, the purpose of which was to relate πᾶν ἑρπετόν to τὰ πάντα, began not with πᾶν ἑρπετόν, but with πληγῇ and νέμεται.

HEIDEGGER: That means that the saying is to be read backwards. How it is possible that we can read πᾶν ἑρπετόν as πάντα ὡς ἑρπετά, developed out of πληγῇ and νέμεται. From πᾶν ἑρπετόν alone, we cannot learn the extent to which πάντα are also mentioned with πᾶν ἑρπετόν. But by means of πληγῇ and νέμεται, which refers back to the lightning-fragment, it becomes understandable why πᾶν ἑρπετόν must be understood as τὰ πάντα.

PARTICIPANT: I would like to ask a foolish question. Can one really understand πᾶν ἑρπετόν as τὰ πάντα? For only the living being is spoken of in πᾶν ἑρπετόν, but τὰ πάντα also encompasses the inanimate.

HEIDEGGER: The explication of Fr. 11 began with the word πληγῇ that was referred to the lightning bolt that steers τὰ πάντα, as is said in Fr. 64. The explication was directed to ἕν. In starting from ἕν in the specific form of the lightning bolt, it was made clear that and how πᾶν ἑρπετόν is to be comprehended as τὰ πάντα. Your question about the inanimate which would also belong to πάντα is in fact foolish, because a specific domain is therewith marked off in opposition to another domain. The present explication of Fr. 11, however, has shown that with πᾶν ἑρπετόν it is not a matter of a demarcated domain but of something universal.

FINK: We must read πᾶν ἑρπετόν as πάντα ὡς ἑρπετά. Crawling does not mean here a property of specific things, namely living things on the earth. Rather, crawling is a character of πάντα in entirety, which does not reveal itself immediately, but only in relation to the suddenness of the lightning which lets τὰ πάντα appear in its brightness. In comparison to the suddenness of the lightning bolt that tears open light, the movement of πάντα that are gathered in the brightness of lightning is a crawling movement. Between the suddenness of lightning and the crawling of πάντα, there is no relationship as between the extratemporal and the intratemporal. On the other hand, it is also not a matter of the relationship of Achilles and the tortoise. Everything that moves about in lightning's dimension of brightness is driven by the blow. In this being driven, πάντα gain the character of crawling in reference back to lightning. Fr. 11 does not mention a shepherd who, turning out to pasture, distributes and guides. Fr. 11 says nothing of a guider, but mentions πάντα in the character of their being struck and being the subject vis-à-vis the lightning bolt. Fr. 11 does not relate to Fr. 64 as a partial domain to the entirety of πάντα. Much more, it expresses something about the relationship of πάντα to naked power which drives and guides.

HEIDEGGER: Explication of Fr. 11 puts before us the question whether πληγῇ and νέμεται actually allow a reference to the lightning bolt, so that πᾶν ἑρπετόν is to be understood, not regionally as a single area within the entirety of πάντα, but as the entirety of πάντα itself.

FINK: We turn to Fr. 100: ὥρας αἳ πάντα φέρουσι. Diels translates: "the seasons, which bring everything." In the context Ἥλιος is mentioned, which is another name for fire as well as lightning. In this fragment there is a connection between Ἥλιος, light and time. We can ask ourselves whether lightning isn't only a momentary fire in contrast to Ἥλιος, which is a fire of greater constancy, if not everlasting, but beginning to glow faintly and become dim. If, now, Ἥλιος in the sense of the long enduring lightning bolt replaces lightning, then we must not forget that this fire not only illuminates, but also measures the times. Ἥλιος is the clock of the world, the world-clock; not an instrument that indicates times, but that which makes the seasons possible, which brings all. We cannot understand the seasons in the sense of fixed spells of time or as stretches in homogeneous time, but as the times of days and of years. These times of years are not the lingering but the bringing. πάντα are not so gathered that they are contemporaneous, but they are in the manner that they arrange themselves κατ' ἔριν and κατὰ τὸν λόγον. πάντα rise, act, and are steered by the begetting, fulfilling, and producing seasons.

HEIDEGGER: Let us try to clarify the extent to which time is mentioned in Fr. 100. What are seasons? Alongside the three Hesiodic seasons, Εὐνομία, Δίκη, and Εἰρήνη [Good Order, Justice, and Prosperous Peace],[15] there is also θαλλώ, Αὐξώ, and Καρπώ. θαλλώ is the springtime, which brings the shoot and blossom. Αὐξώ means summer, ripening and maturing. Καρπώ means autumn, picking of the ripe fruit. These three seasons are not like three time periods; rather, we must understand them as the whole maturation. If we want to speak of movement, which form of Aristotlian movement would come into question? First of all, what are the four forms of movement with Aristotle?

PARTICIPANT: αὔξησις and φθίσις [growth and wasting away], γένεσις and φθορά [genesis and corruption], φορά and as fourth ἀλλοίωσις [productiveness and alteration].[16]

HEIDEGGER: Which form of movement would be most appropriate to the seasons?

PARTICIPANT: αὔξησις and φθίσις as well as γένεσις and φθορά.

HEIDEGGER: ἀλλοίωσις is contained in these forms of movement. Spring, summer and autumn are not intermittent, but something continual. Their maturation has the character of continuity, in which an ἀλλοίωσις is contained.

FINK: The movement of life in nature is, however, growth as well as withering. The first part is an increasing to ἀκμή [acme], the second part a withering.

HEIDEGGER: Do you understand fruit as being already a stage of decline?

FINK: The life of a living being forms a rising and falling bow. Human life is also a steady but arching movement, in its successively following aging.

HEIDEGGER: Age corresponds to fruit in the sense of ripening, which I understand not as a declining but as a kind of self fulfillment. If time comes into play with the seasons, then we must let go of calculated time. We must attempt to understand from other phenomena what time means here. Also, we may not separate the content of time from the form of time. The character of bringing belongs to time. In our language we also say: time will tell.[17] So long as we understand time as bare succession, bringing has no place.

FINK: In order to win an understanding of the maturation character of the seasons, we must disregard homogenous time, which one represents as a line and as bare succession and in which the time content is abstracted. Such an abstraction is impossible with the seasons.

HEIDEGGER: Fr. 100 places us before different questions. To what extent may one take the seasons together with πάντα? How must time be thought, if one wishes to speak of it here, especially if one says of it that it brings. We must simply get clear to ourselves in what sense time brings.

FINK: In this, it is necessary not to think time as a colorless medium in which things swim about. Rather, we must seek to understand time in reference to the γίγνεσθαι of πάντα.

HEIDEGGER: We must think time together with φύσις.

FINK: Presently, we stand before the question whether Fr. 100 is able to give us still further references to the matter that we attempt to think, or whether it is not more appropriate to revert first to Fr. 94.

HEIDEGGER: The 2500 years that separate us from Heraclitus are a perilous affair. With our explication of Heraclitus' fragments, it requires the most intense self-criticism in order to see something here. On the other hand, it also requires a venture. One must risk something, because otherwise one has nothing in hand. So there is no objection to a speculative interpretation. We must therefore presuppose that we can only have a presentiment of Heraclitus, when we ourselves think. Yet, it is a question whether we still can measure up to this task.

4

Ἥλιος, Daylight—Night, μέτρα-τέρματα
(Correlated Fragments: 94, 120, 99, 3, 6, 57, 106, 123).

FINK: In the last seminar session we have let some questions stand un-mastered. Today we are still not in a position to somehow bring the openness of the explication situation to a decision. After discussion of the Ἥλιος-fragment [sun fragment] we attempt to come back to Frs. 11 and 100 in which πᾶν ἑρπετόν and ὧραι [seasons] are mentioned.

We have seen that ὧραι, the hours and the times, are not to be taken as a stream of time or as a temporal relation that, subjected to metric leveling down, is measurable and calculable. Hours and times are also not to be taken as the empty form in contrast to the content of time, but as filled time which begets and produces each thing in its' own time. ὧραι are no hollow forms, but rather the times of the day and of the season. The times of day and seasons apparently stand in connection with a fire that does not, like lightning, suddenly tear open and place everything in the stamp of the outline, but that holds out like the heavenly fire and, in the duration, travels through the hours of the day and the times of the season. The heavenly fire brings forth growth. It nourishes growth and maintains it. The light-fire of Ἥλιος tears open—different from lightning—continually; it opens the brightness of day in which it allows growth and allows time to each thing. This sun-fire, the heaven-illuminating power of Ἥλιος, does not tarry fixed at one single place, but travels along the vault of heaven; and in this passage on the vault of heaven the sun-fire is light- and life-apportioning and time measuring. The metric of the sun's course mentioned here lies before every calculative metric made by humans.

If we now turn to Fr. 94 in which the talk is explicitly about this heaven-fire, then we remain on the trail of fire, which we have already trod with the Κεραυνός-fragment. Fragment 94 runs as follows: Ἥλιος γὰρ οὐχ ὑπερβήσεται μέτρα· εἰ δὲ μή, Ἐρινύες μιν Δίκης ἐπίκουροι ἐξευρήσουσιν. Diels translates: "(For) Helios will not overstep his measures; otherwise the Erinyes, ministers of Dike, will find him out." If we let this fragment work upon us without particularly thorough preparation, what is expressed in it, supposing that we be permitted to take the sayings of Heraclitus as a model of a thematic statement?

First of all, the word μέτρα [measure] is problematic. Which measure does the sun have or set up? Does the sun itself have measures in which it travels along the vault of heaven? And if the sun sets up measures, which measures are these? Can we determine more closely this distinction between the measures that belong to the sun itself and those that it sets up? First, we can understand μέτρα in reference to the passage and course of the sun. Ἥλιος, as the fire that travels the heaven, has specific measures in its course like the measures of morning light, of midday heat and of subdued twilight. If we look only toward the phenomenon of the sun's course, we see that Ἥλιος exhibits no even, homogeneous radiation, but rather timely differences in the way of being luminous. At the same time, however, by the measures through which the sun passes in its passage, the nourishing fire is apportioned in various ways to the growth of the earth that is found in the sun's brightness. The second meaning of μέτρα lies therein: the measures of light and warmth which the sun apportions to growth. We can on one hand distinguish the measures which are exhibited by the course of the sun itself, and on the other hand those measures which the sun sets up to what it shines on in the way that the sun apportions the fiery to it. μέτρα can thus be understood in a two-fold manner: the μέτρα of the sun's course and the μέτρα that works down from the sun's course to what nourishes itself from the sun's light. However, does the sun also have μέτρα in yet a completely different sense? Is Ἥλιος, which is bound to the measures of its course and which apportions from there the nourishing fire to everything found in the sunlight, is this Ἥλιος squeezed into measures in a completely other sense? Is there perhaps also μέτρα in such a manner that the entire double domain of light is determined by measures? When Heraclitus says, "For Ἥλιος will not overstep his measures," a natural law of Ἥλιος is in no way formulated here. It is not a matter of the insight that the sun's course is subject to any inviolable natural law, for then the second sentence would have no meaning. In this sentence it says that in case Ἥλιος should overstep his measures the Erinyes, helpers of Dike, would track him down and bring him to account. But what is a restriction, a holding to measure of Ἥλιος? Ἥλιος will not overstep his measures. Can we imagine at all that he would be able to overstep his measures? We have brought to mind two ways in which he would not take the correct way across the vault of heaven. One could imagine that he suddenly stops, perhaps at the commend of Joshua for the time in which Joshua waged battle against the Amorites. That would be an overstepping of the μέτρα of his own nature. In such a case he would no longer be in accord with his own nature of fiery power. The sun could change her own essence if she traveled along the vault of heaven in a manner other than in accord with nature. The sun could overstep her measures if she ran from north to south instead of from east to west. However, a completely different manner of overstepping the boundary would be supposed if Ἥλιος were to break into a domain of which we could not speak further at the moment, for this domain lies beyond the brightness of Ἥλιος in which the many are gathered. Then Ἥλιος goes out of the sun's domain in which everything is one in another sense. That would also be a going astray of the sun; now, however, not in the manner of deviation from the sun's path, but in the manner of a breaking into the nightly abyss to which Ἥλιος does not belong.

In order to bring this thought somewhat nearer, let us include fragment 120 in which τέρματα [boundaries] and not μέτρα are mentioned: ἠοῦς καὶ ἑσπέρας τέρματα ἡ ἄρκτος καὶ ἀντίον τῆς ἄρκτου οὖρος αἰθρίου Διός. Diels' translation runs: "The boundaries of morning and evening: The bear and, opposite the bear the boundary stone of radiant Zeus." My question now is whether the domain of the sunny is encircled by the τέρματα (which with τερματίζειν = to confine, to connect), that is, encircled on one hand by morning and evening, and on the other hand by the bear and by the boundary stone of radiant Zeus, which lies opposite the bear. I identify the bear with the North Star so that the boundary stone of radiant Zeus, which lies opposite the bear, would lie in the south of the vault of heaven. Fr. 120 implies then that Ἥλιος, which moves across the vault of heaven from morning to evening, is confined in the possibility of its deviation toward north or south by the bear and the boundary stone of radiant Zeus which lies opposite the bear. Therefore, we must think radiant Zeus together with Ἥλιος as the power of day which illuminates the entirety of τὰ πάντα. This entire domain of the sun is closed in four directions of the heaven, in which case we must understand τέρματα as the outer boarders of the domain of light in distinction from μέτρα in the sense of specific places on the familiar path of the sun.

HEIDEGGER: How do you read the genetive: ἠοῦς καὶ ἑσπέρας? Diels translates, "Boundaries of morning and evening," which is to be understood as, "Boundaries for morning and evening." But do you wish to read, "The boundaries which form morning and evening"?

FINK: I stick with the latter, but I ask myself whether the meaning is fundamentally changed by this difference and also by the manner of reading, "Boundaries for morning and evening." If we understand τέρματα as boundary places, the morning as the east boundary, the evening as the west boundary, the bear as north boundary and the boundary stone opposite the bear as the south boundary, then we have, as it were, the four corners of the world as the field of the sun's realm. Thus seen, τέρματα would not be equated with the two meanings of μέτρα just mentioned. That which Fr. 120 says in reference to τέρματα would be a third meaning of μέτρα that we must include with both of the others in order to take in view the full meaning of μέτρα in Fr. 94. In this case—as a deeper-going explication of this fragment will reveal to us—precisely the third meaning plays a prominent role. The first meaning of μέτρα that we accentuated concerned the places and times through which the sun passes from morning through midday to evening. In a second sense, μέτρα means the measures that are sent from the sun for things. A deviation from the measures that are sent would, for growing and living things, mean that the sun is too hot, too close or too far away. The third meaning of μέτρα, which we have picked up out of Fr. 120, signifies τέρματα in which the sun's entire domain of light is enclosed. Were Ἥλιος to overstep the boundary that is fixed by the four corners of the world, the Erinyes, helpers of Dike, would find Ἥλιος out. Such an overstepping would not only mean a deviation from the familiar path; rather, such an overstepping would mean a breaking into a nightly abyss to which the sun's domain does not belong.

HEIDEGGER: When you grasp ἠοῦς καὶ ἑσπέρας as *genitivus subiectivus* [subjective genitive] then you come into proximity of the third meaning of μέτρα.

FINK: I do not want at first to maintain this as a thesis. Rather, I am only concerned to show three possible meanings of μέτρα, whereby the third signifies that which Fr. 120 says about τέρματα.

HEIDEGGER: In ordinary language use, we distinguish, in reference to μέτρα, between the measure and the measured.

FINK: We can understand measure in a topical and in a chronos-related sense. The first significance of μέτρα means the measures that the sun will not overstep, the measures in the sense of the places and times of its path across the vault of heaven. Measures mean here, however, not natural laws, but they concern rather the φύσις of Ἥλιος. The constancy of the sun in its daily and yearly path derives from its φύσις. Ἥλιος remains held in the measures of its path by its own essence. The second meaning of μέτρα signifies the measures, dependent upon the measures of the sun's path, in reference to the growth in the sun's field. Here a growth and decline is possible, above all when one thinks on the ἐκπύρωσις-teaching, on the overstepping of the sun's measures which consumes everything. If Ἥλιος holds in his natural path, the growth that is illuminated by him has its blossoming and its proper times. The third meaning of μέτρα is to be seen in the confinement of the sun's realm by the four corners of morning, evening, the bear and the boundary stone which lies opposite the bear. Inside this encircled domain, Ἥλιος travels and rules. The jurisdiction of Ἥλιος is closed in by the four τέρματα.

HEIDEGGER: Then we must strike the genitive "of" in Diels' translation. Then one must not translate, "boundaries of morning and evening," but rather, "boundaries which form morning and evening."

PARTICIPANT: In the commentary of the Diels-Kranz edition, it is indicated how the translation is to be understood. There we read, "The interpretation of Kranz, Berl. Sitz. Ber., 1916, 1161, is chosen here: Morning and evening land get separated by the communication line of the North Star with the (daily) culmination point of the sun's path which Helios lmay not overstep (B 94) (~ Ζεὺς αἴθριος [radiant Zeus] compare 22 C 1Z. 4, Pherecydes A 9, Empedocles B 6, 2 et al)."

FINK: But then τέρματα would no longer have the sense of boundaries that form morning and evening. In such a view, morning and evening become almost a determination of a region that seems to me questionable.

PARTICIPANT: The translation is oriented around the idea of Orient and Occident, which get separated by the communication line of the North Star with the daily culmination point of the sun's passage. I myself would not follow this interpretation either, since there was not yet the idea of Orient and Occident in Heraclitus' time. Rather, this idea can be assigned only from Herodotus on.

FINK: The Kranz interpretation does away with the boundary character of morning and evening. If one speaks of the one line between the North Star and the daily culmination point of the sun's passage, then also the plural, τέρματα, is no longer quite understandable. Although the explication given by Kranz is a possible answer to the difficulty that Fr. 120 presents, still it seems to me as if the *lectio difficilior* [more difficult rendition] is thereby precluded.

We have brought to mind the ambiguity of μέτρα of Ἥλιος in reference to Frs. 94 and 120. That has been only an attempt. We must now take into consideration the other sun fragments as well as the fragments concerning day and night.

HEIDEGGER: In talking through the three meanings of the μέτρα of Ἥλιος, you wanted to concentrate on the third meaning that you indicated at the beginning of the discussion of Fr. 120. In Fr. 94, this third meaning is given by the second sentence which is started by εἰ δὲ μή [otherwise], and in which Dike and the Erinyes are mentioned.

FINK: Perhaps Ἥλιος, who apportions everything, is himself confined by another power. The jurisdiction that finds him out in a case of overstepping and brings him to account is Dike with her helpers. Dike is the diety of the just, the diety who watches the boundary between the domain of the sun's brightness and of what is found therein, and the domain of the nightly abyss that is denied to us. The guardians of this boundary are the helpmates of Dike. They watch out that Ἥλιος does not overstep his own domain of power and attempt to break into the dark abyss.

HEIDEGGER: On this third possible meaning of μέτρα you point to Fr. 120 as support.

FINK: If we now go back to the phenomena, we find the strange fact that daylight runs out in boundlessness. We have no boundary to daylight. If we speak of the vault of heaven, we do not mean thereby a dome which closes off; rather we mean the sun's domain of daylight which runs out in endless openness. We also know, however, the phenomenon of locking up of the open heavens, the heaven clouded over. But there is still one other boundary of the light domain, and that is the soil on which we walk. Light, as the element of the fiery, together with the element of the air, lies on the earth and in a certain manner also on the ocean. The ocean also forms a boundary for the realm of light, although the ocean lets in the light up to a certain depth. Its transparency is confined. The opaqueness of the earth, which leads to the boundedness of the open domain of light, is a peculiar phenomenon that is not evident to us for the most part. We find ourselves on the opaque earth, at which the domain of light has its boundary. Over us, however, light's domain of power extends in open endlessness. The opaqueness of the earth has a meaning for the passage of the sun. In accord with the immediate phenomenon, Ἥλιος rises out of the bowels of the earth at morning; in daytime he moves along the vault of heaven and he sinks again into the closed ground of earth at evening. That is said as a description of the immediate phenomena without esoteric symbolism.

Now we turn to Fr. 99, which evidences the general structure: εἰ μὴ ἥλιος ἦν, ἕνεκα τῶν ἄλλων ἄστρων εὐφρόνη ἂν ἦν. Diels translates: "Were there no sun, it would be night in spite of the other stars." Ἥλιος is the star that alone brings full brightness. Now, however, he is not only indicated in his power, in his superiority over the other stars, but the structure, which we do not see in Ἥλιος himself, becomes clear in the other stars. The other stars are lights in the night. We have here the noteworthy feature that luminescence exhausts itself in its radiated light space and is walled in by the dark of night. The other stars are gleaming points in the night heaven. The moon can also illuminate the night in a stronger manner than the stars, but the moon cannot extinguish them as alone Ἥλιος can. We must put the following question concerning the other stars in the night. If Ἥλιος presents himself as a realm of light above the opaque ground, and if he seems to go on in open endlessness, can we not also understand the structure of Ἥλιος and τὰ πάντα in terms of the other stars as lights in the darkness of night? That is, can we understand the whole world of the sun as a light in the night which, it is true, is not certified by the phenomena? We would then have to say that as the stars are a light in the night, and as the sun's domain of light has its boundary at the closedness of earth, so the entire world of Ἥλιος, to which the entirety of πάντα belong, is encircled in a deeper sense by a nightly abyss which confines the domain of power of Ἥλιος. The helpmates of Dike watch from the boundary between the light domain of Ἥλιος and the dark abyss. The sun herself we do not see like one of the stars in the night, but only in her own brightness. Fr. 3 speaks thereof: εὖρος ποδὸς ἀνθρωπείου. As phenomenon, the sun has the width of a human foot.

HEIDEGGER: When you speak of "phenomenon," you mean that which shows itself in its immediacy, and not the "phenomenological."

FINK: Fr. 3 also speaks in the manner of allegory. To begin with it says that only a tiny, insignificant place belongs to the sun as a source of light with its own brightness, so that the opening power of Ἥλιος in the opened light space itself appears to be only a negligible affair. What opens veils itself in a certain manner in what is opened by it, and takes a position below the things encircled by it as the light power. To the extent that the sun appears in the firmament in the width of a human foot, ascends, sinks and disappears, she is new on each day, as Fr. 6 says: νέος ἐφ᾿ ἡμέρη ἐστίν. Heraclitus gives no scientific stipulation that each day the sun arises new. The newness of the sun on each day does not contradict the fact that she is the same sun each day. She is the same, but always new. We must hold on to this thought for the question concerning the sun as a form of πῦρ ἀείζωον, which perpetually is, but—as Fr. 30 says—is kindled and quenched according to measures, wherein the constant newness itself comes to expression. When we come to Fr. 30 the concept of μέτρα will allow itself to be determined more precisely.

From Fr. 6 we turn to Fr. 57: διδάσκαλος δὲ πλείστων Ἡσίοδος· τοῦτον ἐπίστανται πλεῖστα εἰδέναι, ὅστις ἡμέρην καὶ εὐφρόνην οὐκ εγίνωσκεν· ἔστι γὰρ ἕν. Diels' translation runs, "Hesiod is teacher of the many. They are pursuaded by him that he knows most; he, who does not know day and night. Yet, one is!" In what does the supposed wisdom of Hesiod consist? To what extent has he, who has written about days and works, not known day and night? Day and night are alternating conditions of the sun's land in which it is bright and dark in rythmic alteration. The darkness of night in the domain of the sun is something other than the closedness of the soil into which no light is able to penetrate. The dark night is illuminated by the glimmering stars. In contrast to the closedness of the earth, the dark of night has by itself fundamental illuminability. Together with the sun fragments we must think the fragments which treat of day and night. Fr. 57 belongs to these. The most difficult phrase in it is ἔστι γὰρ ἕν [Yet, one is]. If day and night are to be one, then wouldn't the plural εἰσί [are] have to stand in place of the singular ἔστι [is]? Is the indistinguishability of day and night meant here, or else something completely different which does not show itself at first glance. Our question is: does Fr. 57, spoken out of ἕν, contain a statement concerning day and night? Are day and night in ἕν, or are they ἕν? Hesiod has evidently understood most of day and night, and yet he is reproved by Heraclitus because he held day and night to be of different kinds. In Hesiod's *Theogony* the contrast of day and night means something other than merely the contrast of two conditions of transparent space in which light can be present or absent.

Perhaps it is too daring if we think in this connection about the strife of the Olympian gods with the Titans. Here a cleft runs through the entirety that draws together for Heraclitus, if not in the evident, then in the unseen harmony. One can read the ἔστι γὰρ ἕν in this sense. Day and night do not comprise any distinction you please, but rather the original form of all distinctions. The contrast of day and night also plays a role with Parmenides (μορφὰς γὰρ κατέθεντο δύο γνώμας ὀνομάζειν) [For they made up their minds to name two forms],[18] however, in reference to mortals. If one understands ἔστι γὰρ ἕν in the sense that day and night are one in ἕν, then wouldn't the plural εἰσί have to stand in place of ἔστι? Seen grammatically, is a plural possible here at all? For me the question is whether, instead of reading, "day and night are one ἕν or are in ἕν," one must read, "there is ἕν." In this case, vanishing of distinctions would have another sense. Hesiod knew his way around, but he did not know of ἕν, that it is. "For there is ἕν." Thus read, ἕν is not to be comprehended as predicative, but as the subject of the sentence.

HEIDEGGER: Then ἔστι γὰρ ἕν is to be taken absolutely. To think of it differently or to believe that Hesiod did not recognize day and night would be an unreasonable suggestion.

FINK: When Heraclitus says that Hesiod has not recognized day and night, that is an intentionally provocative statement.

HEIDEGGER: One does not need to be Hesiod in order to distinguish day and night. When he treated of day and night he did so in a deeper sense than in the manner of a mere distinction that each of us performs. Thus, Heraclitus cannot have wanted to say that Hesiod has distinguished day and night, but that he has erred since day and night are one. We cannot accept Diels' translation, "Yet, one is!"

FINK: "Yet, one is!" sounds like "They are one of a kind." I am unable to connect any sense with this translation. Day and night are familiar to us as the changing conditions, as the basic rhythm of life, as presence and absence of the sun in her light in the domain of the open. The domain of the open can be daylight or dark night. This distinction is familiar to us in its rhythmic return. In the way that the return is adhered to, Ἥλιος shows adherence to measures that he has and that are protected from outside by Dike. When Heraclitus says that Hesiod misunderstood day and night, he does not thereby wish to maintain that Hesiod has overlooked the fact that day and night form no distinction at all. Rather, Heraclitus wishes to maintain that day and night are one in thinking back to ἕν, and that within ἕν they are set apart as opposite relations, as we can also find in Fr. 67, where it says that god is day night, winter summer, war peace, satiety hunger. Heraclitus is much more concerned here with ἕν in quite another manner.

PARTICIPANT: Musn't we also take Fr. 106, in which μία φύσις ἡμέρας [one nature of day] is mentioned, along with Fr. 57?

HEIDEGGER: How do you wish to bring both fragments into connection?

PARTICIPANT: I would think μία φύσις [one nature] together with ἔστι γὰρ ἕν.

FINK: The μία φύσις of day, however, is held against a positing of good and bad, that is, propitious and unpropitious days. The oneness of the nature of day stands against such distinction of the days. This, however, is not to be equated with the ἔστι γὰρ ἕν in reference to day and night. The distinction of good and bad days does not have the same importance as the distinction of day and night. Accordingly, ἕν is in each case different.

HEIDEGGER: Nevertheless, you are in a certain way right in connecting Frs. 57 and 106. In both fragments the talk is about an ignorance in reference to Hesiod. The one time, he misunderstands ἕν in reference to day and night; the other time, he misunderstands the one and the same φύσις of each day. To this extent, ἕν and μία φύσις do hang together.

FINK: Fr. 106 is, rather, only a parallel to Fr. 57. In the latter, Hesiod is found to be unreliable as the teacher of most people. He, who is versed in the fundamental distinction of day and night, has not observed that there is ἕν.

HEIDEGGER: Most people are, for Heraclitus, they who do not know what matters. The πλεῖστοι [the greatest number] are the same as the πολλοί [the many]. We cannot translate φύσις in Fr. 106 with essence.

FINK: When we say "essence," it is not meant in the sense of *essentia* [substance].

HEIDEGGER: If we include Fr. 123, φύσις κρύπτεσθαι φιλεῖ [Nature loves to hide], how then is φύσις to be understood?

PARTICIPANT: In the sense of emerging.

HEIDEGGER: The connection of φύσις and ἕν will concern us in greater detail later.

FINK: For me, the puzzling word in Fr. 57 is ἔστι γὰρ ἕν. We have translated: For there is ἕν. But what kind of ἕν is treated here? Is it ἕν in the sense of a counterword to τὰ πάντα, and thus the ἕν of lightning, of the blow, of the sun and of fire; or is still another ἕν meant here? My supposition tends to be that it is a question here of ἕν in the sense of the oneness of both domains of Ἥλιος and of night, which is guarded by Dike and her helpmates. This new sense of ἕν will first become clearer for us if we include the life and death fragments. The night meant here is the nightly abyss by which the sun's domain is encircled at the four τέρματα as they are called in Fr. 120. Apart from this interpretation, one could also argue as follows. If ἕν is mentioned in Fr. 57 in reference to day and night, it is then a question of the ἕν of the land of sun in which the sun is present and absent in rhythmic change; and indeed in such a manner that in the change of day and night the domain remains in which the sun is present and absent. There is ἕν in so far as the structure of the vault on which the sun moves remains, and in so far as the relation of opposition to the land that lies under the sun remains, even though the sun temporarily is absent and new on each new day. Thus seen, ἕν would be the vault of heaven. However, this explication is not acceptable to me. I do not understand, "there is ἕν," in this sense.

HEIDEGGER: Why do you reject this interpretation?

FINK: Because for me the union of day and night under the vault of heaven is too easy a reading. When Heraclitus says "there is ἕν" in reference to day and night, the land of sun is meant with the day, and the dark abyss that incloses and encircles the land of sun is meant with night. The sun's domain and the nightly abyss together form ἕν.

HEIDEGGER: Is the ἕν that you now have in view something like an over-being that surpasses even being: I suppose that you want to get out of being with your interpretation of ἕν, which departs from the hitherto existing illuminating ἕν of lightning.

PARTICIPANT: I do not believe that ἕν as the double domain of the land of sun and the nightly abyss surpasses being. If the preceding interpretation has, in starting out from the Κεραυνός-fragment, focused first on the structural moment of the light character in being, the uncovering, then the current interpretation, when the nightly abyss is mentioned, focuses on the structural moment of closedness in being, on the concealment that belongs essentially to uncovering. Therefore, the explication does not surpass being; rather, it goes deeper into being than the preceding awareness, since it takes in view the full dimensionality of being.

FINK: Our explication of Heraclitus began by our illuminating the reference of lightning and τὰ πάντα. Lightning tears open the brightness, lets τὰ πάντα come forth to appearance and arranges each thing in its fixed outline. Another name for ἕν is the sun. The sunlight, which runs out over us in open endlessness, finds a boundary at the closedness of the soil. In his own field of light, Ἥλιος has only the width of a human foot. He moves along in fixed measures on the vault of heaven. By his own measures, growth and living creatures, which are shined upon by Ἥλιος, have their specific measures. Within the realm of the sun there is a general distinction between day and night that is posited with the presence and absence of the sun. The domain that is encircled by the four τέρματα remains even when the sun seems to sink away. The structure of ἕν then shifts over from the temporary presence of the sun to οὐρανός [heaven]. One can then say that the distinction of day and night is not so important to grasp because under οὐρανός day and night alternate and the relation of a vault of heaven to the many thereunder remains. Hesiod had distinguished day and night and thereby not considered that day and night is only one distinction within οὐρανός. This interpretation still does not appeal to me. Precisely when we consult the fragments on death and life, the other dimension of closedness will show itself to us beside the already familiar dimensions of the light character and openness. The ἕν which Heraclitus attempts to think in Fr. 57 is the unity of the double domain.

HEIDEGGER: But how do both domains hang together?

FINK: The light space of lightning or of Ἥλιος, in which πάντα come forth to appearance and move into their outline, is encircled by a dark abyss. Ἥλιος is not permitted to overstep the boundary set to his domain of power and go into the nightly foundation, because he will be brought to account by the Erinyes, who guard the boundary of the double domain.

HEIDEGGER: Is it here a question of two domains or of one and the same which is distinguished in itself? Let us put this question aside for the moment. We will come back to it later. I would like once again to go into ἔστι γὰρ ἕν. Can one place the plural εἰσί here at all? Diels sets a semicolon before ἔστι γὰρ ἕν. Seen purely stylistically, a period and not a semicolon would suitably have to be placed in Heraclitus' language. Perhaps Diels was misled into using the semicolon by the subsequent γὰρ [yet]. A period is therefore called for, because in ἔστι γὰρ ἕν something uncommon follows which must be sharply contrasted with what has preceded.

FINK: Most people are familiar with the distinction of night and day. Hesiod, who treated of day and night, also belongs to them. But he did not understand day and night because he did not know ξυνόν. The ἔστι γὰρ ἕν works like a blow. It is intentionally thematic and is said like a dictate.

HEIDEGGER: Because Hesiod did not know ξυνόν, Heraclitus cannot associate with him. They both speak a different language.

FINK: In ἔστι γὰρ ἕν Heraclitus does not think the vanishing of distinctions, but the ἕν of the double domain. There is ἕν. Here ἕν is the subject of the sentence. One must come into the dimension of ἕν as the double domain in order to go beyond the πολλοί. Heraclitus would not say that Hesiod is a blockhead. When he reproves Hesiod it is only because Hesiod is a speculative blockhead. ἔστι γὰρ ἕν is foundation for οὐκ ἐγίνωσκεν [does not know].

HEIDEGGER: Heraclitus does not name the ground but only says that Hesiod does not know it.

FINK: The ignorance of Hesiod is unmasked by the ἔστι γὰρ ἕν.

PARTICIPANT: It remains a difficulty for me to what extent ἔστι γὰρ ἕν should be illuminating about the ignorance of Hesiod, which shows itself in thinking about day and night. It must therefore be determined by us in which relation ἔστι γὰρ ἕν stands to Hesiod's knowledge of day and night.

FINK: You refer γὰρ too directly to Hesiod's misunderstanding about day and night. Hesiod has interpreted the phenomenon of day and night not just differently from Heraclitus. There is not another view of day and night that replaces Hesiod's differentiation of day and night here. Rather, Heraclitus speaks out of the knowledge of ἕν when he says that the partition of day and night contradicts the fundamental character of being.

HEIDEGGER: Hesiod belongs to the people who are named in Fr. 72: καὶ οἷς καθ' ἡμέραν ἐγκυροῦσι, ταῦτα αὐτοῖς ξένα φαίναται. "And those things with which they jostle every day seem strange to them." Hesoid jostles daily with the distinction of day and night.

FINK: Day and night are for him the most daily and the most nightly . . .

HEIDEGGER: . . . but it remains strange to him in what they actually are, when thought from ἕν.

FINK: If we finally view the Helios and the day/night fragments together, we can say the following. The heaven-fire of the sun behaves similarly toward everything that has continuence by the sun's passage, as the lightning toward πάντα. The sun gives light, outline and growth and brings the time for everything that grows. The sun is determined in her passage by μέτρα, which has to check her, because she is otherwise brought to account by the helpmates of Dike. The sun also determines the μέτρα for the increase and growth of things. She will not overstep the μέτρα but will remain within her domain of power, which is confined by the four τέρματα. The deeper meaning of Dike still remains obscure for the present. Till now, Dike is clear only as a power superior to the power of Ἥλιος. Although Ἥλιος and Zeus are the highest powers on earth, Ἥλιος has a power on the earth that overpowers brightness. The μέτρα of Ἥλιος have been explained to us in a three-fold sense. First we distinguish the μέτρα of the sun's course, second the μέτρα of things under the sun's course and third the μέτρα, which encircle the entire domain of the sun's brightness. Reference to Fr. 3 has shown us the structure of the emplacement of Ἥλιος in the brightness proper to him. Fr. 6 thinks the daily newness and always-the-sameness of the sun together. The one φύσις of day is the same φύσις also with respect to the well known distinction of good and bad, propitious and unpropitious days. We must take all these thought motifs together, without rashly identifying them. Still it becomes constantly more difficult for us to hold in view the manifold of relations. This difficulty already shows itself in reference to the differences of the immediate phenomena we have considered and the paths of thought determined by them.

5

The Problem of a Speculative
Explication.—πῦρ ἀείζωον and
Time? (Fragment 30).

HEIDEGGER: When Professor Fink interpreted πῦρ ἀείζωον, which occurs in Fr. 11, I asked what he was actually doing. I wanted to drive at
the question of how this attempt to think with Heraclitus should be
made. In this connection, there was mention of a speculative leap that
suggested itself in a certain way in so far as we start reading the text from
the immediacy of the expressed content and, in so doing, arrive through
the process of thinking at the expression of something that cannot be
verified by way of immediate intuition. If one thinks schematically, one
can say that we go from a statement according to perception to an unsensuous statement. But what does "speculative" mean?

PARTICIPANT: "Speculative" is a derivative from *speculum* (mirror)
and *speculari* (to look in or by means of the mirror). The speculative,
then, is evidently a relationship of mirroring.

HEIDEGGER: Presumably, the mirror plays a role. But what does the
word "speculative" mean in ordinary terminological use? Where in philosophy is Latin written and spoken?

PARTICIPANT: In the Middle Ages.

HEIDEGGER: There *existimatio speculativa* [speculative judgment] is
mentioned in distinction from *existimatio practica* or also *operativa* [practi-
cal or operative judgment]. *Existimatio speculativa* is synonymous with
existimatio theoretica [theoretical judgment], which is oriented toward the
species [type]. *Species* is the Latin translation of εἶδος [form]. What is
meant here is, therefore, a seeing, a θεωρεῖν that is, a theoretical consid-
ering. Kant also speaks of the speculative in the sense of theoretical
reason. But how does this affair stand with Hegel? What does Hegel call
speculation and dialectic?

PARTICIPANT: The speculative and dialectic designate Hegel's
method of thinking.

PARTICIPANT: With speculation, Hegel attempted to reach beyond
the finite into infinity.

HEIDEGGER: Hegel does not first start out with the finite in order
then to reach infinity; rather, he begins in infinity. He is in infinity from
the start. With my question about the speculative, I only wish to make
clear that the attempt to rethink Heraclitus is not a matter of the speculative in the proper sense of Hegel or in the sense of the theoretical. First
of all, we must renounce talking in any manner about the method ac-

cording to which Heraclitus would think. On the one hand, we must see to it—as Professor Fink has done up to this point—that we make clarifications with the intention of helping the participants follow more clearly and precisely the steps that we have made thus far while reading and thinking the text and that we will make later on. We can clarify the problem which stands behind that when Professor Fink gives us an example.

FINK: The manner of our reading and procedure is characterized in that we start out from what is made present to us of the matter named in Heraclitus' sayings, as though this matter were lying immediately before our eyes. In his fragments, Heraclitus does not speak in any veiled manner like the god in Delphi, of whom Heraclitus says: οὔτε λέγει οὔτε κρύπτει ἀλλὰ σημαίνει.[19] His manner of speaking cannot be equated with that of the god in Delphi. In reading the fragments, we first pick up the phenomenal findings and attempt their clarification. We do not, however, make the phenomenal findings clear in their full extent; rather, our clarification is already selectively steered.

HEIDEGGER: By what is it selectively determined?

FINK: The selection is determined in that we always come back from Heraclitus' saying and seek each feature in the immediate phenomena that are mentioned in the fragment. An empirical phenomenology of the sun would yield an abundance of phenomenal features which would not be meaningful at all for the sense of the sun fragments. First we read the fragment with a certain naïveté. We attempt to bring into relief a few features in reference to the things which are correlates of our sensuous perceptions in order, in a second step toward the features and references thus extracted, to ask how they can be thought in a deeper sense. From immediate seeing of sensuous phenomena, we go over to an unsensuous, though not transcendent, domain. Here, we may not utilize the scheme, which we find in metaphysics, of phenomenal, i.e., sensible, and intelligible world, and operate with a two-world doctrine of metaphysics. Talk about a sensible and intelligible domain is highly dangerous and doubtful.

HEIDEGGER: It would be more appropriate if we designate the phenomenal domain as ontic . . .

FINK: . . . and the unsensuous domain as allied with being. What is remarkable, however, is that we can comprehend the fragments of Heraclitus in a naïve manner also, and then still connect a deep sense [einen tiefen Sinn] with them, so that we cannot even call the genuine philosophical sense a deep sense [Tiefsinn].

HEIDEGGER: Can one speak of a philosophical sense at all?

FINK: Certainly we may not speak of a conceptual meaning of Heraclitus' sayings. Since we have the language of metaphysics behind us, we must attempt to avoid being misled by the developed thought paths of metaphysics. In order to indicate the manner of our procedure, let us go once again into Fr. 11. Translated, it runs: Everything that crawls is driven to pasture or tended with the blow. An image is mentioned there that we know from the phenomenal environment and that we can easily bring to mind. In a rural region or in an agrarian state, the beast is driven to pasture with the whip blow. We can then read πᾶν ἑρπετόν as pasture animals. The image that Heraclitus mentions implies that the pasture animals will be driven to pasture by the shepard with the whip blow, indeed so that they change pasture ground from time to time.

HEIDEGGER: Tending is a driving as well as a leading.

FINK: For our explication of νέμεται, driving and leading are the meaningful moments of sense. Now, when we also hear Νέμεσις in νέμεται as the power that allots and fatefully determines, then we have left the immediate phenomenon of tending and entered thoughtfully upon the unsensuous domain. We understand νέμεται no more as the driving and leading of the shepard in the sense of alloting and dispensing of what is appropriate to actual pasture animals, but as an alloting and dispensing reign. Then the question suggests itself whether that which is said in small scale in the fragment cannot also be said in large scale. The microcosmic and macrocosmic relationship suggests itself as perhaps a most harmless expression. The thoughtful transposition of phenomenal structures into another dimension, however, brings with it a transformation of the structures from which we first start out.

HEIDEGGER: Yet, the thoughtful transposition implies a specific kind of thinking about the appearance of which we are still ignorant.

FINK: When I speak of thoughtful transposition into another dimension, that is only a first attempt to circumscribe the manner of our procedure, because we still do not know what it means to go over into another dimension. If we wish to speak of an analogy in this connection, then we must think it in a specific way. In this analogy, only one side is given to us, namely the phenomenal one. As we hold selectively to specific phenomenal structures, we translate them into large scale in an adventurous attempt. In Fr. 11, we translate the way and manner in which a herd is lead to pasture into the large scale of the entire actuality in which a tending and alloting reign of things and elements happens. The enlargement of a special individual phenomenon into the whole would perhaps be a form under which we could speak of the way of our attempt to think with Heraclitus.

HEIDEGGER: I regard this formulation of your procedure as dangerous. Perhaps we can say that Heraclitus does not see the large scale from the small but, the other way round, sees the small scale from the large. We must distinguish on one hand our attempt to rethink the fragments of Heraclitus and on the other hand the way that Heraclitus himself has thought.

FINK: What Heraclitus thinks in large scale, he can only say in small scale.

HEIDEGGER: Thinking and saying have their special difficulties. Is it a question of two different matters? Is saying only the expression of thinking?

FINK: The distinction between inner thinking and the articulation of thinking in language is an idea that we have from the history of philosophy. There is the view that philosophical thinking cannot say completely everything that it thinks; so that, in a certain way, what philosophy thinks remains behind the linguistic expression. The deepest thoughts are then ἄρρητον [unspeakable]. This model does not apply to Heraclitus. His sayings are no hierophantic, withholding speech about the linguistically inscrutable mystery. Heraclitus does not know the opposition of the linguistically open and the impenetrable mystery that gets thought as *refugium* or *asylum ignorantiae* [refuge or asylum of ignorance]. It is something else when we think the mystery in a completely different manner. Heraclitus speaks in a language which does not know the stark difference between inner thinking and outward saying.

HEIDEGGER: But how about thinking and saying? We will also have to say for Heraclitus that there is a saying to which the unsaid belongs, but not the unsayable. The unsaid, however, is no lack and no barrier for saying.

FINK: With Heraclitus we must always have in view the multidimensionality of speaking that we cannot fix at one dimension. Seen from the immediate statement, only the pasture animals in their manner of movement are named in πᾶν ἑρπετόν. But now we have attempted to read and interpret πᾶν ἑρπετόν as πάντα ὡς ἑρπετά, and we have referred πληγή to the lightning bolt. In this consists our jump-off into the nonphenomenal domain. Measured by the tremendously sudden movement, everything that stands under the lightning in its light-shine and is brought into its stamp has the character of an animallike, i.e., slow movement. It is to be asked, however, whether it is a matter of two levels, so that we can say: as in the sensory domain the animal herd is put to pasture by the whip blow, so in the whole all things are steered by lightning. I would like to think that we may not set both these levels off so sharply in contrast from each other. If we speak of two levels, then there is the danger that we make comparisons from the phenomenal level and begin to move into unrestricted analogies. If we suppose the two levels to be sharply distinguished, then we miss precisely their interplay. Heraclitus knows no fixed levels; but we must precisely notice, with interpretation of his fragments, that and how they interplay. The force of his sayings consists in the fact that working from the large scale, Heraclitus can also say something in reference to the everyday.

HEIDEGGER: Perhaps you have already said too much.

FINK: Our starting point, however, in explicating the fragments, consists in the more or less known traits of the phenomena. I want to attempt to clarify still another fragment which has already concerned us. Fr. 99 reads in translation, "If the sun were not, it would be night on account of the other stars." Here is pronounced not only a eulogy of the power, of the strength of Ἥλιος which drives out darkness, but we see in the other stars the possibility of being lights in the darkness. Light shines in the darkness. That means that the circuit of lights is surrounded by the night. The stars and the moon indicate the possibility of the lights being imbedded in the dark of night. Here lies the jump-off for our question. Could it not be that as the stars are imbedded in the night, the open-endless domain of the sun is also imbedded in a nonphenomenal night?

HEIDEGGER: When you speak of "endless," that is no Greek idea.

FINK: With the expression "open-endless" I mean only the phenomenal feature that we see no wall when looking up, but rather only the character of running out and of not arriving. The phenomenal state of affairs addressed in Fr. 99, that lights can be imbedded in the dark of night, has put before us the question whether or not the sun's domain, and thus Ἥλιος in his reference to τὰ πάντα, can have μέτρα on his part which we cannot immediately see. In jumping-off from the phenomenal imbeddedness of the stars in the night, we have attempted to take in view the nonphenomenal encirclement of the sun's domain by a nonphenomenal night. We have attempted to clarify what the μέτρα of the sun pertain to in three ways: first, as the μέτρα of the sun in her course; second, as the μέτρα which are apportioned by the sun to everything lying under her; and finally, as the μέτρα in the sense of the τέρματα named in Fr. 120, which encircle the sun's domain, the domain of the sun's brightness and the πάντα found in it.

HEIDEGGER: In this connection, you have spoken of the night. But how do you understand the night?

FINK: The four τέρματα confine the sunny world at its four ends. This encircled domain is characterized by the temporary presence and absence of the sun, from which the problem of day and night arises. As seen from the phenomenon itself, we are all of Hesiod's opinion. Immediate seeing indicates that day and night alternate. Against this, Heraclitus formulates the provocative sentence and says: although Hesiod appears to understand most about human works and days, he has not understood that day and night are one. For our part, we have asked whether this being one is to be read directly as it is said, or whether we must avail ourselves of a more difficult rendition. In the latter case we must say: Hesiod had held day and night distinguished; however, there is ἕν. So understood, day and night do not coincide; but from knowledge of ἕν even the most conspicuous distinction between day and night cannot in the end be accepted as such. There is the one, and if there is success in coming into knowledge of the one (ὁμολογεῖν), then that which is torn asunder in opposition is suffused by the single unity of ἕν. So far as Heraclitus thinks from out of ἕν, he cannot allow the demarcation made between day and night by the most knowledgeable teacher.

HEIDEGGER: You thus distinguish a manifold essence of night. On one hand, you distinguish the night from the daily day, and then you understand night also as the closedness of earth, . . .

FINK: . . . whereby the closedness of earth is the boundary of the sun's domain. The realm of the sun in her reference to τὰ πάντα is the domain of openness in which day and night are in exchange, . . .

HEIDEGGER: . . . and day and night in their exchange are still in another night?

FINK: Perhaps.

HEIDEGGER: With my questions, I would only like to get at the place from which you speak of another night.

FINK: If I have spoken of another, more original night, of the nightly abyss in explication of the sun fragment, I did so in preview of the death-life fragments. From there I have viewed the deeper sense of the phenomenon of closedness of the earth and in a certain way also of the sea as the boundary of the sun's domain. Only when we first consider the relation of life and death will we see how the realm of life is the sun's domain and how a new dimension breaks open with the reference to death. The new dimension is neither the domain of openness nor only the closedness of the earth, although the earth is an excellent symbol for the dimension of the more original night. Hegel speaks of the earth as the elementary *individuum* into which the dead return. The dimension of the more original night is denoted by death. That dimension, however, is the realm of death, which is no land and has no extension, the no-man's-land, . . .

HEIDEGGER: . . . that cannot be traversed and that also is no dimension. The difficulty lies in addressing the domain denoted by death.

FINK: Perhaps language in its articulation is at home in the domain that is itself articulated, in the domain of the sun, in which one thing is separated from the other and set into relief against the other, and in which the individual has specific outline. If now, however, we understand ἕν not only in the sense of the dimension of openness, of the brightness of lightning and the πάντα found in it, but also as the more original night, as the mountain range of being [*das Gebirg des Seins*] which is no countryside, which has no name and is unspeakable—although not in the sense of a limit of language—then we must also take in view a second dimension in ἕν, alongside the dimension of the sun's domain. The dimension of brightness is imbedded in this second dimension, and death points to it. Still, that at which death points is a domain that nobody can find in life-time. The more fragments we read, the more the question marks accumulate for us.

HEIDEGGER: In connection with what has been said concerning language, I would like to refer to the lecture "*Sprache als Rythmus*" ["Language as Rhythm] by Thrasybulos Georgiades, delivered in the lecture series "*Die Sprache*" ["Language"] of the Bavarian Academy of Fine Arts and the Berlin Academy of Arts, as well as in his book *Musik und Rythmus bei den Griechen.*[20] In both works, he has spoken excellently about langauge. Among other things, he asks about rhythm, and shows that ῥυσμός has nothing to do with ῥέω (flow), but is to be understood as imprint. In recourse to Werner Jaeger, he appeals to a verse of Archilochos, Fr. 67a, where ῥυσμός has this meaning. The verse reads: γίγνωσκε δ᾽ οἷος ῥυσμὸς ἀνθρώπους ἔχει. "Recognize which rhythm holds men." Moreover, he cites a passage from Aeschylus' *Prometheus,* to which Jaeger likewise has referred and in which the ῥυσμός or ῥυθμίζω [bring into a measure of time or proportion] has the same meaning as in the Archilochos fragment: ὧδ᾽ ἐρρύθμισμαι (*Prometheus* 241). Here Prometheus says of himself, "... in this rhythm I am bound." He, who is held immobile in the iron chains of his confinement, is "rhythmed," that is, joined. Georgiades points out that humans do not make rhythm; rather, for the Greeks, the ῥυθμός [measure] is the substrate of language, namely the language that approaches us. Georgiades understands the archaic language in this way. We must also have the old language of the fifth century in view in order to approximate understanding of Heraclitus. This language knows no sentences...

FINK: ... that have a specific meaning.

HEIDEGGER: In the sentences of the archaic language, the state of affairs speaks, not the conceptual meaning.

FINK: We have begun our explication of Heraclitus with the lightning fragment. We have turned then to Fr. 11, in which it is said that everything which crawls is tended by the blow, whereby we brought the blow into connection with the lightning bolt. Finally, we have taken the sun and the day-night fragments into view. Here it was above all the three-fold sense of μέτρα, the reference of sun and time and the imbeddedness of the sun's domain in an original night. The boundaries between the sun's domain and the nightly abyss are the four τέρματα. In the sun we have seen a time-determining power which proportions the measures of time. The next fragment in our series is Fr. 30. κόσμον τόνδε, τὸν αὐτὸν ἁπάντων, οὔτε τις θεῶν οὔτε ἀνθρώπων ἐποίησεν, ἀλλ᾽ ἦν ἀεὶ καὶ ἔστιν καὶ ἔσται πῦρ ἀείζωον, ἁπτόμενον μέτρα καὶ ἀποσβεννύμενον μέτρα. Diels translates, "This world order, the same for all beings, was created neither by gods nor by humans; rather, it was always and is and will be eternal living fire kindled in measures and quenched in measures." At first we interpret only the second half of the fragment. Lightning, we could say, is the sudden fire, the sun is the fire in orderly passage of the course of time, but πῦϱ ἀείζωον [eternal living fire] is something that we do not find in the phenomenon like the lightning and the sun.

HEIDEGGER: How do you wish to translate κόσμος?

FINK: I would like to pass over the first half of Fr. 30 and attempt to interpret only the second half. If we translate κόσμος with world order or ornament, then we must bring that translation into connection with Fr. 124, where the talk is of the most beautiful κόσμος as a junk heap. When we now attempt to read and interpret Fr. 30 from the end, we must also return to naivete. A phenomenal fire continues in burning. The conflagration of fire is a process in time. The fire was yesterday, is today and will be tomorrow. Now, however, my question is: are ἦν ἀεί [was always], ἔστιν [is], and ἔσται [will be], in reference to πῦϱ ἀείζωον, determinations of the ways of fire's being-in-time? Is the ἀείζωον [eternal living] of fire thought by always-having-been, being-now, and coming-to-be? But must we think the fire in terms of the familiar way that we specify duration, with only the difference that the usual fire that is ignited lasts a while and goes out again and thus has not always been, is not always, and will not always be? How is ἀείζωον to be understood? Does it mean the perdurance of fire through the whole time? Do we not then think the fire named here by Heraclitus too naïvely, if we suppose that its distinct character would be that it always was, is present and will always be? I would rather suppose that we must think the other way around. The fire is not always past, present, and coming; rather, it is fire that first tears open having-been, being-now, and coming-to-be.

HEIDEGGER: But what is the subject of the second half of the sentence on your interpretation? For Diels it is κόσμος, of which he says that it has been brought forth neither by gods nor humans. Rather κόσμος always was, is, and will be eternal living fire.

FINK: I reject this translation. I understand πῦϱ [fire] as the subject of the second half of the sentence.

HEIDEGGER: Do you make a break before ἀλλ' [rather], so that the following has nothing to do with the preceding?

FINK: The κόσμος as the beautiful joining of πάντα is that which shines in fire. To this extent the first and second halves of the sentence have much to do with one another. The fire is the productive power of bringing-forth. Gods and humans shine up and are brought to unconcealed being only because there is fire to which they stand in a preeminent relation.

HEIDEGGER: Then we must also put "the eternal living fire" as the subject of the second half of the sentence instead of Diels' translation "she" (i.e., the world order).

FINK: When Heraclitus now says of eternal living fire that it is kindled after measures and quenched after measures, that appears to contradict the ἀεί [eternal], and sounds like a shocking specification to us.

HEIDEGGER: Let us at first leave this question out of account. In order to stay with what you have first said: do you reject saying that the world order is the fire?

FINK: The world order is no work of gods and humans, but the work of the eternal living fire. It is not, however, the work of the fire that always was and is and will be, because the eternal living fire first tears open the three time dimensions of having-been, being-now, and coming-to-be. Heraclitus speaks in Fr. 30 first in a denial: the κόσμος is not brought forth (Diels' translation, "created," is out of place) by one of the gods or one of the humans. We can also say: the κόσμος is not brought forth to appearance by one of the gods or by a human. Therein, we already hear the fiery character of fire. The κόσμος as the beautiful joining of πάντα comes forth to appearance in the shine of fire. That the κόσμος as the beautiful jointed order is not brought forth to appearance by one of the gods or by a human, is first only to be understood in the sense that gods and humans have a share in the power of fire among all the beings of the κόσμος; and they are productive. Gods and humans are productive, however, not in the manner of the most original ποίησις [production], which produces the πῦρ ἀείζωον. In the explication of Fr. 30, however, I wish first to question whether time characteristics are asserted in the term πῦρ ἀείζωον. The πῦρ ἀείζωον is neither like a process within time, nor is it comparable with what Kant calls the world stuff as the basis of the constantly extant time. The fire mentioned by Heraclitus is not in time, but is itself the time-allowing time that first and foremost lets ἦν [was], ἔστι [is] and ἔσται [will be] break out; it does not stand under these. If we tentatively take πῦρ ἀείζωον as the time-allowing, time-opening, then ἀεί stands in a taut relationship to ἦν, ἔστι, and ἔσται, and furthermore to what the concluding phrase of Fr. 30 concerns, in a taut relationship to the kindling after measures and quenching after measures.

HEIDEGGER: For me the central question now is where you start out. Do you start out from ἦν, ἔστι, and ἔσται or rather from πῦρ ἀείζωον?

FINK: I start out with πῦρ ἀείζωον and go from it to ἦν, ἔστι, and ἔσται. If one reads word for word, the three-fold of time is said from ἀείζωον.

HEIDEGGER: In other words, it is said out of what is perpetually, that it was, is, and will be.

FINK: This thought is hard to carry through. So long as we read the fragment naïvely, we must say that the talk is of an eternal living fire that always was and is and will be.

HEIDEGGER: The ἦν and ἔσται have no sense in reference to ἀείζωον.

FINK: The ἦν means what is gone; the ἔσται means being not yet. It is not fire that is past and will be; rather, fire first and foremost opens the way for arising in time, tarrying in time, and going under in time. Fire as the time-allowing time first and foremost breaks open the three time ecstacies of past, present, and future.

HEIDEGGER: There is the possibility for passing, so that it itself cannot always have been. But when you speak of time-allowing, in what sense do you mean that?

FINK: In the sense of apportioning of time.

HEIDEGGER: You understand the allowing as apportioning. But how is time meant in the time-allowing?

FINK: We must distinguish time-allowing and the apportioned time that things have in such a way that they have already been for a while, are present, and will also be yet a while. This manner of being-in-time belongs only to things; it does not, however, belong to the eternal living fire which first lets the three time ecstasies break out. πῦρ ἀείζωον is the tearing open of having-been, being-now and coming-to-be. That which stands in the shine of fire receives the time apportioned to its tarrying from this original opening of time. The fire sets measures. The hardness of the problem would disappear if one supposed that πῦρ ἀείζωον were determined by the temporal evidence of being-in-time. The question, however, is whether it is meant that the fire always was and is and will be, or whether a productive relation is to be thought between the fire and ἦν, ἔστι, and ἔσται.

HEIDEGGER: When you speak of the time-allowing of πῦρ ἀείζωον, don't you mean that in the ordinary sense, as we sometimes say, "someone allows another time"?

FINK: The time that the fire allows, by apportioning time to things, is no empty time form, no medium separated from content, but is, so to speak, time with its content.

HEIDEGGER: Of the time thus given, one must say: it tarries. It is not a depository in which things appear as dispensed; rather, time as apportioned is already referred to that which tarries.

FINK: To what is individual.

HEIDEGGER: Let us leave aside what is individual. But do you wish to say that we go beyond the ordinary comprehension of time with your interpretation of time and of time-allowing?

FINK: I proceed first from the strangeness that πῦρ ἀείζωον in Fr. 30 is mentioned as a process in time, while it is precisely not in time;

rather, it is the time-forming in the sense of the apportioning of time for all that is in time. We have previously thought this apportioning of time in the driving lightningbolt and in the fire of Ἥλιος. We may not determine the time of fire, which forms the times for τὰ πάντα, in a captious reference from concepts of being-in-time back to the most original time. The easy version runs: Fire was always and is and will be. Comprehended thus, fire is something standing, extant and merely lying there, which subsists through the course of time. This remaining is characterized by the temporal dimensions of having-been, being-now and coming-to-be. But then one already has time, and one brings temporal concepts to bear on the time-forming fire. The more difficult version, on the contrary, runs: That the ἦν, ἔστι, and ἔσται first arise from the time-allowing of fire.

HEIDEGGER: Fire is, thereby, not only as glow, but as light and warmth. . .

FINK: . . . and is, therefore, to be understood as the nourishing.

HEIDEGGER: Above all, the moment of shining is important to πῦρ ἀείζωον.

FINK: The fire is that which brings-forth-to-appearance.

HEIDEGGER: If we understand fire only as a flash in the pan, it would yield no shining.

FINK: From out of shining we must think back to κόσμος. It is what shines up in the shine of fire. First we must ask ourselves how, by way of the innertemporal characteristic of πῦρ ἀείζωον, can πῦρ ἀείζωον be referred to as that which first of all releases past, present, and future from out of itself?

HEIDEGGER: You speak of releasing. How is this usage to be understood more closely? Nature is also released with Hegel. How does πῦρ ἀείζωον release past, present, and future? For me the question is whether that which subsequently comes in any way supports your interpretation, or whether that which comes makes your interpretation possible.

FINK: What troubles me is the taut relationship between ἀείζωον and ἦν, ἔστι, and ἔσται. The ἀεί of πῦρ and the three time determinations don't appear to me to go together so easily. What has been, is, and comes to be do not refer to fire. Rather, we must understand the springing up of having-been, being-now, and coming-to-be for τὰ πάντα from out of fire.

HEIDEGGER: I would like to have a clue for this step of your interpretation. So long as I do not see this clue, one could say that the step from παν ἑρπετόν to πάντα ὡς ἑρπετά and from the night, which surrounds the stars and moon, to a more original night, which confines the domain of the sun, is indeed to be carried through. It is to be carried through because a clue is given, however, that the step from πῦρ ἀείζωον and the three time determinations toward the time forming of πῦϱ ἀείζωον, in the sense of the letting spring up of having-been, being-present, and coming-to-be, has no clue, and cannot, therefore, be rightly carried through.

FINK: For me the clue is this, that it is impossible to talk of πῦϱ ἀείζωον as within time. Otherwise, it becomes a thing that happens in the world, perhaps also the highest thing, the *summum ens,* which, however, is an *ens* in the midst of things. Seen thus, it would be subordinate to time. My question is, however, whether the determinations of being-in-time are not subordinated to πῦϱ ἀείζωον.

HEIDEGGER: So far as I can see, there is only this clue, that πῦϱ ἀείζωον is no thing and that, therefore, no "was," "is" and "will be" can be predicated of it, . . .

FINK: . . . and also no perpetuity in the ordinary sense.

HEIDEGGER: We stand before the question of how πῦϱ ἀείζωον relates itself to time. One does not get further. In the summer semester of 1923 in Marburg, while working out *Being and Time,* I held a lecture on the history of the concept of time. As I investigated the archaic idea of time with Pindar and Sophocles, it was striking that nowhere is time spoken of in the sense of the sequence. Rather, time is there taken in view as that which first grants the sequence—similarly as in the last paragraphs of *Being and Time,* although the problem is there viewed from Dasein.——I look at my watch and find that it is three minutes before 7 P.M. Where is the time there? Try to find it.

6

πῦϱ and πάντα (Correlated
Fragments: 30, 124, 66, 76, 31).

The seminar began with the report of one of the participants on Hermann Fränkel, *"Die Zeitauffassung in der Frühgriechischen Literatur,"* printed in *Wege und Formen frühgriechischen Denkens,* 1960.[21]

FINK: In her report, she has shown that in Homer χϱόνος [time] means the long, lingering time, the endurance of time understood in awaiting, or rather the time that still remains for mortals who suffer long. Both are specific forms of time.

HEIDEGGER: It is important for us that there is no theoretical conceptual determination of time as time with Homer and Hesiod. Rather, both speak of time only out of experience.

FINK: Professor Heidegger's question started out from Fränkel's expression of day as a unity of encounter, i.e., from the idea of a manner of givenness according to the encounter. The question was whether time refers to an encountering subject, or is rather to be understood as concrete time in the sense of the different ways that we are in time, excepting that we encounter time. It is dangerous if we speak about the encounter of time, because it is then referred to consciousness. Then we move into the distinction of the time of consciousness, in which we live, and objective time, which is separated from subjectively encountered time. The question was what specific time is; whether the specificity of time is to be grasped from its encountered character or from another approach, which lies outside the distinction of subjective and objective time.

HEIDEGGER: I object to the expression "unity of encounter." When it was said by one of the participants that Homer presents a specific idea of time, and that this specificity rests in the encounter of long tarrying and waiting, this is correct. I object only to the formulation. For the Greeks did not "encounter." Let us break off discussion connected with the report, because we lose too much time otherwise. But what does it mean when we say that we lose time? On what presupposition can we lose time at all?

PARTICIPANT: Only when time is limited to us can we lose time.

HEIDEGGER: Being limited is not decisive. Rather, in order to lose something, we must have it. I can only lose time, if I have time. If I say that I have no time, how is time then characterized?

PARTICIPANT: I presuppose that time is available to me.

HEIDEGGER: Regarding time, that means that it is characterized as time for . . . .

PARTICIPANT: As time for this, time is not the time for something else. For it is time to do this rather than something else.

HEIDEGGER: Time, as "not the time," is the privative characterization of time. The one character of time that we have emphasized is time as time for.... Another character of time to which I would like to refer shows itself when I look at the clock and say that it is 5:45 P.M. Now I ask, where is time?

PARTICIPANT: Therewith, time shows itself as clock-time or measured time.

HEIDEGGER: When I look at the clock and say that it is 5:45 P.M., and ask where time is, does this question make sense at all?

PARTICIPANT: It is a problem whether one can ask where time is.

HEIDEGGER: Hence, I ask you, can one ask at all where time is?

PARTICIPANT: In 1962, in your lecture "*Zeit und Sein,*" you have said that time is prespatial.[22] Accordingly, that would mean that one cannot ask where time is.

HEIDEGGER: On the other hand, we read off the time from the clock. I look at the clock and read that it is 5:45 P.M. Clearly something doesn't make sense here. With Hegel, we must write it on a sheet of paper. But how? We must write that now it is 5:45 P.M. In the now, we thus have time. I do mean time with the now. We will come back to this question when we enter into Fr. 30 and observe the difficulty that lies in the saying of ἦν, ἔστιν, and ἔσται in reference to πῦρ ἀείζωον. It seems to me that here would be the place to consider whether time is mentioned at all in Fr. 30.

FINK: Yet Heraclitus speaks of ἀεί ἦν, ἔστι, and ἔσται.

HEIDEGGER: If we say that Fr. 30 speaks of time, do we go beyond the text?

FINK: But still, Heraclitus clearly used time determinations.

HEIDEGGER: That means, therefore, that he did not speak thematically about time. This observation is important in order to follow up the step that you pursue in your interpretation of Fr. 30, the step in which you determine the relationship of πῦρ ἀείζωον and κόσμος. We can read the fragment also trivially, if we say that ἦν, ἔστι and ἔσται are the anticipatory interpretation of ἀείζωον. In this case, what would ἀεί mean?

PARTICIPANT: The ἀεί would be understood as a connection of εἶναι [to be], ἔσεσθαι [about to be], and γενέσθαι [to have been].

HEIDEGGER: What kind of a connection is that? If we read Fr. 30 almost trivially and understand ἦν, ἔστι, and ἔσται as anticipatory interpretation of ἀεί, what does it then mean? Is time presupposed in "always"?

PARTICIPANT: The "always" can be an innertemporal determination.

HEIDEGGER: The "always" is then understood as "at all times," "permanent." In Latin one speaks of the *sempiternitas* [always-eternity]. That we do not really make progress here is based on the fact that in the fragment time is not spoken about thematically; nevertheless, the interpretation attempts to take time into view in a decisive sense. Only thus, I believe, can we make clear to ourselves the way of your interpretation. While, according to the trivial rendition, the first half of the sentence says that the κόσμος is brought forth neither by one of the gods nor by a human, and the second half, which begins with ἀλλά, says that the κόσμος always was, is, and will be eternal-living fire, according to your interpretation the subject of the second half of the sentence is not κόσμος but πῦρ.

FINK: According to the smoother version, as Diels proposes, fire is a predicative determination of κόσμος. Yet the antecedent phrase should already draw attention. If we translate, "this κόσμος is brought forth to appearance neither by one of the gods nor by a human," then κόσμος—although spoken negatively—moves into view as something brought forth. Thereby, the connection to fire as that which brings forth is already given. We do not understand fire as a predicative determination of κόσμος; rather, we understand κόσμος from out of fire as the beautiful joining of τὰ πάντα which is brought forth to appearance neither by one of the gods nor by a human. There was always and is and will be eternal-living fire in the light-shine of which the beautiful joining of τὰ πάντα shines up. "It always was and is and will be" we must understand in the sense of "there is." Thus seen, κόσμος is comprehended from out of fire, and not fire from out of κόσμος. This rendition would fit in with the trail in which we have interpreted the connection of lightning and sun to τὰ πάντα up to now. The reference of πῦρ and κόσμος would be a special relationship of ἕν and πάντα, according to which τὰ πάντα stand in the light-shine of fire. The smoother rendition has the advantage that the subject remains the same in both halves of the sentence. Thus, fire becomes a determination of κόσμος instead of, the other way around, κόσμος being brought forth to appearance in the shine of fire. Only if the subject in the second half of the sentence is not κόσμος, is there a superiority of fire vis-à-vis κόσμος. Here we could also point to Fr. 124: ὥσπερ σάρμα εἰκῆ κεχυμένων ὁ κάλλιστος (ὁ) κόσμος. Diels translates: "(Like) a heap of things (?) scattered at random, the most beautiful (world) order." Here the most beautiful world order is said to be like a junk heap.

HEIDEGGER: One could translate κάλλιστος κόσμος: the κόσμος as it can only be in general.

FINK: The most beautiful κόσμος, the most beautiful ordered entirety of all πάντα, comes forth to appearance in the shine of fire. If this κόσμος is like a junk heap, we have a hard contrast between κάλλιστος,

which is referred to κόσμος, and the derogatory manner of talking about
σάρμα. To what extent can the most beautiful κοσμος be compared to a
heap of scattered things? To the extent that we compare it with the πῦρ
that brings forth. Compared with the fire that brings forth to appearance, the most beautiful κόσμος seems like a heap of scattered things. If
we read Fr. 124 in this way, it can support our interpretation of Fr. 30,
which depends on the superiority of fire vis-à-vis the κόσμος.

HEIDEGGER: It is difficult for me to comprehend that the most
beautiful κόσμος stands in need of yet another determination.

FINK: I understand the fragment such that the most beautiful
κόσμος receives the negative character of a heap of scattered things in
reference to the ἕν of πῦρ.

HEIDEGGER: Thus, the question is whether Fr. 124 can be used as
support for the explication of Fr. 30.

FINK: The κάλλιστος κόσμος can be characterized as a confused
heap not only in reference to the ἕν of πῦρ, but also in reference to the
other ἕν, which first comes to view with the dimension of death.

HEIDEGGER: Above all, I am concerned to make clear to the participants the manner in which you proceed. You set yourself off from the
more naïve, smoother version and prefer the more difficult version. If
we read Fr. 30 smoothly, then it concerns a statement about the κόσμος
that is brought forth neither by one of the gods nor by a human, but that
always was, is, and will be eternal-living fire. Then the κόσμος is something that is. This statement is then, as you wish to say, completely
unphilosophical.

FINK: A certain philosophical element would then lie only in the
ἀεί, in the eternalness of the world.

HEIDEGGER: You say that, however, under the presupposition that
Heraclitus is a philosopher. In Heraclitus' time, however, there were as
yet no philosophers.

FINK: To be sure, Heraclitus is no philosopher, but he is still a φίλος
τοῦ σοφοῦ, a friend of σοφόν.

HEIDEGGER: That means that you do not interpret Heraclitus
metaphysically. As against the naïve rendition, you require a philosophical rendition that is not yet metaphysical. From what hermeneutical
position do you attempt that?

FINK: It puzzles me that πῦρ ἀείζωον should be spoken of as the
essential predicate of κόσμος, while κόσμος, as the joining of πάντα,
steered by lightning and standing in the light-shine of Ἥλιος, can not
itself be the fire but is the work of fire. In the antecedent phrase it is said
that this κόσμος is brought forth to appearance neither by one of the
gods nor by a human. Surprisingly, we must now ask to what extent it
can be said that no human has brought forth the entire order of things.
This negation is only possible because humans are distinguished by a

productive [*poietische*] power. But this negation sounds paradoxical, because it would never readily occur to anybody that a human has brought
forth the entire order of πάντα. Humans do not bring forth the κόσμος
in the sense of the entire joining of πάντα, except the κόσμος in the sense
of the πόλις [city]; while the gods bring forth the κόσμος in the sense of
the world-rule, though in a limited manner in so far as they cannot
intervene in the power of Μοῖρα [goddess of fate]. Humans and gods are
productive because they partake of the productive power of fire in an
extraordinary manner. Humans make only little κόσμοι and not great
ones, but only because they partake in the ποίησις of πῦρ. Gods and
humans are distinguished beings in the κόσμος, while gods are determined by a still greater nearness to πῦρ ἀείζωον. Out of participation in
the productive power of fire, humans have the capacity of τέχνη and of
establishing states. Gods bring forth no state, but rather world dominion.
Gods and humans are enfeoffed with their own productive power by the
productive dominion of fire, which overrules them, and only therefore
can it be said of them in a denial that they have not brought forth the
great κόσμος. Before ἀλλά in Fr. 30, I would put a semicolon, and then
translate further: but it was always and is and will be eternal-living fire.
The ποίησις of fire is the διακόσμησις [setting in order]. What was
earlier spoken of as οἰακίζει and ἐκυβέρνησε is now the productive
power of fire for the κόσμος.

HEIDEGGER: You do not think power metaphysically. You do not
think metaphysically any longer. Heraclitus does not yet think metaphysically. Is that the same? Is it a question of the same situation of thinking?

FINK: Presumably not. For we, in distinction from Heraclitus, are
stamped by the conceptual language of metaphysics. Perhaps, with the
fundamental ideas of metaphysics, we get scarcely beyond metaphysics.

HEIDEGGER: That is to be noticed for the interpretation, and also
for the connection of the not-yet-metaphysical and the no-more-
metaphysical, which is a special, historical connection. The expression
"not metaphysical" is insufficient. We no longer interpret metaphysically
a text that is not yet metaphysical. In back of that a question hides that is
not now to be raised but that will be necessary in order to be able to make
the way of your interpretation clear.

FINK: Now we can refer to the less smooth explanation to the concluding phrase: ἁπτόμενον μέτρα καὶ ἀποσβεννύμενον, μέτρα. If fire is
always living, it is not quenched as such. Rather, it is kindling and
quenching in reference to the κόσμος, and it sets measures for day and
night and all things that stand in the openness of the alternation of day
and night. The ἁπτόμενον μέτρα καὶ ἀποσβεννύμενον μέτρα is no determined state of fire. It is not something that happens to fire. Rather,
the kindling and quenching according to measures happens in reference
to that which comes and goes in the shine of fire. The ἦν, ἔστιν, and

ἔσται also pertains to what shines up in the shine of fire. We understand the three time determinations not as temporal marks of distinction of πῦρ ἀείζωον but, the other way around, from out of the ἀεί of πῦρ we understand the having been, the now, and the coming of things that come forth to appearance in the shine of fire. Things have their being-in-time in the manner of originating, tarrying, and disappearing. While they tarry, they spread themselves out between the now, the having been, and the coming.

HEIDEGGER: In the fragment, "was," "is," and "will be" are mentioned. You, however, speak of having-been, being-present, and coming-to-be. Clearly, it is a matter of something different. While time determinations are used in the fragment, in your interpretation you take time as such to be thematic.

FINK: The always living source of time can only be addressed with names taken from τὰ πάντα.

HEIDEGGER: I agree with that, but what concerns me now is the hint that ἦν does not mean having-been as having-been.

FINK: I am amazed at the hard bond of πῦρ ἀείζωον and ἦν, ἔστιν, and ἔσται. Perhaps we can say that in a certain manner it cannot be said of πῦρ ἀείζωον that it only is, because it is not eternal. Rather, we must say that as the brightness of the lightning and sun brings πάντα forth to appearance and into the outline of its gestalt, so it is the ἀεί of πῦρ that brings it about that πάντα, which stand in the light-shine of fire, were, are, and will be. However, the difficulty lies in the fact that the characteristic of being-in-time of πάντα places itself back upon πῦρ ἀείζωον as the source of the ways of being-in-time. Of πῦρ ἀείζωον, however, one cannot say that it was, is, and will be. For then one comprehends it like something extant. What would it mean to say that πῦρ ἀείζωον is now? Does it have a specific age, so that it is older in each moment? And what would it mean to say that it always was and will be? Always having-been means that it has past times behind it, just as coming-to-be means that it has a future before it. Can one say of πῦρ ἀείζωον that it has past times behind it, that it now has presence and has a coming presence in the future? Here πῦρ ἀείζωον is mentioned in the manner in which things are in time, spring forth, tarry, and disappear, have past, present, and future. But πῦρ ἀείζωον, on its part, lets past, present, and coming spring forth. We must be wary of comprehending πῦρ ἀείζωον as a perpetual stock.

HEIDEGGER: For me, the question is, what is the reason for this reversed step of the interpretation. For you, the ἀεί becomes the source for ἦν, ἔστιν, and ἔσται.

FINK: As to the source of the three time determinations, the reason for my reversed interpretive step lies in the fact that πῦρ ἀείζωον, which is not itself innertemporal, is addressed by means of what is first made

possible through it. Herein lies a covering of the original by the derivative. Were we to appease ourselves with the immediate wording of the
fragment, and give preference to the smoother rendition, then πῦρ
ἀείζωον would have past and future; and it would now no longer be
what it was, and not yet be that which it is coming to be.

HEIDEGGER: We have said that we no longer interpret metaphysically a text that is not yet metaphysical. Is the no-longer-metaphysical
already included in the not-yet-metaphysical.

FINK: That would be Heraclitus interpreted by Heidegger.

HEIDEGGER: It does not concern me to interpret Heraclitus by
Heidegger; rather, the elaboration of the reasons for your interpretation
concerns me. Both of us are in agreement that if we speak with a thinker,
we must heed what is unsaid in what is said. The question is only which
way leads to this, and of what kind is the foundation of the interpretive
step. To answer this question seems to me especially difficult in reference to time in Fr. 30. Consequently, I have asked about the "always."
How should we understand it? In the setting of your interpretation,
what does "always" mean? If I ask you, is it the *nunc stans* [the standing
now], and you answer no, then I ask, what is it? Here we are faced with a
question mark.

FINK: The special difficulty lies in the fact that what precedes as the
source of time cannot be said at all in appropriate manner. In reference
to the source of time, we find ourselves in a special predicament.

HEIDEGGER: You rightly emphasize the predicament in which we
find ourselves. The difficulty before which we stand consists not only in
the step of thought but also in our rethinking. We must have sufficient
clarity about what is to be thought in order to hear Heraclitus in the
correct manner. Nevertheless we cannot resolve what has to be thought
in terms of one fragment; rather, we must—as you have already said—
have all the fragments in view for the interpretation of one fragment. I
am again and again concerned to make clear the sequence of steps of
your interpretation. Therefore, I have indicated that time becomes
thematic with your step of thought, while in Fr. 30 time comes to view
only as an understanding of time, without becoming thematic for Heraclitus.

FINK: Concerning the phrase, ἦν ἀεὶ καὶ ἔστιν καὶ ἔσται πῦρ
ἀείζωον [it was always and is and will be eternal-living fire], I will not
contend that we have within easy reach an interpretive possibility that will
allow us to address the source of time, which is hidden by intratemporal
determinations, without intratemporal determinations. For that would
mean that we would already be able to retrieve the premetaphysical
language.

In this connection, let us glance at Fr. 66, which should be correlated
now only in order to indicate the superiority of πῦρ vis-à-vis χόσμος and

τὰ πάντα. It runs: πάντα γὰρ τὸ πῦρ ἐπελθὸν κρινεῖ καὶ καταλήψεται. Diels translates: "For fire, having come upon them, will judge and apprehend (condemn) all things." In this translation it is questionable whether κρινεῖ must be translated as "will judge" in the sense of an end situation, or whether it must not rather be translated as "will divide." And it is questionable whether καταλήψεται must be comprehended as "will be struck into its imprint." We must then say that fire will, at the time it brings τὰ πάντα forth to appearance, divide them and strike each thing into its imprint. Thus, the superiority of fire is also indicated here vis-à-vis τὰ πάντα, which are mentioned in Fr. 30 by the name of the κόσμος, that is, the entire order. The more difficult rendition of Fr. 30, suggested by me, requires that the subject of the first and second halves of the sentence changes. According to the smoother rendition, the subject of the antecedent phrase, κόσμος, will also be retained in the second half. Seen linguistically, this version might be the more easy; but seen thoughtfully, it appears to me objectionable. The more difficult rendition implies that in the antecedent κόσμος comes into view and is named as something brought forth, but κόσμος is held away from the power of gods ;and humans to bring forth. As something brought forth, the κόσμος, which arises neither from the ποίησις of gods nor of humans, points to fire's bringing-forth-to-appearance. Therefore, the subject can no longer be κόσμος in the second half of the sentence. For otherwise πῦρ ἀείζωον would be a predicative determination of κόσμος, notwithstanding the fact that κόσμος is something brought forth by fire. Thus, we must read: neither a god nor a human brought the κόσμος forth to appearance; rather, it was always and is and will always be living fire— which brings the κόσμος forth to appearance. We can understand the phrase, "was always and is and will be," almost in the sense of "there is." But the way in which there is πῦρ ἀείζωον is the manner in which πῦρ ἀείζωον bestows the three ways of being-in-time on πάντα. If we read Fr. 30 thus, a decisive advantage of fire over κόσμος emerges, an advantage that is supported by Fr. 66. The question, however, is whether we may read Fr. 30 such that πῦρ ἀείζωον, which is mentioned in the three time determinations, is the decisive factor. In this connection, we can ask whether we can also draw the superiority of fire from Fr. 31—although it includes new motifs of thought.

PARTICIPANT: Musn't we also include Fr. 76 here: ζῇ πῦρ τὸν γῆς θάνατον καὶ ἀὴρ ζῇ τὸν πυρὸς θάνατον, ὕδωρ ζῇ τὸν ἀέρος θάνατον, γῆ τὸν ὕδατος. Translated by Diels, it runs: "Fire lives the death of earth and air lives the death of fire; water lives the death of air and earth that of water."

FINK: In this fragment the movement is spoken in the joining of words: fire lives the death of earth. That means that it is not a question here of a simple going over; rather, it is a question of the interlocking of life and death—a problem to which we will pay attention separately. Also concerning Fr. 31, we wish to use here only the words of Heraclitus himself in our consideration: πυρὸς τροπαὶ πρῶτον θάλασσα, θαλάσσης δὲ τὸ μὲν ἥμισυ γῆ, τὸ δὲ ἥμισυ πρηστήρ. (γῆ) θάλλασσα διαχέεται, καὶ μετρέεται εἰς τὸν αὐτὸν λόγον, ὁκοῖος πρόσθεν ἦν ἢ γενέσθαι γῆ. Diels translates: "Change of fire: first sea; of sea, however, one half earth, the other half breath of fire. The earth melts as sea, and this receives its measure according to the same sense (relationship) as it acknowledged before it became earth."

IIEIDEGGER: Let me refer at this point to an essay by Bruno Snell on τροπή in *Hermes* 61, 1926.

FINK: Diels translates, "Change of fire," while Heraclitus speaks in the plural of τροπαί, changes, transformations. But how should we understand the transition of fire into sea and from sea into earth and breath of fire, as well as from earth into sea and sea into fire? Is it here a question of the familiar phenomenon of one aggregate state passing over into the other? Is it intended here that some elements go over and turn themselves into others? Does Heraclitus speak of transformations of elements, such as we see aggregate states going over; as, for instance, liquid goes over into steam or fire into smoke? What are the τροπαί? Does Heraclitus speak of a multitude because fire converts itself into a series of different things? At first, it looks like a series: fire converts itself into sea, sea converts itself half into earth and half into breath of fire. Can we inquire here at all about everyday, familiar kinds of events? From the phenomenon, we know only the change of aggregate states. However, we are not witnesses of a cosmogonic process. What is very difficult to see is the conversion of fire into sea, while the sea, that is, water, is nevertheless that which most quenches fire. The general question is whether we are right if we take the transformations of fire as if everything were first fire, and as if there were then a separation of water, of which one half would be earth and the other half the breath of fire. Presumably, we are not dealing at all with a relationship of mixing in sequence and at the level of πάντα. Rather, I would suppose that the fire is opposed to the sea, the earth, and the breath of fire, that the fire thus relates itself in opposition to the sea, the earth and the breath of fire as κεραυνός and Ἥλιος are in opposition to πάντα. The fire, as the ἕν, would then turn about in different ways, as τὰ πάντα show themselves. This interpretation should at first be formulated only as a question. If we understand τροπή only as turning over in a local motion, Fr. 31 is not at all intelligible. For we cannot say that fire turns into water, earth, and breath of fire in a local motion. If τροπή means turning in a local motion, what then do the overturnings of fire mean? Nevertheless, Heraclitus says that fire turns first into sea. Yet here a local motion is evidently not thought. Does fire move in such a way that it first becomes water, and does water move in such a way that half becomes earth and the other half becomes breath of fire? If we understand τροπαί in this sense, then we take fire as a kind of primary substance, which assumes different forms of appearance in sequence. My question, however, is whether one can make πυρὸς τροπαί clear by the changeover of aggregate states familiar to us.

HEIDEGGER: Would you say that fire stands behind everything? What is questionable, however, is what "behind" means here; above all, whether fire stands behind everything in the manner of a primary substance, . . .

FINK: . . . or whether one must not begin here also from the relatedness of ἕν and πάντα, and whether one must give up the thought of a basic matter. Our task here will again be to work out the more difficult rendition.

7

Difference of Interpretation: Truth of Being
(Fragment 16) or Cosmological
Perspective (Fragment 64).—Heraclitus and the
Matter of Thinking.
—The Not-Yet-Metaphysical and the
No-Longer-Metaphysical.—Hegel's
Relationship to the Greeks.—πυϱὸς τϱοπαί and
Dawn.
(Correlated Fragments: 31, 76).

HEIDEGGER: Since we have interrupted our seminar for three weeks over Christmas, a short synopsis of the way of our undertaking till now might prove useful. If an outsider were to ask you what we work at in our seminar, how would you answer such a question?

PARTICIPANT: Discussion of the problem of time in Fr. 30 was central in the last hours before Christmas.

HEIDEGGER: In other words, you have indeed let yourself be misled by the explication of Fr. 30 which Mr. Fink has given. For—as we have emphasized again and again—time does not come to the fore at all with Heraclitus.

PARTICIPANT: But Fr. 30 leads to time determinations, and our question was how these ought to be understood.

HEIDEGGER: With that, you go into a special question. But if somebody asked you what we work at in our Heraclitus seminar, and if he wanted to hear not about individual questions but about the whole; if he asked what we have begun with, what would your answer be?

PARTICIPANT: We have begun with a methodical preliminary consideration, that is, with the question of how Heraclitus is to be understood.

HEIDEGGER: What has Mr. Fink done at the beginning of his interpretation?

PARTICIPANT: He has started with a consideration of τὰ πάντα.

HEIDEGGER: But how does he come to τὰ πάντα?—If I speak with you now, I thus speak with everyone.—

PARTICIPANT: Through Fr. 64: τὰ δὲ πάντα οἰακίζει Κεϱαυνός.

HEIDEGGER: In the explication, have we begun with τὰ πάντα or with lightning? For it is important to distinguish that.

PARTICIPANT: First, we have asked ourselves how τὰ πάντα is to be translated; then, we turned to the lightning; and finally, we have looked at all the fragments in which τὰ πάντα is mentioned.

HEIDEGGER: Mr. Fink has thus begun the explication of Heraclitus with the lightning. Is this beginning a matter of course? Is it not surprising?

PARTICIPANT: If one considers the starting points made elsewhere, this beginning is unusual.

HEIDEGGER: Mr. Fink, who begins with the lightning, is, as it were, struck by lightning. With what does Heidegger begin?

PARTICIPANT: With the Λόγος [gathering-process].

HEIDEGGER: And beside that . . .

PARTICIPANT: . . . with 'Αλήθεια [nonconcealment].[23]

HEIDEGGER: But how does Heidegger come to 'Αλήθεια?

PARTICIPANT: By Fr. 16: τὸ μὴ δῦνόν ποτε πῶς ἄν τις λάθοι.[24]

HEIDEGGER: Where this fragment is used as a basis for a Heraclitus explication, one must also read it as the first fragment. But how do Frs. 64 and 16 come together, or how is Fr. 64 distinguished from Fr. 16? Wherein lies the distinction between both beginnings?

PARTICIPANT: In Fr. 16, τὸ μὴ δῦνον ποτε [that which never sets] stands at the central point; in Fr. 64, it is κεραυνός [lightning].

HEIDEGGER: Are both fragments, and thus both beginnings, identical?

PARTICIPANT: No.

HEIDEGGER: Take Fr. 16 entire, and compare it with Fr. 64.

PARTICIPANT: The distinction between the two fragments consists in this, that only τὰ πάντα is mentioned in Fr. 64, while the human being comes into play in Fr. 16.

HEIDEGGER: We are thus concerned with a great difference. The question will be what the different starting point of Frs. 64 and 16, respectively, signifies; whether or not an opposition is displayed here. We will have to ask this question explicitly. But what could one reply if it were said that the human becomes thematic in Fr. 16, while he is not mentioned in Fr. 64?

PARTICIPANT: If τὰ πάντα comprehends all entities, then the human is co-thought as an entity.

PARTICIPANT: Fundamentally, I agree with that. But then it is not said in Fr. 64 how a human, in distinction to all nonhuman πάντα, is and stands in relationship to lightning. On the contrary, Fr. 16 expressly names the way that a human behaves toward τὸ μὴ δῦνόν ποτε.

HEIDEGGER: A human is also named in Fr. 64 in so far as he is and belongs as an entity to τὰ πάντα. But the question is whether we already think of a human when we take him as an entity which belongs to τὰ πάντα like all other entities, whether we must not think of him otherwise as an entity in the midst of πάντα. Let us, therefore, keep in mind that the beginning of Mr. Fink's Heraclitus explication is surprising. This beginning with the lightning then leads to . . .

PARTICIPANT: ... our taking into view the relationship between lightning and τὰ πάντα.

HEIDEGGER: What follows after that?

PARTICIPANT: An explication of Fr. 11.

HEIDEGGER: But how do we come to this fragment? What is the pertinent motif that leads us from Fr. 64 to Fr. 11?

PARTICIPANT: What Heraclitus himself said gave us support for this transition. In Fr. 64, he speaks of τὰ πάντα, in Fr. 11 of πᾶν ἑρπετον, which we have understood as πάντα ὡς ἑρπετά.

HEIDEGGER: But where lay the pertinent support for such a procedure?

PARTICIPANT: Lightning (lightning bolt) led us to πλγή (blow).

HEIDEGGER: Besides, we saw a relevant connection between steering (οἰακίζει) and driving (νέμεται). Therefore, we took up first the relationship of lightning and τὰ πάντα, and finally, we took up the relationship of πληγή and πᾶν ἑρπετόν. Then we turned ...

PARTICIPANT: ... to the sun fragments.

HEIDEGGER: The explication began with the lightning or lightning bolt, then turned to the sun, and after that to πῦρ ἀείζωον. Later, we must specify more exactly the references of lightning, sun, and fire. What we have thematically treated up to this point has now become clear. But how does Mr. Fink proceed in explication of the fragments?

PARTICIPANT: The explication has become a problem for us.

HEIDEGGER: To what extent is the explication a problem? How would you characterize the procedure of Mr. Fink? The manner of his explication is by no means to be taken for granted, but is rather to be designated as venturesome.

PARTICIPANT: More has been said in the interpretation of the fragments than stands in them.

HEIDEGGER: The interpretation is hazardous. But Mr. Fink does not interpret arbitrarily; rather, he has his grounds for preferring the more difficult rendition and the hardness of the problem. What is the problem we are concerned with here? With what right does he prefer the more difficult rendition? Let us take Fr. 30 as an example.

PARTICIPANT: In each case we have preferred the more difficult rendition so that the subject matter comes to the fore.

HEIDEGGER: What matter is that?

PARTICIPANT: The matter is already suggested in a manifold, perhaps most explicitly in reference to the time question.

HEIDEGGER: I do not allow talk about time now. Let us bracket being and time now. What matter is treated that should come to the fore? Think of Mr. Fink's introductory remarks.

PARTICIPANT: The matter of thinking.

HEIDEGGER: And the matter of thinking is? We must say that the matter of thinking is that which we seek, that of which we still do not know. The same outsider, after he has listened to what you answer to his question, could reply to you that when we deal with Heraclitus we sit, as it were, in an ivory tower. For what we are doing would have nothing to do with technology and industrial society; rather, it is nothing but worn-out stories. What would be the answer here?

PARTICIPANT: It is doubtful that we are dealing here with worn out stories. For we do not take Heraclitus as a thinker of the past. It is rather our intention to bring something to the fore in the exposition of Heraclitus that is possibly something other or quite the same. For us, there is no concern for an exposition that has to do with a past matter.

HEIDEGGER: Do we thus provide no contribution to Heraclitus research?

PARTICIPANT: I would not say that, because our problematic can also be helpful for research.

HEIDEGGER: We seek the determination of the matter of thinking in conversation with Heraclitus. We intend thereby no thematic contribution to Heraclitus research. We are not interested in this direction. Perhaps what we are doing is also inaccessible for Heraclitus research. The way and manner in which we speak with the fragments and listen to them is not the simple, everyday way and manner of forming an opinion, as when we read the newspaper. Mr. Fink forces you to think otherwise. The greater difficulty of the more difficult rendition is not only related by degrees to our capacity of apprehension. What seems here like a grammatical comparative is presumably another distinction.

PARTICIPANT: A comparative presupposes that something which stands in a context gets compared. Between the simple, everyday thinking and understanding and that which is called the more difficult rendition, there is clearly a gulf that is worthy of emphasis.

HEIDEGGER: We have thus looked at the reference of τὰ πάντα and lightning, τὰ πάντα and sun, τὰ πάντα and fire. In Fr. 7, πάντα τὰ ὄντα was mentioned. In the reference of τὰ πάντα to lightning, to the sun, to fire and to ἕν, which we have come across, what is the greater difficulty of the more difficult rendition in distinction to the naïve manner of reading?

PARTICIPANT: The question is whether the reference of πάντα to lightning, to the sun, to fire, to ἕν, to πόλεμος, or to λόγος is in each case different, or whether the expressed multiplicity of that to which τὰ πάντα refers is only the name of a manifold.

HEIDEGGER: The difficulty before which we stand is the manifold of lightning, the sun, fire, ἕν, war and λόγος in their relationship to τὰ πάντα, or to τὰ ὄντα. The manifold does not belong to πάντα or to ὄντα. But to what does it then belong?

PARTICIPANT: I see the difficulty in this, that on one hand τὰ πάντα form a totality, and that on the other hand τὰ πάντα are supposed to stand in a reference to something that does not belong to the totality.

HEIDEGGER: You would say that with the totality we have everything, that with it we are at the end of thinking. On the other hand, a manifold is mentioned that exceeds the totality. If τὰ πάντα is the totality of ὄντα, what is as a whole, is there still something which leads further?

PARTICIPANT: Although you have said that the word "being" should be bracketed, we cannot now refrain from naming being as what leads further than what is as a whole.

HEIDEGGER: Till now, the conversation was not about being. Being is something that is not an entity and that does not belong to what is as a whole. The more difficult rendition consists in this, that we do not read the fragments ontically, as we read the newspaper, that reading of the fragments is not concerned with things that become clear simply. Rather, the difficulty is that here it is obviously a matter of a kind of thinking that lets itself into something that is inaccessible to direct representation and thought: that is the genuine background.

Another difficulty is the following. The kind of thinking that thinks what is as a whole in regard to being is the way of thought of metaphysics. Now we said in the last seminar that Heraclitus does not yet think metaphysically, whereas we no longer attempt to think metaphysically. Has the "not-yet-metaphysical" no reference at all to metaphysics? One could suppose the "not-yet" to be cut off from what follows, from metaphysics. The "not-yet" could, however, also be an "already," a certain preparation, which only we see as we do, and must see as we do, whereas Heraclitus could not see it. But what about the "no-longer-metaphysical"?

PARTICIPANT: This characterization of our thinking is temporarily unavoidable, because we simply cannot put aside the history of metaphysics from which we come. On the other hand, regarding what the "not-yet-metaphysical" deals with, perhaps too much is already said in this characterization.

HEIDEGGER: If Heraclitus cannot say that his thinking is not yet metaphysical because he cannot yet preview the coming metaphysics, so must we say of ourselves that we no longer attempt to think metaphysically, and indeed because we come from metaphysics.

PARTICIPANT: An ambiguity lies in "no-longer." On one hand, it can be comprehended in the sense of a superficial, temporal determination. Then it implies that metaphysics lies behind us. On the other hand, it can also be understood such that the bearing on metaphysics is maintained, although not in the manner of a metaphysical counterposition within metaphysics.

HEIDEGGER: You wish to say that "no-longer-metaphysical" does not mean that we have dismissed metaphysics; rather, it implies that metaphysics still clings to us, that we are not free of it. Where within Western philosophy is the relationship of epochs to each other thought in most decisive manner?

PARTICIPANT: With Hegel.

HEIDEGGER: If we say that we no longer attempt to think metaphysically, but remain nevertheless referred to metaphysics, then we could designate this relationship in Hegelian fashion as sublation. None of us knows whether metaphysics will reappear. In any case, the "no-longer-metaphysical" is more difficult to specify than the "not-yet-metaphysical." But what about Hegel and the Greeks? Doesn't he take them to some extent all in the same breath?

PARTICIPANT: With Hegel, another understanding is presented of what a beginning is.

HEIDEGGER: The question about the beginning is too difficult for us now. The answer which I wish is simpler. What character, according to Hegel, has Greek thinking for philosophy?

PARTICIPANT: A character of preparation.

HEIDEGGER: This answer is too general. More specifically said . . .

PARTICIPANT: In the preface to the *Phenomenology of Mind,* Hegel says that everything depends on comprehending and expressing truth not only as substance, but just as much as subject.

HEIDEGGER: How is that to be understood? But first: is the "Preface" you mention the preface to the *Phenomenology?*

PARTICIPANT: It is the preface to the system of science, whereas the "Introduction" is the real preface to the *Phenomenology.*

HEIDEGGER: The "Preface" thus pertains to the *Logic,* and not only to the *Phenomenology of Mind.* In the "Preface" Hegel says something fundamental about philosophy, that it should think the truth not only as substance, but also as subject. In Greek, substance means . . .

PARTICIPANT: . . . ὑποκείμενον, and what is underlying.

HEIDEGGER: How is substance thought by Hegel? If I say that the house is big or tall, how is the manner of thinking that only thinks substance to be characterized? What is not thought here?

PARTICIPANT: The movement between the house and being tall.

HEIDEGGER: The Greeks, who according to Hegel think only of substance, ὑποκείμενον, have categories for this.

PARTICIPANT: The movement can only come into view when yet another basis supervenes, the subject.

HEIDEGGER: When it is said that the house is tall, what is not thought therein?

PARTICIPANT: The one who thinks.

HEIDEGGER: Thus, what kind of thinking is that which simply views ὑποκείμενον and not the subject?

PARTICIPANT: I hesitate to say the overused words.

HEIDEGGER: In philosophy no word or concept is overused. We

must think the concepts new each day. We have, for example, the statement that this glass is full. Something is said, therewith, about what lies before us, but the reference to an I is not thought. When this reference becomes thematic for thinking, for the I, then what lies before us becomes what lies opposite us, that is, it becomes an object. In Greek there are no objects. What does object mean in the Middle Ages? What does it mean literally?

PARTICIPANT: What is thrown up against.

HEIDEGGER: The object is what is thrown up against whom? Can you throw the glass up against yourself? How can I throw something up against myself, without something happening? What does *subiectum* [substance] mean in the Middle Ages? What does it mean literally?

PARTICIPANT: What is thrown under.

HEIDEGGER: For medieval thinking, the glass is a *subiectum,* which is the translation of ὑποκείμενον. *Obiectum* [representation], for the Middle Ages, meant, on the contrary, what is represented. A golden mountain is an object. Thus the object here is that which is precisely not objective. It is subjective. I have asked how the Greeks think according to Hegel's interpretation. We have said that in their thinking the reference to the subject does not become thematic. But were the Greeks still thoughtful? For Hegel, nevertheless, their thinking was a turning toward what lies before and what underlies, which Hegel called the thinking of the immediate. The immediate is that between which nothing intervenes. Hegel characterized all of Greek thought as a phase of immediacy. For him, philosophy first reaches solid land with Descartes, by beginning with the I.

PARTICIPANT: But Hegel saw a break already with Socrates, a turning toward subjectivity that goes along with mores, in so far as these become morality.

HEIDEGGER: That Hegel sees a break with Socrates has a still simpler ground. When he characterizes Greek thinking as a whole as a phase of immediacy, he does not level down inner distinctions like that between Anaxagoras and Aristotle. Within the phase of immediacy, he sees a division comprehended by the same three-fold scheme of immediacy—mediation—unity. He does not, thereby, apply an arbitrary scheme; rather, he thinks out of that which is for him the truth in the sense of the absolute certainty of the absolute spirit. Nevertheless, the classification of metaphysics and Greek thinking is not so easy for us, because the question about the determination of Greek thinking is something that we must first put to question and awaken as a question.

The question from the seminar before last, concerning what the speculative means with Hegel, still remains unanswered.

PARTICIPANT: Speculation for Hegel means the view [*Anschauung*] of eternal truth.

HEIDEGGER: This answer is too general and sounds only approximate. With such academic questions, one has no recourse to an index, but to the *Encyclopedia*. There the speculative is a determination of the logical. How many determinations are there and what are the remaining ones?

PARTICIPANT: In all there are three dimensions of the logical, which correspond to the three determinations already named, immediacy, mediation, and unity.

HEIDEGGER: Are the three determinations of the logical three things side-by-side? Evidently not. The first moment, which corresponds to immediacy, is the abstract. What does abstract mean with Hegel?

PARTICIPANT: What is separated and isolated.

HEIDEGGER: Better: the thinking of one-sidedness, which only thinks one side. It is peculiar that the immediate should be the abstract, while for us the immediate is rather the concrete. But Hegel calls the immediate abstract in so far as one looks at the side of givenness and not at the side of the I. The second moment of the logical is the dialectical, the third is the speculative. The Hegelian determination of the speculative will be significant for us, when we will be concerned at an important part of the seminar with the apparent opposition of beginning with κεραυνός or with τὸ μὴ δῦνόν ποτε πῶς ἄν τις λάθοι.

Now I still have a question for you, Mr. Fink, which concerns Fr. 30. Do I understand you correctly when you comprehend κόσμος as identical with τὰ πάντα in your interpretation?

FINK: κόσμος and τὰ πάντα are not identical, but κόσμος does indeed mean the jointed whole of τὰ πάντα, the whole stamping, which is not fixed but moved. Heraclitus speaks of manifold ways of movement, as in strife or war.

HEIDEGGER: Does κόσμος then belong in the sequence of lightning, sun, and fire?

FINK: Not without further consideration. That could only be said if κόσμος were thought not as the order brought forth by fire, but as the ordering fire. If κόσμος had the function of διακόσμησις, then it would also belong in the sequence of basic words.

HEIDEGGER: In Fr. 30, κόσμον τόνδε is mentioned. If we hold that together with κατὰ τὸν λόγον τόνδε, then couldn't κόσμον τόνδε, corresponding with λόγον τόνδε, mean the same as this κόσμος, which is still to be treated, which is still to be thematized?

FINK: Above all, the demonstrative τόνδε does not mean an individual this, not this κόσμος, which is now as opposed to other κόσμοι. When it is said that the κόσμος is brought forth as the jointed order, a κόσμος in the singular, which belongs to a plurality of κόσμοι, is not meant thereby. Of this κόσμος it is said: τὸν αὐτὸν ἁπάντων [the same for all beings]. Whether this is Heraclitus' phrase, we leave aside now. Diels translates ἁπάντων as "all living beings." I reject this translation. I also reject the interpretation that thinks this phrase together with Fr. 89, in which it says that those who are awake have one common world, while those who sleep turn each one to his own world. I do not understand τὸν αὐτὸν ἁπάντων as the same, that is, the one and common world of those who are awake (κοινὸς κόσμος) in opposition to the private world (ἴδιος κόσμος) of those who sleep. I interpret ἅπαντα in the sense of τὰ πάντα. Although ἅπαντες customarily refers to humans and living beings, ἁπάντων, just as much as πάντων, here means only that Heraclitus speaks by reason of the flow of language, instead of from πάντων ἁπάντων.

HEIDEGGER: But what then does πάντα mean?

FINK: πάντα form a joining and come forth in the shining up of fire in their determination and character.

HEIDEGGER: Can't one also start from a plural, where κόσμοι are the many states of an entire order of πάντα? κόσμον τόνδε would then be this one state in distinction to others.

FINK: But there is no passage in Heraclitus in which he speaks of many κόσμοι.

HEIDEGGER: However, the τόνδε marks a place at which a new theme begins. On your interpretation, κόσμος is to be understood ontologically as much as ontically.

FINK: Heraclitus stands neither on the side of πάντα nor on the side of fire; rather, he takes up a curious position between them.

HEIDEGGER: With that we can now return to Fr. 31.

FINK: I attempt first to expose a thought that contains a proposal for an interpretation of Fr. 31. In the last seminar we expressed our doubt as to whether transformations or overturnings are meant with τροπαί. If it is a question of transformations, then we think of the ἀλλοίωσις, of a basic substance. If we translate τροπαί with overturnings, then—we could ask—do we mean the turning points in the way of the sun-fire in the firmament which measure time?

HEIDEGGER: Is πυρὸς τροπαί a *genitivus subiectus* or a *genitivus obiectus* [subjective genitive or objective genitive]?

FINK: The τροπαί are asserted of fire. However, a difficulty lies in the fact that we have from the history of metaphysics familiar and common ideas and developed and general ways of thought in which we are always already moving, and from which we are also apt at first to interpret Fr. 31. One such idea, already given to us from metaphysics, is the idea of an underlying substance that shows itself in many disguises.

HEIDEGGER: πυρός is then *genitivus obiectivus*.

FINK: *Genitivus obiectivus* and *subiectivus*. Another scheme presents itself to us from ancient speculation on the elements, in which one or another element is declared to be the original element. Does πῦρ also have the function of a basic element that converts itself through that which emenates out of it? Two common schemes with which we could attempt to interpret πυρός τροπαί are the αλλοίωσις of an underlying substance and the emenation of an original element. But I believe that we must entertain an extreme distrust of such conceptions. In the text it says: overturnings of fire, first into sea. The fire turns itself over into sea, that is, into that which we understand as a power opposed to fire. At first, we could suppose that it is a question of the sharp, ontic opposition of fire and water that is familiar to us. In the small domain of the human environment, there is the phenomenon that water quenches fire and that fire can vaporize water. But such reciprocal contest and annihilation is only possible on the soil of earth. Clearly, the fragment does not refer to this small domain, but rather to the great domain of the world. Here we have a view of fire in the heavens, the sea, and the earth—the sea that girds the earth. In the great domain of the world, the domain that presents itself to us in the view of the world, fire and water do not annihilate each other.

The view of the world [*Welt-Anschauung*] is not understood here ideologically; rather, it means the immediate view of the great relationships of the heavenly stars, the sea that lies under them and the earth. When Heraclitus says that fire first turns itself over into sea, we suspend the schemata of αλλοίωσις and emanation, even though we are still not able to think what "turning over" means. The sea turns itself half into earth, half into breath of fire. Then we read that the earth is passed into sea and that earth dissolves in the measure in which sea was before, when sea became earth. Nothing more is said in the fragment concerning whether and how the breath of fire turns further. With the breath of fire, the overturning is brought to a close. All that is spoken of is the turning of fire into sea and the sea's turning half into earth and half into breath of fire, and finally of earth turning into sea. Fire turns itself over into sea, this splits into earth and breath of fire, and half of the earth turns back into sea. Apparently a reciprocal exchange of water and earth, of fluidity and solidity, is mentioned. What is for us a familiar distinction of opposites dissolves itself. No further turning and no returning to fire is declared concerning the breath of fire. The differences of sea, earth, and breath of fire are referred back to a common origin, to a genesis which is posited step by step; but we still do not know the character of the genesis. If now we cannot apply the familiar scheme of ἀλλοίωσις, that is, the scheme of the original substance with its states and modes and the scheme of emanation, then we get into a difficulty. How then should we interpret the πυρὸς τροπαί? We must ask what Heraclitus has thoughtfully experienced and caught sight of. I attempt now—if you will—to give a fantastic meaning to πυρὸς τροπαί, which is thought as a possible answer to the question of what Heraclitus has thoughtfully caught sight of. We could make the turning of fire intelligible to ourselves by starting out from the phenomenon of the break of day, from the phenomenon of dawn on the Ionian coast. At dawn, the expanse of the sea flashes up out of the fire which breaks out from night and drives out night; and opposite the sea there flashes up the shore and land, and above the sea and land the zone of the vault of heaven which is filled by the breath of fire. A deeper sense would lie in what is familiar to us as the break of day, if we do not now think the relationship of fire to sea, earth, and breath of fire, namely the bringing-forth-to-appearance that is the basic event of fire, simply as the casting of light to and letting-be-seen of that which is already determined thus and so. A deeper sense would lie in that which is familiar to us as the break of day, if we also do not understand bringing-forth in the sense of a building manufacture or of a creative bringing-forth, but attempt to advance thoughtfully behind the two expressive forms, coming-forth-to-appearance in the sense of technical and creative achievement and casting of light. In order to win a deeper sense of the break of day, it would depend on avoiding the scheme of technical bringing-forth in the sense of a material transformation and also the scheme of creative bringing-forth; and beside that, it would depend on taking away from the letting-shine-up in the light of fire the basic trait of impotence. If we could succeed in thinking back behind the familiar schemata of making, bringing-forth, and casting light or letting-be-seen, then we could understand the break of day in a deeper sense. We could then say that in the breaking of the world-day the basic distinctions of the world area, sea, earth, and vault of heaven, first come forth to appearance. For this deeper thought we have an immediate phenomenon in the break of day. But nowhere do we have a phenomenon corresponding to the return course of earth into sea.

HEIDEGGER: How would you translate τροπαί in your projection, which you yourself call fantastic, but which is not at all so fantastic because it includes reference to immediate phenomena.

FINK: We see the arising of fire, and in its arising the τροπαί are the turnings of fire around toward that which shows itself in the fire shine. τροπαί signify no material transformations . . .

HEIDEGGER: . . . and also no mere illumination.

FINK: In announcement of the deeper sense of πυρὸς τροπαί, I was concentrating on a commonness, not known in ontic relationships, of bringing-forth into visibility and letting-arise in the sense of φύσις. That is an attempt to avoid the scheme in which fire converts like an original element over into other elements like water and earth. And I attempt to think this in a simile between the arising of the articulated world in the light-shine of the world illuminating fire, and the regions of πάντα laying themselves out.

HEIDEGGER: You thus take the phenomenon of dawn as the basis of your interpretation . . .

FINK: ... in order to avoid the phenomenon of transformation.

HEIDEGGER: You mean thereby the dawn of the world and not of a specific day, just as you have in view the world-fire and not the sun.

FINK: But in the phenomenal sun, we can think fire.

HEIDEGGER: How should we think fire? In order to heighten the difficulty, I refer to Fr. 54, in which the word ἀφανής [invisible] comes to the fore. The fire is invisible; it is the fire which does not appear.

FINK: As we have said at the outset: the fire is that which is not there in τὰ πάντα.

HEIDEGGER: If you proceed from day to world-day, so we could think from the sun thither to fire.

FINK: Nowhere do we find the sudden change of fire into sea as an ontic phenomenon.

PARTICIPANT: To what is θαλάσσης referred?

FINK: To τροπαί. For the turning over of sea into earth and breath of fire is a continuation of τροπαί.

HEIDEGGER: I propose that we bracket Fr. 31. The difficulty we got into lies in this, that we have not spoken clearly enough about πῦρ, which we still have to do. I understand neither the interpretation which is accompanied by chemical ideas nor can I follow through the attempted correspondence of day and world-day. For me, there is a hole here.

FINK: The difficulty will perhaps clear itself up if we come to Fr. 76, in which fire, sea, and earth appear in repeated sequence. The most important thing there is the manner in which τροπαί are characterized. What is named only as turning over in Fr. 31, is here spoken of as "to live the death of the other." With that, we meet a new, surprising thought. At first, it should sound noteworthy to us that the dark formula of death, which first becomes clear to us in the domain of the living, is referred to such entities as neither live or die, like water or earth. In the small domain of human ambit, we know well the phenomenon that fire vaporizes water and water quenches fire. Here we can say that fire lives the destruction of water and water lives the destruction of fire.

HEIDEGGER: To live would mean here "to survive" ...

FINK: ... to survive the passing of the other, to survive in the annihilation of the other. But we have here only a poetic metaphor. In order to understand the τροπή-character, we must get away from the idea of a chemical change. Starting from the life-death fragments, we must represent to ourselves what Heraclitus thinks by life and death. From there we can also understand the ἀνταμοιβή, that is, the exchange of πάντα for fire and of fire for πάντα. This is a relationship like that of gold and goods, in which connection it is more a matter of light than the value of gold. We do not understand the turning over of fire into what is not fire in the sense of a chemical change or in the sense of an original substance that changes (ἀλλοίωσις) or in the sense of an original element that masks itself through its emanations. Rather, we will view the entire range that binds fire, sea, earth, and breath of fire in connection with life and death. Apparently, we revert to anthropological fragments in opposition to cosmological fragments. In truth, however, it is not a question of a restriction to human phenomena; rather, what pertains to being human, such as life and death, becomes in a distinctive sense the clue for understanding of the entirety of the opposing relatedness of ἕν and πάντα.

8

Intertwining of Life and Death
(Correlated Fragments: 76, 36, 77).
—Relation of Humans and Gods
(Correlated Fragments: 62, 67, 88).

FINK: Fragment 31 remained closed to us for many reasons: first, because the plural τροπαί proves itself to be a matter of dispute, on the one
hand, as a technical term, and on the other, as a plurality of turns that
happen in sequence; and second, because of the resulting problem of
whether the concept of turn can be thought in the usual circle of ideas of
the transformation of an original stuff (ἀλλοίωσις) or emanation of an
original element that conceals itself in its manifold appearances as alien
forms. I am of the opinion that we must mobilize a mistrust of all the
usual schemes of thought that are familiar to us from the conceptual
tradition of metaphysical thinking. Here, these are above all the two
schemes of ἀλλοίωσις and emanation. The attempt to clarify Fr. 31 from
the phenomenon of dawn on the Ionian coast falls short, in the characterization of the letting-arise and shining-up of the world regions of sea,
earth, heaven, and breath of fire, of the task of thinking this neither as a
real transformation of an original substance, nor as the emanation of an
original element, nor as bringing-forth in the technical or creative sense,
nor as the impotent illumination of already-existing entities by the light-
shine of fire. Perhaps it is necessary to go back behind the distinction of
actual manufacture and creative bringing-forth and of bare casting of
light and illumination, if we wish to think the shining-up of entities in an
all encompassing shine of lightning, of the sun, or of eternal living fire.

HEIDEGGER: You say that the coming-forth-to-appearance of what
is is no actual making, no creative bringing-forth and also no bare illumination. In this connection, you have some time ago referred to the
fact that a similar predicament is hidden in Husserl's concept of constitution.

FINK: The problem of constitution in Husserl's phenomenology has
its place in the subject/object-reference. The perception [*Gewahren*] of
the unity of an object in the multiplicity of ways of being given is consti-
tuted in the interplay of aspects of the object. With the concept of constitution Husserl attempts, to begin with, to avoid a complete realism and
idealism. Complete realism holds that perception is only a comprehension according to consciousness of what is independent of consciousness.
As against this, complete idealism holds that the subject makes things.

The predicament of finding a concept that does not refer to building, creation or bare representation always presents itself with Husserl. In distinction to ancient philosophy, modern philosophy does not think appearance so much from the issue of what is in the openness of a general presencing, but rather as becoming an object and presenting itself for a subject. In the general concept of appearance, nevertheless, self-presentation belongs to each entity. But each entity presents itself to everything that is, and, among others, to the entity that is characterized by cognition. Presentation, then, is a collision among what is, or a representation of what is by the one who represents. But what is cannot be understood with the categories of attraction and repulsion.

HEIDEGGER: Another manner of explaining representation occurs in reference to receptivity and spontaniety.

FINK: Kant speaks of receptivity in reference to sensory data, and in a certain manner also in reference to the pure forms of intuition, space and time. Spontaniety is based on the categorical synthesis of transcendental apperception.

HEIDEGGER: Which moment do you see now in Husserl's doctrine of constitution?

FINK: In his concept of constitution, Husserl means neither making nor bare perception of things which are independent of consciousness. Nevertheless, the positive characterization of the concept of constituion remains difficult. When Husserl strove to think back behind the distinction of making and bare perception, this problem remained in the path of cognition, that is, in the relationship of the subject to an entity that is already posited from the beginning. The prior question, however, is whether...

HEIDEGGER: ... objectivity necessarily belongs...

FINK: ... to the being of what is, or whether objectivity first becomes a universal approach to what is in modern philosophy, with which another, more original approach is covered up.

HEIDEGGER: From this it follows once again that we may not interpret Heraclitus from a later time.

FINK: All the concepts that arise in the dispute over idealism and realism are insufficient to characterize the shining-forth, the coming-forth-to-appearance, of what is. It seems to me more propitious to speak of shining-forth than of shining-up. For we are easily led by the idea of shining-up into thinking as if what is already were, and were subsequently illuminated. ἀλήθεια would then be only an elicitation of what already is in a light. However, the light, as ἀλήθεια and fire, is productive in a sense still unknown to us. We know only this much, that the "producitivity" of fire is neither a making nor a generative bringing-forth nor an impotent casting of light.

HEIDEGGER: One could then say that coming-forth-to-appearance is neither *creatio* [creation] nor *illuminatio* [illumination] nor constitution . . .

FINK: . . . nor τέχνη as bringing forth. For τέχνη is the bringing-forth of a specific form out of the substratum of an available, though not manufactured, material . . .

HEIDEGGER: . . . in distinction to *creatio* . . .

FINK: . . . which brings-forth living creatures. We must thus bracket out an entire catalog of current ways of thinking in order not to think coming-forth-to-appearance in an inappropriate manner. But such a procedure has only the character of a *via negationis* [way of negation], and does not lead a step nearer to an understanding of what the shining-forth of τὰ πάντα or ὄντα in the ἕν of fire, sun or λογός means.

HEIDEGGER: Coming-forth-to-appearance concerns a general reference . . .

FINK: . . . the puzzling reference of ἕν and πάντα. This reference is puzzling because the ἕν never occurs among τὰ πάντα. τὰ πάντα means all of what is. But what kind of allness is that? We know relative, specific allness like that of genus and species. For example, we think an allness of species in the concept "all living things." τὰ πάντα, however, form no relative allness, but rather the allness of everything which is. Yet ἕν does not fall under the allness of τὰ πάντα. Rather, the other way around, τὰ πάντα are housed in ἕν, but not—as you have once said in a lecture—like potatoes in a sack, but rather in the sense of what is in being.

HEIDEGGER: We must ask still more closely about τὰ πάντα and ὄντα. How should we interpret ὄντα? What are τὰ πάντα?

FINK: For one thing, we could make the attempt to enumerate whatever there is. What is, for instance, is not just nature and her things. We could begin an enumeration with the elements: sea, earth, heaven.

HEIDEGGER: The gods belong to what is.

FINK: But with that, you already refer to what is and is unphenomenal. At first, let us stay with what is phenomenal. After the elements, we could name the things made up out of them. But there are not only things of nature. Rather, there are also artificial things that we do not come across in nature and for which there is no pattern in nature. A human shares in bringing-forth. A human begets a human, says Aristotle. That means that he has a part in the creative power of nature. Beside that, a human brings forth artificial objects. It is an open problem whether the Aristotelian analysis of the things manufactured in τέχνη, with the help of the scheme of the four causes, is a sufficient determination of the artifact. It is questionable whether artificial things have a random character or whether they have a character of necessity. Some time ago, you asked whether there are shoes because there are shoemakers or whether there are shoemakers because there are shoes. To human Dasein belong such things as are bound up with Dasein's manner of being, and those are necessary things. Alongside these, there are also luxury items. Also the political orders, like states, cities, settlements, laws, belong to what is, but also idols and ideals. This rough overview refers to a great many entities. We do not, however, know straight away how all that we have mentioned coincides in its common feature of being which, nevertheless, makes it different. But an ever more complete overview of all that is would never lead to uncovering ἕν with or alongside τὰ πάντα. Rather, understanding ἕν in its unique character in distinction to τὰ πάντα depends on a τροπή of our spirit.

HEIDEGGER: When we speak of τὰ πάντα, do we suppose τὰ ὄντα from the start, or is there a distinction between the two?

FINK: We think the being of what is in an inexplicit manner when we talk about τὰ πάντα. If the being of what is is referred to explicitly, if τὰ πάντα are designated as ὄντα, then it can mean that they stand in the horizon of questionability, whether they are actual or supposed entities. Images, for example, which are perceived by εἰκασία [apprehension of or by phantasms], are also entities, but they are not that which they represent. Among things, there are grades of being of what is. There are possibilities of the appearance of things which exhibit themselves as other than what they are, without this appearance having to be seen as subjective deception. Reflection on water, for example, is such a phe nomenon of appearance. But it is not easy to describe the manner of being of the reflection on water. If τὰ πάντα are designated as ὄντα, that can mean, on the one hand, that they have proved their quality of actual being, and on the other hand it can mean that the being of what is should be expressly named.

HEIDEGGER: It seems to me that still another question conceals itself behind this one. Are πάντα τὰ πάντα in so far as they are ὄντα, or are ὄντα ὄντα in so far as they are τὰ πάντα?

FINK: A decisive question is now raised, in which two ways of philosophical thinking are indicated. When we think ὄντα from out of τὰ πάντα, we move into an explicit relation to the world, but without al ready thinking of the world. But if we understand τὰ πάντα from out of ὄντα, we move in an understanding of being and think toward its wholeness. Two possible points of departure for thinking have revealed themselves to us.

HEIDEGGER: You touched on the problem of the reflection in water and the appearance connected with it. Another problem about which I am still not clear is the perception of the sunset and the Copernican revolution. The question is whether the sunset is a necessary representation, or whether a seeing is possible for which the sun does not set.

FINK: Perception of the sunset is the right of the naïvely encountered world as against the scientific interpretation of the world. Through cultivation and indirect knowledge, a human can come to the point where he no longer sees what lies before his eyes, to the point, for instance, where he no longer sees the sunset as that which displays itself immediately to his view, but displays itself only in the manner seen in scientific explanation.

HEIDEGGER: The truth of the immediate experience of the world disappears by reason of the scientific interpretation of the world.

FINK: In earlier times, two hundred years ago for instance, life was still centered in the nearby region. Information about life at that time came out of the neighboring world. That has fundamentally changed today in the age of world wide transmission of news. Hans Freyer, in his book *Theorie des gegenwärtigen Zeitalters,* describes the technical world as an environment of surrogates.[25] For him, scientific knowledge of the environment is a surrogate. I regard this description as an inappropriate view, because in the meantime technological things have become a new source of human experience. Today a human exists in the omnipresence of complete global information. The world is no longer divided into neighboring zones, distant and more distant zones; rather, the world that was once thus divided today becomes covered over by technology that, through its skilled intelligence service, makes it possible to live in the omnipresence of all information.

HEIDEGGER: It is difficult to comprehend how the world, divided into near and distant zones, gets covered over by the technological environment. For me, there is a breach here.

FINK: To a certain extent, modern man lives schizophrenically.

HEIDEGGER: If we only knew what this schizophrenia meant. But what we have said up to now is sufficient to see that we are not talking about out of the way matters. The problem for us is the reference of ἕν and πάντα. From where do we experience this reference, from πάντα or from ἕν or from the to and fro in the Hegelian sense? How would you answer this problem with reference to Heraclitus?

FINK: The beginning of our interpretation of Heraclitus by way of lightning was supposed to indicate that there is the basic experience of the outbreak of the whole. In the everyday manner of life, this experience is hidden. In everyday life we are not interested in such experience. In everyday living we do not expressly comport ourselves toward the whole, and also not when we knowingly penetrate into the distant Milky Way. But a human has the possibility of letting become explicit that implicit relationship to the whole as which relationship he always already exists. He exists essentially as a relationship to being, to the whole. For the most part, however, this relationship stagnates. In dealing with the thinker Heraclitus, one can perhaps come to such an experience in

which the whole, to which we always already implicitly comport ourselves, suddenly flashes up.

HEIDEGGER: Thereby we turn our questioning to the reference of
ἕν and its many forms, and to its inner reference to τὰ πάντα. It is always
a difficulty for me that too little is said about τὰ πάντα in the text of
Heraclitus. We are forced to supplement what we do not learn about τὰ
πάντα from Heraclitus with what we know about the Greek world, and
perhaps we let τὰ πάντα be expressed by the poets.

FINK: I said that we still do not have the possibility of declaring what
the coming-forth-to-appearance of τὰ πάντα is in the always living fire.
In order to investigate this problem further, we cite Fr. 76, which appears to be one of the least certain fragments. There are more versions
of it in which a turning (τροπή) is thought. The Greek text handed down
by Maximus Tyrius runs: ζῇ πῦρ τὸν γῆς θάνατον καὶ ἀὴρ ζῇ τὸν πυρὸς
θάνατον, ὕδωρ ζῇ τὸν ἀέρος θάνατον, γῆ τὸν ὕδατος. Diels translates:
"Fire lives the death of earth, and air lives the death of fire; water lives
the death of air, and the earth that of water (?)."

What is surprising in the fragment is that the turning of earth into fire
is mentioned in the formula: to live the death of something else. What is
disconcerting is not so much the talk of arising and birth, but rather the
pronouncement that fire lives the death of earth, air lives the death of
fire, water lives the death of air, and earth lives the death of water. The
most important thing seems to me to be that the annihilation of what
precedes is the birth and arising of what follows. What follows comes
forth in that it lives the death of what precedes. The fall of what precedes appears to be the way on which the new and other comes forth. It
is not, thereby, a question of a superiority of annihilation over what is
arising. That is of significance, because later when we consider in greater
detail the formula, "to live the death of something other," we will not be
able to say that it is a matter of a circular argument. For life turns into
death, but death does not turn into life.

In Fr. 76, it says that the death of what precedes is the life of what
follows. An amendment that Tocco (*Studi Ital.* IV 5) has made in the
text, which is handed down by Maximus and which makes the relationship ambiguous, runs: Fire lives the death of air and air lives the death of
fire. Water lives the death of earth, earth lives the death of water. Here
the connections of fire and air and water and earth are posited as mutual
relations. In the comments of Diels-Kranz we read that ἀὴρ [air] is presumably smuggled in by the stoics. The following is given as a further
variant from this: Fire leaves the death of water, water lives the death of
fire or the death of earth, earth lives the death of water. We have no
familiar phenomena of a change over of elements. When sea and earth
are talked about, it is a matter of elements on a large scale, a matter of
the world regions. If water is mentioned, however, it is not clear whether

the sea is also meant. In Fr. 76, a revolution of fire, air, water, and earth is perhaps mentioned. The overturnings mentioned here cannot quite be followed through by us.

In this connection, we look at Fr. 36: ψυχῇσιν θάνατος ὕδωρ γενέσθαι, ὕδατι δὲ θάνατος γῆν γενέσθαι, ἐκ γῆς δὲ ὕδωρ γίνεται, ἐξ ὕδατος δὲ ψυχή. Diels translates: "It is death for souls to become water, but for water, death to become earth. But out of earth comes water, and out of water comes soul." The turnover is here named with the hard and obscure word, γένεσις [to become]. The issuance and the hard change of soul over into water, of water into earth, of earth into water, of water into soul, do not allow the idea that the same original substance lies behind its transubstantiations. The fragment mentions γενέσθαι and γίνεται and the hard word ἐκ [out of]. We must ask ourselves whether ἐκ in the sense of the issuance of something is also to be understood in the sense of the whence or else in the sense of the Aristotelian ἐξ οὗ [out of itself], as that which lies at the base and would change over in a μεταβολή [change]. At first, it is striking that in Fr. 36 the four elements are not clarified more. Rather, ψυχαί [souls] are mentioned. What could ψυχαί be? What is thought by ψυχαί? Do we abandon the apparent way of alternating change over of elements when the rubric ψυχαί now emerges in issuance and passage? I am of the opinion that the soul in the sense of the human soul is not primarily meant by ψυχαί. An element of endowment with consciousness does not enter into the activity of the elements with ψυχαί.

Perhaps we can ascertain this in a reference to Fr. 77: ψυχῇσι τέρψιν ἢ θάνατον ὑγρῇσι γενέσθαι. The second part runs: ζῆν ἡμᾶς τὸν ἐκείνων θάνατον καὶ ζῆν ἐκείνας τὸν ἡμέτερον θάνατον. Diels' translation is: "For souls it is desire or (?) death to become wet. We live the death of those souls and they live our death." When it says that we live the death of the souls and that the souls live our death, when, in other words, the souls stand in relationship to us so that they live our death and vice versa, then they cannot easily be identified as humans. But we also have no motive for determining ψυχαί. We could at first only say that a new thought motif in the turning of fire appears with ψυχαί.

HEIDEGGER: The difficulty here is that one does not know where the matter under consideration belongs, and where it has its place in Heraclitus' thought.

FINK: I have taken up this fragment because the formula, "to live the death of something," also occurs in it, even though we still do not know who or what lives death as ψυχαί. This strange, most surprising formula must be thought explicitly by us, if we wish to keep away from pure ideas of chemical transmutation, the ἀλλοίωσις and the emanation of the turns of fire.

We turn to a first consideration of Fr. 62: ἀθάνατοι θνητοί, θνητοὶ ἀθάνατοι, ζῶντες τὸν ἐκείνων θάνατον, τὸν δὲ ἐκείνων βίον τεθνεῶτες. Diels translates: "Immortal: mortal, mortal: immortal, for the life of these is the death of those, and the life of those is the death of these." Heraclitus speaks here in a short, tightly worded way. Here we have the formula, "to live the death of something other," in a special way. Diels-Kranz separate the "immortal mortal" and "mortal immortal," each time with a colon. One could suppose that in one instance it is a matter of a determination of θνητοί [mortals] and in the other a determination of ἀθάνατοι [immortals]. In the first case ἀθάνατοι would be the subject and θνητοί the predicate; in the second case θνητοί would be the subject and ἀθάνατοι the predicate. Does it mean that there are immortal mortals and mortal immortals? Doesn't the phrase contradict itself? Or is a relationship of the immortals to the mortals thought here, a relationship which is fixed by their being placed together?

HEIDEGGER: It is noteworthy that θνητοί stands between the ἀθάνατοι.

FINK: Do you take ἀθάνατοι as the subject of the sentence? One could ask what kind of a distinction is thought in ἀθάνατοι and θνητοί? A simple answer would be that ἀθανατίζειν [to be mortal] is the negation of θάνατος [death].

HEIDEGGER: How is θάνατος to be determined in reference to what we have said up to this point?

FINK: We cannot give such a determination yet, because we have moved till now in the domain of τὰ πάντα in reference to πῦρ ἀείζωον. Perhaps one could view death from ἀείζωον, if one thinks it as the always living, in contrast to the experience that every living thing is finite. But it is difficult to think the ἀείζωον.

HEIDEGGER: Don't we learn from Fr. 76 that θάνατος is distinguished in contrast to γένεσις?

FINK: There it is said that through the death of one, another comes forth.

HEIDEGGER: Does θάνατος mean φθορά?

FINK: I regard this identification as doubtful. Death and life are not normally referred to fire, air, water, and earth, in any case so long as one does not understand fire in the sense of Heraclitus. Looked at from the phenomenon, we speak of life and death only in the domain of living things. In reference to the domain of what is lifeless, we could speak only in a figurative sense of death and life.

But let us remain at first with Fr. 62, in which ἀθάνατοι and ονητοί are mentioned. We could say that the immortals are the gods, and that the mortals are humans. The gods are not deathless in the sense of an α-*privitum* [alpha-privative]. They are not unrelated to the fate of death. Rather, they are in a certain way referred to the death of mortals through the reverse relation to death, from which they are free. As coobservers, the gods have a realtion to death, which relation we can say though not comprehend. Their reverse relation to death has only the character of exclusion. As ἀ-θάνατοι, the gods have a relation to mortals, which relation appears in the form that the life of the immortals is the death of mortals. We are accustomed to understanding life and death in hard opposition, the hardness of which cannot be surpassed. The opposition of life and death is not the same as that of warm and cold, or of young and old. In the oppositions familiar to us, there are transitions, for example, the transition of being warm to being cold, and the transition of being young into being old. Still, taken strictly, there is no transition of being warm into being cold. Rather, that which at first has a share in being warm maintains a share in being cold. Also, being young does not turn, strictly speaking, into being old. Rather, that which at first is young turns into something old, becomes old. Such transitions are in part reversible, so that they can return their course, and in part one way and irreversible. What at first has a share in being warm and then turns cold can also turn again into being warm. However, what is first young and then old cannot become young again. In Fr. 67, which says that god is day-night, winter-summer, war-peace, satiety-hunger, Heraclitus names different oppositions that are familiar to us; however, they all have a character fundamentally other than the opposition of life and death. Is the juxtaposition of life and death in any way still measurable and comparable to the juxtapositions familiar to us? In the phenomenon, the fall of living things into death is irrevocable and final. True, it is hoped in myth and religion that a new life awaits us after death, and that death is only an entrance door. This postmortal life is not the same life as the premortal life here on earth. But it is questionable whether talk of "afterwards" and "previously" continues to have any sense here at all. Evidently, there is expressed in this only a perspective of those who are living and who fill the no-man's-land with ideas of a life to be hoped for. With familiar oppositions, which we know and which have transitions, we find a going under of one into another and, roughly, the birth of the warm out of the cold and of the cold out of the warm. But do we also find in the phenomenon a birth of life out of death? Clearly not. The birth of what lives is an issue out of the union of the two sexes. The new life is born out of a special intensity of being alive. Thereby, we do not need to share the same view with Aristotle, that the new life is already preformed as a seed in the parents, and that birth is then only the ἀλλοίωσις of a still germinal kind of being into a developed kind of being. But could we imagine how life and death are intertwined, and indeed not in the sense that life turns into death, but in the sense that the transition is thought as "to live the death of something other"? That does not mean: to come out of death into life. Let us begin with the form of speech. We are accustomed to saying that life lives, that death dies. That is not meant in the sense of a redundant manner of expression. For we could say that the individual dies his or rather another's death, or rather that the individual lives his life in his separation against the alienation that each one experiences from the practices and institutions and the social situation. In such formulations the reference of an intransitive verb to an inner accusative is at once familiar to us.

HEIDEGGER: In order to clarify the inner accusative that you name, we could think about Hegel's speculative sentence. Hegel gives the example: "God is being." At first, it appears to be a normal declarative sentence in which God is the subject and "being" is the predicate. If this sentence is comprehended as a speculative sentence, however, then the distinction of subject and predicate is cancelled in that the subject turns into the predicate. God disappears in being; being is what God is. In the speculative sentence, "God is being," the "is" has a transitive character: *ipsum esse est deus* [being itself is God]. This relationship of the speculative sentence is nevertheless only a remote, risky analogy to the problem that now occupies us.

FINK: But "God is being," thought speculatively, is a certain analogy only to the formula, "to live life," but not to the other formula, "to live the death of something other." Here "to live" is not referred to life, but to something that appears to be the contrary.

HEIDEGGER: But the question is what "death" means here. We do not know which opposition is thought between life and death.

FINK: That depends on the conception of whether death is the process of dying, of becoming dead, or completed death. This distinction makes the problem still more difficult.

HEIDEGGER: What is astonishing is that the matter that is so estranging to us appears to be so glibly said by Heraclitus.

FINK: What Heraclitus says here about life and death is in general most estranging. If we represent the state of affairs symmetrically, then we could not only say that the immortals live the death of the mortals, but we could also ask whether there is a transitive dying of something. The entanglement of life and death has its place only on the constant foundation of life. That precludes a verbal dying.

HEIDEGGER: If τεθνεῶτες is to be understood in the present, then Heraclitus would say that they die the life of those.

FINK: Thus seen, the matter to be thought by us becomes still more complicated. It would not only be a matter of "to live the death of something other," but also a matter of the contrary course in a transitive dying. ζῶντες means to live another's death, whereas τεθνεῶτες means being dead. If we make the transition from life and death to being alive and being dead, we must ask what "being" actually means in reference to death. Is being dead a manner of being? An act is mentioned in ζῶντες: living the death of those. That corresponds to the formula of Fr. 76: Fire lives the death of earth.

HEIDEGGER: In order to clarify τεθνεῶτες, understood in the active sense, we are reminded of Rilke's phrase, "to achieve death." But the question is whether τεθνεῶτες refers to an active dying in the present or to being dead (finished) in the perfect.

FINK: Dying in the present is the end phase of life. What is questionable is who or what lives or dies. In the phrase ἀθάνατοι θνητοί it is not decided whether ἀθάνατοι is a predicative determination of θνητοί or, conversely, whether θνητοί is a predicative determination of ἀθάνατοι. At first, the immortals and the mortals are confronted with one another and tied up with one another . . .

HEIDEGGER: . . . and after that follows the illustration.

FINK: The phrase ἀθάνατοι θνητοί is no enumeration. For in that case, the reverse formulation would not be possible. We see that the immortals and the mortals stand in a relation. The concept of the gods is untouched by death and nevertheless we conjecture a relationship to death. For it is said: while they live the death of those. To what does this phrase refer? What is the subject of ζῶντες? Is it the immortals or the mortals? And what is the subject of τεθνεῶτες? The gods live the death of humans. The gods are spectators and witnesses who accept the death of humans as offerings.

HEIDEGGER: And humans die the life of the gods.

FINK: Let us also include Fr. 88: ταὐτό τ̓ ἔνι ζῶν καὶ τεθνηκὸς καὶ (τὸ) ἐγρηγορὸς καὶ καθεῦδον καὶ νέον καὶ γηραιόν· τάδε γὰρ μεταπεσόντα ἐκεῖνά ἐστι κάκεῖνα πάλιν μεταπεσόντα ταῦτα. Diels translates: "And it is always one and the same, what dwells (?) within us: living and dead and waking and sleeping and young and old. For this is changed over to that and that changes back over to this." When Heraclitus says ταὐτό τ̓ ἔνι ζῶν καὶ τεθνηκός, is living and dying or being dead . . .

HEIDEGGER: . . . or being able to die meant?

FINK: If the living and the dead are paralleled with the waking and sleeping, the young and old, then no ability is meant. Waking and sleeping, as alternating states, are the most alternating forms of the course of human life. Being young and being old are the initial and final times of the human course of life. The relation of waking and sleep, and of young and old, are certain parallels to the relationship of life and death. The relationship of life and death becomes still more complicated by them, . . .

HEIDEGGER: . . . because the kind of the three distinctions is quite different.

FINK: Living and dying are one and the same; waking and sleeping are the same; young and old are the same. Heraclitus declares the sameness of what seems to be different. How is ταὐτό [the same] to be understood here?

HEIDEGGER: We could understand it as "belonging together."

FINK: Indeed, each pair, living and dying, waking and sleeping, young and old, belongs together. But how do living and dying, for example, belong together in a "same"?

HEIDEGGER: In reference to what is same.

FINK: If being alive and being dead are the same, then they form a sameness that hides itself. The distinctness of life and death becomes clear for the most part when they are posited as analogous to the former two relationships. Sleeping and waking, as well as being young and being old are familiar differences to us, which are referred to the course of time of our lives. Waking and sleeping are alternating states in the course of time, being young and being old are two distinctive phases in the course of time of our lives. Against that, life and death is a relationship of the entire lifetime to something that overshadows it but that does not occur in the lifetime.

Is the saying of the thinker Heraclitus a slap in the face to the current opinion that insists on the distinctness of life and death as well as on the difference between waking and sleep, being young and being old? Is it a matter of directing the thrust of his thinking against the trend toward a world that is divided up in differences, and doing so with respect to a sameness? This would not mean that phenomena would loose their distinctions; rather, it would mean that they are ταὐτό in relation to ἕν. Heraclitus says that being alive—being dead, waking—sleeping, and being young—being old, are the same. He does not say, as Diels-Kranz translate and therewith interpret: "the same which dwells in us." ἡμῖν [us] is added to ἔνι [within] by Diels. It is precisely questionable whether we are the place of the sameness of great oppositions of life and death or whether the place of sameness must not rather be sought in ἕν, to which humans comport themselves and which they thus resemble in a certain sense. Certainly it is at first a matter of a dictatorial assertion that the living and the dead, waking and sleeping, the young and the old, are the same. It is not said that the three opposing pairs of opposites are the same, but rather Heraclitus names three oppositions that stand in a specified correspondence and he thinks the ταὐτό in relation to each one of the oppositions. The lifetime forms the common basis for the threefold opposites. The entire lifetime is confined by death. Within life, sleep is the analog to death, being old has a specific reference to death, and waking and being young are most related to being alive. But in Fr. 88, there is no mention of life and death, but of what is alive and what is dead. But how are the expressions "the living" and "the dead" to be understood? If we say the just (τὸ δίκαιον) and the beautiful (τὸ καλόν), then do we mean what is just or being just, what is beautiful or being beautiful?

HEIDEGGER: Your interpretation thus goes in the direction not of understanding the three distinctions as three cases of a species, but rather in the direction of classifying the three distinctions in reference to the phenomenon of time . . .

FINK: . . . and thus toward constructing an analogical relationship. Here it is not a question of fixed distinctions. Nevertheless, we are concerned with differences that form distinctions. Being alive and being dead do not stand in a gradual relationship to one another, because being dead does not allow of degrees. As against that, we are accustomed to intensifying being alive, and to distinguishing inert and high forms of life-performance. Waking and sleep, however, turn almost unnoticeably into one another. Life and death do not form an opposition like beautiful and ugly, nor is their distinction one of degree. The nature of their being different is the problem. As soon as we attempt to be clear about the all-too-familiar dialectical interpenetration the questionable character of the text disappears. If we start from the fact that each analogy is a likeness of what is unlike, then we could say that sleeping and waking, as well as being old and being young, relate in a certain sense to being dead and being alive. Perhaps it is a comparison all too full of hope, nevertheless, when we call sleep the brother of death and when we regard sleep as an in-between phenomenon. Also, regarding the question about the sense of the fomula, "to live the death of something," the tying together of life and death is the strange thing in the transitive use of "to live." It is a matter of interpretation whether the current model can also be applied; so that we not only say that death lives, but also that life dies.

We came to no result, and perhaps we will come to no final result at all. But the all too familiar explication of τροπή has wandered into the foreignness and darkness of the formula, "to live the death of something." We could perhaps think the relationship of fire to earth, to air, and to water rather in reference to life and death, so that, with reference to the difficult relationship of tension of life and death, we could come to a certain anthropological key for the nonanthropological foundational relatedness of ἕν and πάντα.

9

Immortal: Mortal (Fragment 62).—
ἓν τὸ σοφόν (Correlated Fragments: 32, 90).

FINK: Mr. Heidegger cannot come today since he is prevented by an important trip. He asks us, however, to continue explication of the text, so that we make some further progress in our interpretation of the fragments. By means of the summary, he will inform himself about the progress of this session in order then to express an opinion.

Let us bring to mind the way of thought, better, the gist of open questionabilities, that has led us in the last session. We started out from the problem of the transformations of fire with the question whether the change of an original stuff is thereby thought, or whether a relatedness of ἕν and πάντα is aimed at. Finally, we arrived in Fr. 76 at the dark formula, difficult to comprehend, that something lives the death of another. This formula is then used in Fr. 62 as a mark of the relationship of immortals to mortals, or mortals to immortals. Is it only a matter here of another domain for the employment of the problematic formula, "to live the death of something"? Is the formula also meant here in the fundamental breadth, as we have learned it in Fr. 76 in the relationship of the elements, fire, air, water, and earth? Is it a matter of cosmological references, or of cosmological counterreferences in so far as the formula is here applied to things that stand open in a special manner to the whole, that is, to gods and humans? Is the above mentioned formula applied here to cosmological living beings? Perhaps that happens, because the relationship of immortal to mortal is analogous to the reference of ἕν in the form of lightning, of sun, and of fire, to the πάντα. Is the fundamental relatedness, ever disconcerting to us, of ἕν and πάντα rather sayable from out of its reflection? Is the world-relatedness of ἕν and πάντα rather sayable from out of the relationship of gods and humans who understand being? With this, the path of our problem situation is first of all indicated. Let us now attempt to clarify the structure of Fr. 62. For we cannot say that its structure has become clear and distinct at this point.

The fragment runs: ἀθάνατοι θνητοί, θνητοὶ ἀθάνατοι, ζῶντες τὸν ἐκείνων θάνατον, τὸν δὲ ἐκείνων βίον τεθνεῶτες. We could translate, "Immortal: mortal, mortal: immortal." Diels thereby brings immortals into a relationship to mortals and mortals into a reference to immortals. In addition, this relationship is explained by the dark problem-formula that Diels translates as follows: "for the life of these is the death of those, and the life of those is the death of these." This translation appears to me to be too free. For it does say: ζῶντες τὸν ἐκείνων θάνατον, τὸν δὲ ἐκείνων βίον τεθνεῶτες, "in that they live the death of those and in that they die the life of those." If we interpret ἀθάνατοι in the familiar sense as gods and θνητοί as humans, then it is a matter of an interpretive step that we cannot assert with unconditioned certainty. To be sure, the immortals are the gods in Greek myth. But there are also intermediate beings, the heroes, who are born as mortal, half gods, and are elevated to become immortals. Is the milieu of immortals and mortals familiar with reliability and certainty? The problem is what is indicated by ἀθάνατοι and θνητοί. But first we take up the mythological meaning, and comprehend the immortals as the gods and the mortals as humans.

The gods are also characterized in Fr. 62 from out of death. True, immortals are indeed removed from death. They are not delivered over to death, but they stand open to it. As immortals they must know themselves as the ones who win their self-understanding in the negation of dying. They know themselves as the beings who are open to death, but who do not encounter death, the beings who observe the death of humans, and the beings who come to know their own permanence in the sight of the passing away of transient humans. The mortals are humans who know that they are delivered over to death in reference alone to the gods who always are and are removed from death. θνητοί is not some objective designation which is spoken from an extra-human point of view; it points, rather, to the self-understanding of humans in understanding that they are delivered over to death, in so far as they know themselves as *morituri* [those about to die]. Humans know themselves as transient in view of and in reference to the everlasting gods who are removed from death. With immortals and mortals the greatest innerworldly distance is named between innerworldly beings, the taut bow stretching between gods and humans who, however, are nevertheless referred to one another in their self-understanding and understanding of being. Mortals know their own disappearing being in view of and in reference to the everlasting being of the gods; and the gods win their perpetual being in contrast and in confrontation with humans who are constantly disappearing in time. The distinction of immortals and mortals is characterized from out of death. But this distinction is not one like the distinction between life and death itself. For, in their self-understanding, the immortals and the mortals live and comport themselves toward the being of the other. The relationship of the gods to humans is not to be equated with the relationship of the living to the dead, and yet the taut bow stretching between ἀθάνατοι-θνητοί and θνητοί-ἀθάνατοι is thought out of the reference to life and death. The most widely stretched out distinction between gods and humans, immortals and mortals, is intertwined and is tightened together with its opposite extreme—perhaps in an analogy to the relatedness of ἕν and πάντα.

The question which leads us is whether, with the admission of the relationship of immortals to mortals, more than just an anthropological clue is found for indicating how the fire, the sun, the lightning, as special forms of ἕν, comport themselves toward πάντα. There is not ἕν and τὰ πάντα next to one another. They do not lie on the same plane, do not lie on a comparable plane of the usual sort, but they are unique in their relatedness. Their relatedness can be indicated with no known relationship. ἕν is not among πάντα; it is not already thought when we think τὰ πάντα strictly and include in this quintessence everything that is at all. When we ourselves think τὰ πάντα as quintessence, it is not inclusive of ἕν. It remains separated from τὰ πάντα, but not in the manner, familiar to us, of being separated by spatial and temporal boarders or by belonging to another kind of species. All usual kinds of separation are inapplicable to the fundamental relatedness of ἕν and πάντα. But at the same time we must also say that the unique belonging-together of ἕν and πάντα, the intertwining of what is separated, must also be seen in the unique separation of ἕν and τὰ πάντα. ἕν and τὰ πάντα are tightened together in their intertwining.

Up to now we have met with a manifold of similies; for example, as in the night, things shine up in the light-shine of the lightning flash and show their relief, so in an original sense, the entirety of things comes forth to appearance in the outbreaking light-shine of ἕν, thought as lightning. Or again: as the things that stand in sunlight shine up in their imprint in the light of the sun, so the entirety of inner-worldly things comes forth to appearance in the ἕν thought as sunlight. Here, things do not come forth side by side with the sunlight, but the sunlight surrounds the things and is thus separated from them and at the same time bound with them in the manner of an including light. Just so, there is also an entirety of the many τὰ πάντα, not side by side with the light of shining-forth; rather, the light of shining-forth envelops the entirety of πάντα and is "separated" from it and "bound" with it in a manner difficult to comprehend, which we could probably best clarify for ourselves in comparison with the all-embracing light. Are immortals and mortals now also referred to each other like ἕν and τὰ πάντα with their greatest separation? Thereby we understand the immortals as those who know their own perpetual being only on the background of the temporal perishing of humans. And we understand the mortals as humans who only know their transient being by having a relationship to the immortals who always are and who know their perpetual being. We could read ἀθάνατοι θνητοί, θνητοί ἀθάνατοι in many ways; either with Diels or else in the following way: immortal mortals, mortal immortals. This hard phrase appears to be self-contradictory. But one does not go especially far off base with a paradoxical concept of immortal mortals and mortal immortals. The gods live the death of mortal humans.

Does that mean that the life of the gods is the slaying of humans? And on the other side, do humans die the life of the gods? Neither could we connect any correct sense with this rendition. I would, therefore, rather believe that the following suggests itself. The gods live in comparing themselves with mortal humans who experience death. They live the death of mortals in that, in their self-understanding and their understanding of being, they hold themselves over against the transience of humans and the all-too-finite manner in which humans understand what is. But it is more difficult if we ask ourselves how we should translate τὸν δὲ ἐκείνων βίον τεθνεῶτες [in that they die the life of those]. Could we set τεθνεῶτες [they, having died] parallel to ζῶντες [those living]? But the question is whether the perfect participle has the meaning of the perfect or whether it is to be translated as in the present participial form like ἀποθνήσκοντες [those who are dying]. This question can only be decided by the philologists. The life of the immortals is the death of mortals. The gods live the death of the mortals, and the mortals die the life of the gods or become atrophied in reference to the life of the gods. We also use the phrase: to die a death, to live a life. In Fr. 62, however, it says: to live the death of the other, to die the life of the other. If we wish to make clear to ourselves what it means that the gods live the death of humans, we could at first reject the radical interpretation according to which the gods would be cannibalistic beings. They do not live the death of humans in the sense that they devour them. For they do not need humans as food nor, in the final analysis, do they need the offerings and prayers of humans. But what then does the formula mean: the gods live the death of humans. I am able to connect only one sense with this sentence. I say that the gods understand themselves in their own everlasting being in express reference to mortal humans. The constant being of the gods signifies a persistence in view of humans' being constantly delivered over to time. In this manner the gods live the death of humans. And in the same way I am able to connect only one sense with the sentence which says that humans die the life of the gods, or that they atrophy in reference to the life of the gods; namely, it is thereby said that humans, by understanding themselves as the ones who most disappear, always comport themselves toward the permanence that the life of the gods appears to us to be.

Humans die as the transient ones not only in so far as they stand in association with transients. They are not only the ones who most disappear in the realm of what disappears, but rather they are at the same time understandingly open to the permanence of the gods. A fundamental reference to that which never perishes belongs to the relation of

humans to themselves and to everything around them. Thus we understand "to live the death of humans" and "to die the life of the gods" as a
reciprocal, intertwining relationship of the self-understanding and
understanding of being of gods and humans. The gods live the death of
humans in the sense that they could only understand themselves as
immortals in their perpetual being against the background of what is
transient. They are only perpetual when, at the same time, they are
referred to the sphere of change in time.

According to Fr. 62, gods and humans behave precisely not as in
Hölderlin's poem, "Hyperion's Song of Fate." "You walk above in the
light, / Weightless tread a soft floor, blessed genii! / Radiant the gods'
mild breezes / Gently play on you / As the girl artist's fingers / On holy
strings. — Fateless the Heavenly breathe / Like an unweaned infant
asleep; / Chastely preserved / In modest bud / For ever their minds / Are
in flower / And their blissful eyes / Eternally tranquil gaze, / Eternally
clear. — But we are fated / to find no foothold, no rest, / And suffering
mortals / Dwindle and fall / Headlong from one / Hour to the next, /
Hurled like water / From ledge to ledge / Downward for years to the
vague abyss."[26] Here the domain of the gods and the domain of humans
are separated like two spheres that do not intertwine with each other, but
lie opposite one another without mutual reference. High above in the
light, the gods wander without destiny, their spirit eternally in bloom,
while humans lead a restless life and fall into the cataract of time and
disappear. The way in which Hölderlin here views the eternal life of the
gods indicates that the view of mortals does not necessarily belong to the
self-understanding of the gods. But if gods and humans do not form two
separated domains, but rather form two domains turned toward each
other, then we could apply the intertwining relationship to the beginning of Fr. 62, which ties mortals and immortals together with each
other in a hard manner.

PARTICIPANT: The tying together of the gods' perpetual being and
the being of humans wandering in time has its analogy in Goethe's
thought of perdurance in oscillation [*Dauer im Wechsel*].

FINK: There is, however, a perdurance as constancy in time. Kant,
for example, thought the continuation of the world stuff in roughly this
manner.

PARTICIPANT: Goethe's thought of perdurance in oscillation does
not mean constancy in time, but goes in the direction of Heraclitus'
thoughts.

FINK: Still, we would first have to know to which passage of
Goethe's you refer. For there is also perdurance that stands throughout
oscillation like, for example, the world stuff of Kant, which does not
itself pass away or come into being, but only appears as different. Thus,
however, we think the relationship between substance and its attributes.

PARTICIPANT: For Goethe, perdurance constitutes itself first and foremost in oscillation.

FINK: That is also true in regard to substantial perdurance. But Heraclitus means precisely not that something endures in temporal changing. For then we would have only the relationship of an original stuff to its forms of appearance. But that was precisely the question, whether the relationship of fire, sea, and earth is the relationship of a perduring original stuff (fire) in the oscillations of its conditions or appearances as alien forms, or whether it is a matter of quite another unique distinction. All inner-worldly entities have the structure of relatively perduring substances with changing conditions, or they belong to a unique substance as the continuous substrate that goes on and neither passes away nor comes into being. If we apply this scheme of thought for the turning over of fire, then fire behaves toward sea and earth no differently than an original stuff to its many forms of appearance. However, we have sought after another relationship of fire to sea and earth that pertains to the relatedness of ἕν and πάντα. The relationship of immortal gods and mortal humans takes on an analogous representation for this relatedness of ἕν and πάντα. Thereby, we think gods and humans not only in reference to the opposition of power and fragility, but such that gods and humans, in order to know their own being, have to know one another. If ἕν is ἕν τὸ σοφόν [the one, which alone is wise], it can only know itself in its highest opposition to τὰ πάντα and at the same time also as that which steers and guides τὰ πάντα. With this, we view a relatedness not of the kind in which a supertemporal sphere of entities realtes itself to a temporal sphere of things. It is not a matter of a two-world doctrine of Platonic kind, but rather of a theory of the world, of the unity of the ἕν and of the individual things found in the passage of time. When Goethe speaks of perdurance in oscillation, he means, perhaps, the constancy of nature over against the appearances of nature. But he thereby finds himself in the neighborhood of the thought of an original stuff.

PARTICIPANT: I cannot associate myself with this conception. I am of the opinion that Goethe's thought of perdurance in oscillation comes into the neighborhood of your interpretation of Heraclitus.

FINK: In Fr. 30, ἕν is mentioned as πῦρ ἀείζωον, which is an immortal fire. The immortal gods are the analogical keepers of the immortal fire. In Fr. 100 it says: ὧρας αἳ πάντα φέρουσι [the seasons which bring all things]. Accordingly, πάντα, which is brought forth by the seasons, is therefore not perpetual, but something that abides in time. From there, ἕν behaves toward τὰ πάντα as πῦρ ἀείζωον or—since Professor Heidegger is not present today, we could dare say—as being itself, thought as time, behaves toward what is driven in time, temporally determined things. I did not say either that ἀθάνατοι and θνητοί are to be identified with ἕν and πάντα, but that they represent symbolically the relatedness of ἕν and πάντα. Immortal and mortal are not themselves cosmic moments that are separated and at the same time embraced like ἕν and πάντα. Rather both are cosmological beings who understand the whole, the gods from above and humans from below. If we want to speak here of an analogy, we must be clear that it is always thoroughly a matter of similarity by means of unsimilarity, whereby the unsimilarity is always greater. Talk about humans as *imago dei* [image of God] does not mean that a human is a mirror image of the Godhead and similar to the Godhead like a mirror image to the original image. A human is an image of God through the infinity of distance. We have no language for the purpose of addressing the relatedness of ἕν το τὰ πάντα. The ἕν lights up to us only in lightning, in sun, in the seasons, in fire. Fire, however, is not the phenomenal, but the unphenomenal fire, in the shine of which τὰ πάντα come forth to appearance.

Because we have no language to characterize the fundamental relatedness of ἕν and πάντα, and because we wish to keep πυρὸς τροπαί away from the traditional blunt schemes of thought, according to which an always extant original stuff changes its conditions or disguises itself in its forms of appearance, we have started out from Fr. 76, in which the fundamental relatedness of ἕν and πάντα is addressed in the formula, "to live the death of another." From there, we turned to Fr. 62 in which the formula, "to live the death" and "to die the life" is said, not of fire, air, water, and earth, but of immortals and mortals. Application of that formula to gods and humans appears at first to stand closer to our human power of comprehension. The transition from Fr. 76 to Fr. 62 is no narrowing of a general cosmological reference to an anthroplogical-theological relationship. The anthropological-theological relationship is no reference of two kinds of beings, but rather the relationship of how the two different kinds of beings understand themselves and that which is. The gods understand their own perpetual being in reference to the death of humans. If the gods did not have before them the fall of humans and πάντα into time, could they live their life, which is never broken off, in blissful self-indulgence, and could they become aware of their divinity? Could ἕν, which is represented by the immortals, be by itself without the view of πάντα; could πάντα, which are represented by mortals and their understanding of being, be without knowing of the endlessness of πῦρ ἀείζωον? I would like to repeat again that the relationship of immortals to mortals is not to be equated with that of ἕν and πάντα. I was only concerned to point out that one can find an index to the relatedness of ἕν and πάντα in the intertwining relationship of gods and humans in their self-knowledge and knowledge of the other. Thus, it is a matter neither of a parallel nor of an analogy in the usual sense. All the fragments of Heraclitus' theology speak of god only like one could speak of ἕν. All distinctions fall away in the god. Thereby, not only a sublimity of the god vis-à-vis the other living beings is expressed, but that which Heraclitus says about the god must be thought from the peculiar analogous relationship of the god to ἕν τὸ σοφὸν.

In Fr. 32, Heraclitus says the following: ἓν τὸ σοφὸν μοῦνον λέγεσθαι οὐκ ἐθέλει καὶ ἐθέλει Ζηνὸς ὄνομα. "The one, which alone is wise, is not willing and yet willing to be called by the name Zeus." In a certain manner we could think ἕν in Zeus, if the surrounding ἕν of the whole is also represented by Zeus as the highest innerworldly being. It is important, therefore, that Heraclitus says οὐκ ἐθέλει [is not willing] first and then ἐθέλει [is willing]. Only after the negation can a certain analogical correspondence be said of the god and ἕν.

PARTICIPANT: In order to carry out your interpretation of ἕν, one must understand ἕν in a two-fold meaning. On one hand, ἕν is in opposition to τὰ πάντα, and on the other, ἕν is as the unity of opposites of ἕν and πάντα. One cannot posit the opposition between ἕν and πάντα without presupposing a bridging unity between them. Perhaps I can clarify myself by a reference to Schelling. Schelling says that the absolute is not only the unity, but the unity of unity and of opposition. Thereby it is meant that behind each opposition stands a bridging unity. If we wish to avoid a two-world doctrine, then ἕν stands not only in opposition to τὰ πάντα, but we must think ἕν at the same time as bridging unity.

FINK: ἕν is the unity within which there first is the entirety of πάντα in their manifold oppositions. You argue formally with the scheme of concepts from German idealism, that the absolute is the identity of identity and nonidentity. This relationship can be developed in other fashions. Thereby, we do not, however, come into the dimension of Heraclitus. ἕν and πάντα form a unique distinction. It is better if we speak here of distinction and not of opposition. Otherwise, we think all too easily of the usual oppositions like warm-cold, male-female, and so on, and thus of reversible and irreversible oppositions. One could project here an entire logic of oppositions. Our question is directed toward ἕν. We came onto its trace in departure from lightning. In the view of natural science, lightning is nothing other than a specific electrical appearance. But Heraclitus thinks the nonphenomenal rising of the entirety of πάντα in it. Although we have uncovered more nuances of the ἕν-πάντα relatedness in going through various fragments, we still cannot comprehend this relatedness completely. After we have learned about the ἕν in the form of lightning, lightning bolt, sun, and seasons, we also met with the determination of ἕν as fire. Since we did not want to comprehend πυρὸς τροπαί in a blunt physiological sense, we had to search for another comprehension.

In Fr. 76, we learned for the first time the formula, "to live the death of something." In Fr. 62, we found the formula again as the relationship of immortals to mortals. We attempted with this formula of counterreference, i.e., "to live the death of the other" and "to die the life of another," to think toward the relationship of gods and humans. Gods do not live the death of humans in the sense that a slaying of humans belongs to their life. We interpret "to live the death of mortals" as a life of the gods in sight of the being of living beings who understand being in a finite, temporal manner. In sight of humans who are delivered over to death and who are not sheltered by perpetual being, the gods understand their ἀεί εἶναι [to be always] and are, as it were, the πῦρ ἀείζωον, even if they are never ἀεί in the strict sense like πῦρ ἀείζωον is. Against this, humans die the life of the gods. In understanding of the perpetual being of the gods, they are not allowed thereby to partake of it. Humans win no share of the perpetual being of the immortals, but they understand themselves and their disappearance in reference to the fact that the gods are not delivered over to death. I attempt to give one sense to the formulas, "to live the death of mortals" and "to die the life of immortals," in which I interpret them as the intertwining of the self-understanding and understanding of being of gods and humans. This intertwining relationship represents the counter reference of ἕν, the always living fire, and the temporally finite being of πάντα in general which are brought forth by the seasons. The immortal gods are the reflection, the innerworldly representations, of the always living fire as a form of ἕν. In this interpretation, I see a possibility of understanding how the gods live the death of humans. They live the death of humans not in the sense of an encounter; rather, they are referred to the death of humans in the encounter of their own perpetual being.

In the first and second versions of "Mnemosyne," Hölderlin says: "For the heavenly ones are unable / To do everything. Namely, the mortals / Reach the abyss. Thus, the echo returns / With them. Long is / the time, but / What is true happens." That means that the gods, those who do not stand in need, nevertheless need one thing, namely mortals who pass further into the abyss. We have a simile of ἕν to the πάντα, which are constantly driven about in time, in that we see how the gods cannot, in their perpetuity, self-sufficiently enjoy their infinity, and how they are in need of the counter reference to mortals. We have a simile of ἕν and πάντα in that we see how humans, driven about in time, are in need of the counter reference to perpetual gods for the sake of knowledge of their own finitude. Humans and gods have the commonality that they are not only entities in the world, but that they live in the manner of understanding relationships to being. Humans understand being in a finite way, the gods in infinite manner. The gods exceed humans not only in force generally, but in the power of their understanding of what is. The πᾶν is mortal immortal. The πᾶν is, however, no *coincidentia oppositorum*, no night in which all oppositions are obliterated. τό πᾶν is the word in which ἕν and πάντα are comprehended together. We can apply paradoxical phrases to it alone.

We turn now to Fr. 90: πυρός τε ἀνταμοιβὴ τὰ πάντα καὶ πῦρ ἁπάντων ὅκωσπερ χρυσοῦ χρήματα καὶ χρημάτων χρυσός. Diels translates: "Alternating change: of everything for fire and fire for everything, like goods for gold and gold for goods." We appear to interrupt the line of interpretation with this fragment. Here the exchange relationship is thought, which we could more or less think and which does not seem to go along with the way that gods and humans alternately understand themselves and being. At first the fragment seems to offer no special difficulty. The fragment speaks of an alternate counterexchange, of a counterrelationship, where the one is replaced by the other and enters the place of the other. It appears that here the relationship of πῦρ and πάντα is spoken of in comparison to an event in the market. We know a market of natural exchange, or else in the more developed form of the exchange of money, in which goods are exchanged for money and money for goods. The goods, as multitude and variety, behave toward the single form of gold like the multitude in general behaves to that which is simple, but that corresponds, nevertheless, to the multitude of goods. Is this relationship also a form of the fundamental relatedness of ἕν and πάντα? The ἕν, as the most simple and all embracing, stands in a relatedness of opposition to τὰ πάντα. In the fragment, we read: exchange of τὰ πάντα for fire and of fire for ἅπαντα. We also understand ἅπαντα here in the sense of πάντα as in Fr. 30, in which we have conceived ἅπαντα not as living beings, but as synonymous with πάντα. Heraclitus speaks of an alternating exchange of τὰ πάντα for fire and of fire for τὰ πάντα. What we could say about the relationship of goods and gold, nevertheless, does not hold in the same way regarding the exchange-relationship of τὰ πάντα and fire. In reference to τὰ πάντα and fire, we could not say that there, where the one is, the other will go. The vendor in the market gives up the goods and receives money for them. Where previously the goods were, money comes in and, the other way around, where the money was, goods come in.

May we comprehend the relatedness of ἕν and πάντα so bluntly? Clearly not. The comparison becomes clearer, if we do not take gold only as a specific coinage, as a form of gold, but if we rather notice the glimmer of gold which is a symbol of the sunny. Then the sunny, illuminated gold behaves to the goods like ἕν to τὰ πάντα and, the other way around, τὰ πάντα behaves toward ἕν like the goods to the sunny, illuminated gold. The glimmer of gold suggests that it is not a question here of any simile you please, in which we could replace gold with money. In our simile it is less a matter of alternate exchange of real and token values; rather, it is a matter of the relationship of the glimmer of gold to goods. The gold stands for the glimmer of fire of πῦρ ἀείζωον, the goods for τὰ πάντα. The πῦρ ἀείζωον and τὰ πάντα in their relationship of exchange could not intelligibly be directly expressed. Likewise, the simile of gold and goods in their relationship of exchange will ultimately fail. Nevertheless, the relatedness of πῦρ ἀείζωον (ἕν) and πάντα receives a direction through the failure of that simile.

If one thinks here of the ἐκπύρωσις-doctrine, then one must characterize the relationship of transposition as follows: in place of πάντα, fire steps in and—what διακόσμησις [ordering] is about—in place of fire τὰ πάντα step in. In this case, we would understand the relationship of fire and τὰ πάντα in a strict analogy to the relationship of gold and goods. In the sense of the ἐκπύρωσις-doctrine, in the rigid style of the Stoa, one could say that πάντα disappears in the ἐκπύρωσις of fire, and in the διακόσμησις the fire turns into τὰ πάντα. But in that case we declare the fundamental structure of a perpetual happening to be a temporal process.

The difficulty we are confronted with in the simile of gold and goods in alternating relationship consists in the fact that the simile indicates something essential in the relationship of πῦρ ἀείζωον and πάντα, but that as soon as we adopt it and comprehend it in a strict sense, it does not sound right any longer. The πῦρ ἀείζωον as a form of ἕν is in a constant reference to τὰ πάντα, just as the gods stand in a constant reference to humans. This constant reference gets lost, if we wish to understand the relationship of the eternal living fire to πάντα in terms of the ἐκπύρωσις-doctrine, radically comprehended. The Diels translation of τὰ πάντα and ἁπάντων with "the all" is questionable. It points in the direction of the ἐκπύρωσις. Heraclitus, however, does not say τό πᾶν or τοῦ παντός, but τὰ πάντα and ἁπάντων (πάντων). τὰ πάντα, however, apply to the entirety of entities. The exchange of fire into τὰ πάντα and of τὰ πάντα into fire behaves analogously to the alternate exchange of the glimmering gold into goods and of goods into glimmering fire of gold.

The question that we must first leave open is the characterization of the relatedness of ἕν and πάντα as a relatedness of transmutation. When we try to illustrate the relatedness of ἕν and πάντα by the example of the market, certain features of the fundamental relatedness in question come to light. Nevertheless, this relatedness eludes us throughout all similes indicating comparisons, and it brings us close to the boundary not only of the sayable, but also of the thinkable. In Fr. 62, the intertwining relationship of gods and humans represents the relatedness of ἕν and πάντα. The gods, in their counterreference to humans, are in a specific sense the representatives of ἕν in its relatedness to πάντα, and indeed because they understand most about πῦρ ἀείζωον. Finally, we could say that an unhappy consciousness befalls us not only as the interpreters of the sayings of Heraclitus; rather, it lies above all in the sayings themselves.

10

The Standing Open of Gods and Humans
(Fragment 62). The "Speculative" in Hegel.—
Hegel's Relationship to Heraclitus.—
Life - Death (Correlated Fragments: 88, 62).

HEIDEGGER: I was not present at the last seminar session. I am asked to express myself on the course of thought. That, however, is a different matter from immediate participation in the discussion. For there is the danger that I approach the matter from the outside.

First, I would like to touch on the difficulty that was prevalent in the last session: the determination of the relationship of gods and humans in relation to the relatedness of ἕν and πάντα. It is thus a question of a relation between relationships. I intentionally speak formally now in order to let the structure be seen that lies at the basis of the thoughts of the last session. If we notice the approach and the course of the sessions till now, the difficulty appears to me to have been to find the transition from a relationship, still undetermined, of lightning, sun, seasons, and fire to τὰ πάντα, to the relationship of gods and humans in their relation to the relatedness of ἕν and πάντα. The difficulty can be seen in the way ἕν suddenly reveals another character. So far as I have understood the course that Mr. Fink has in view for the seminar, it is that of deliberately setting out from the fire-fragments and only then to bring into view all that which one knows as logos-fragments and as specifically Heraclitean. In this, I see the difficulty that by the interpretation of the peculiar state of affairs, "to live death, to die life," which is said of gods and humans, a correspondence—and not an equation—becomes visable to the actual, thematic relatedness in question of ἕν and πάντα. When we speak of the "relatedness of ἕν and πάντα," then it seems as if we were thinking about a connection between both which we have localized concretely and for which relatedness we then sought a bow which spanned them. In the end, however, the matter stands in such a way that ἕν is the relatedness, and that it relates to τὰ πάντα by letting them be what they are. So understood, the relatedness is, in my opinion, the decisive point that our determination must reach; thereby the idea of two terms is eliminated. Precisely this idea must henceforth be held off, even though it is not yet settled what all the references are which belong in the wholeness of πάντα, and what the reference is of all the references to ἕν or in ἕν itself.

Something is conspicuous to me terminologically in the summary of the last session. You, Mr. Fink, make a distinction between "cosmic" and "cosmological," and you speak of cosmic moments and cosmological entities.

FINK: One could bluntly conceive the relationship of gods and humans, which has been formulated in the dark formula "to live death, to die life," and say that the gods win the substance of their lives out of the death of humans, as humans win their life out of the death of animals they consume. To live the death of another would then be a process, a perpetual style of the process of life. We cannot connect any meaning with the idea that the gods need the life of mortals like they need the sacrificial animals of mortals in early religion. If one wants to disregard the blunt idea, one must turn from a mere cosmic relationship between gods and humans to the cosmological reference of humans and gods. Gods and humans are not only like other living things; rather, they are both determined by an understanding relationship to themselves and to each other. The understanding relationship does not encapsulate the gods by themselves. The gods do not refer only to themselves; rather, they can experience their own perpetual being only in reference to the changeable being and being bound to death of humans. In order to understand their own perpetual being in their self-understanding, they must understandingly hold themselves close to the death of humans. Understood thus, holding close is not to be understood as ontic but as ontological or cosmological. Vice versa, humans, who relate to their own wasting away, must understandingly hold themselves close to the perpetual being of the gods. This ontological understanding contains an analogy to the original relatedness of ἕν and πάντα.

HEIDEGGER: If you reject the cosmic relationship as ontic and speak of a cosmological relationship instead of an ontological one, then you use the word "cosmological" in a special sense. In your use of the word "cosmological," you do not mean the common meaning of cosmology as the doctrine of the cosmos. But what, then, do you have in view?

FINK: The holding [verhaltende] ἕν, which contains all πάντα, and not the cosmos, for instance, as a system of spatial points.

HEIDEGGER: Thus, you do not use the word "cosmology" in the sense of natural science. It only concerns me to see the justification on account of which you speak of cosmology. You have your grounds, because you do not say "ontic" and "ontological," but rather "cosmic" and "cosmological."

FINK: The criterion lies there, where you yourself criticize ontology.

HEIDEGGER: You speak about the relatedness of ἕν and πάντα as a world-relationship.

FINK: I do not thereby understand it as a relationship of two terms. I think the ἕν as the one which lets everything arise as many in the sense of πάντα, but which takes them back again.

HEIDEGGER: I don't want to tie you down to Heidegger, but ἕν-πάντα as world-relationship indeed implies that ἕν, like the world, worlds.

FINK: The ἕν is the gathering, letting-be, and also annihilating power. Beside the moment of gathering and letting-be, the moment of taking back again and annihilating is important for me.

HEIDEGGER: If we think now of Fr. 30, which speaks of κόσμον τόνδε, what is the use of κόσμος here in comparison to your use of the word "cosmology"?

FINK: κόσμον τόνδε does not mean the gathering of πάντα in ἕν, but rather the jointed whole of πάντα.

HEIDEGGER: Thus, you do not use "cosmological" in the sense of the Greek κόσμος. But why, then, do you speak of the "cosmological"?

FINK: I do not think the cosmological from out of Heraclitus, but rather from out of Kant and from the antinomy of pure reason. Pure reason attempts to think the whole. The whole is a concept that is first oriented toward things. In this manner, however, we can never thoughtfully experience the gathered whole. Kant exhibits the aporias of an attempt at thought that believes itself able to think the whole on the model of a spatial thing. Because the attempt does not manage with this approach, Kant subjectivizes the whole as a subjective principle in the process of experience, which is complimented by the regulative idea of the totality of all appearances.

HEIDEGGER: The justification of your use of "cosmic-cosmological" in distinction to "ontic-ontological" is thus the allness . . .

FINK: . . . which, however, is the allness of ἕν, of the self-gathering, letting-arise, and letting-pass-away. In reference to the clamping together of letting-arise and letting-pass-away, I refer to Nietzsche's motif of the coupling of building and breaking, joining and undoing, of the negation in the sway of the world.

HEIDEGGER: I would like to touch on yet another difficulty. I share your interpretation of Fr. 62. For me also it is the sole possible way to interpret the formula, "to live the death of another, to die the life of another," in the manner you indicated. For me the question is how much we know, according to the purest sources, about the gods in their relationship to humans with the Greeks. In reference to your interpretation of the relationship of the gods and humans, one could bluntly say that you impute an existenz-ontology to the gods. According to its sense, your interpretation goes in the direction of an existenz-ontology not just of humans in relationship to the gods, but also, vice versa, of the gods in their relationship to humans.

FINK: In the world of religion we find the strict demarcation between gods and humans. Professor Heidegger means to say, however, that when I ascribe an existenz-ontology to the gods, this would be because the gods are not only distinguished from humans, but because they distinguish themselves in their own being from humans by holding themselves understandingly toward the death of mortals...

HEIDEGGER: ... and because they experience themselves as perpetual beings only in their self-distinction from mortals.

FINK: Only because they have view of mortals can they experience themselves as perpetually being. The immortals are those who do not meet death; mortals are those who are bound to death. But Heraclitus converts this customary comprehension of Greek mythology, which lets mortals and gods be for themselves, and which lets them turn toward each other only occasionally. He makes this occasional relationship into a relationship constituting gods and humans in their own being. The immortal being of the gods is only possible if they relate themselves toward the mortal being of humans. The knowledge of human being bound to death constitutes the understanding of imperishable being proper, and vice versa, the knowledge of the perpetual being of the gods constitutes the understanding of mortal being proper. Gods and humans do not form two separated spheres. It depends on seeing not the *chorismos* [separation], but the intertwining of the godly and human understanding of self and of being.

HEIDEGGER: It is not a question of speaking in a blunt manner of gods and humans as of different living beings, of whom the former are immortal, the other mortal. Spoken in the terminology of *Being and Time,* immortality is no category, but rather an existentiale, a way that the gods relate themselves toward their being.

FINK: The godly knowledge of the being bound to death of humans is no mere consciousness, but rather an understanding relationship. With Athena, who appears as mentor to mortals in order to bring help to them, it is perhaps a matter of still another theme. The epiphany of the gods is no actual mortal being of the gods, but a masking. When Aristotle says that the life of θεωρία [contemplation], which exceeds φρόνησις [practical wisdom], is a kind of godly life, an ἀθανατίζειν [to be immortal] (whereby ἀθανατίζειν is formed like ἑλληνίζειν [to be Greek]), that implies that in θεωρία we comport ourselves like immortals. In θεωρία, mortals reach up to the life of the gods. Correspondingly, we must say of the gods, that their comportment toward humans is a "θανατίζειν" [to be mortal], presupposing that one could form this word. The emphasis lies in this, that the relationship of humans to gods cannot be described externally, but rather that they themselves exist as their alternate and counterrelationship, except that the gods, to a certain extent, have the more favorable existenz-ontology and humans, on the contrary, the less favorable. The godly and human understanding of self and being must project itself in mutual understanding.

HEIDEGGER: In the relationship of gods and humans, it depends on a phenomenon that had not been treated till now in regard to ἕν and πάντα: the standing open of gods and humans. You called the open-standing relationship between gods and humans a representative of the relatedness of ἕν and πάντα.

FINK: With this, the σοφόν-character of ἕν is foreshadowed. The ἕν is gathering unity in the manner of λόγος and σοφόν. We may not interpret the σοφόν-character of ἕν as knowledge. In it, the moment of understanding reference of ἕν to πάντα is thought. In the light-character of lightning, sun, and fire, we first have a foreshadowing of the σοφόν-character of ἕν. But we must also warn against an explication of ἕν as world-reason and as the absolute.

HEIDEGGER: Let me just characterize your way of thinking. You prepare the understanding of σοφόν or πῦρ φρόνιμον [sagacious fire] in Fr. 64a in a departure from lightning, from sun, from the seasons, from fire, light, radiance, and shine. In this manner, it is somewhat more difficult to make the transition from the thingly reference of ἕν as lightning, sun, and fire, to πάντα, over to the open-standing reference of gods and humans to each other, which the reference of ἕν τὸ σοφὸν to πάντα represents. Your way of Heraclitus interpretation starts out from fire toward λόγος; my way of Heraclitus interpretation starts out from λόγος toward fire. A difficulty is hidden behind that which is still not unraveled by us, but which we have already touched on in various forms. For your interpretation of the mutual relationship of gods and humans you have drawn upon Hölderlin as a comparison, that is, firstly on "Hyperion's Song of Fate," in which the gods are separated from humans and are not referred to one another.

FINK: Without fate, like the sleeping infant, breath the heavenly ones. This poem speaks of the gods' indifference toward humans.

HEIDEGGER: You have then interpreted Hölderlin a second time, and alluded to one verse out of "Mnemosyne," which expresses the reverse thought, that the immortals have need of mortals. Still, both poems of Hölderlin stand close by one another. The thought of "Mnemosyne" is already found in the "Rhine Hymn" (Strophe 8), in which it says that the gods stand in need of "heroes and humans / And other mortals." This noteworthy concept of standing in need concerns only the reference of gods to humans in Hölderlin. Where does the rubric of "need" occur as term in philosophy?

FINK: With Hegel in the writing "The Difference of Fichte's and Schelling's System of Philosophy" (1801), in which Hegel speaks of the "need of philosophy."

HEIDEGGER: Thus, in the same time that Hölderlin lived in Frankfurt. In the question about that which Hegel and Hölderlin call "need," we have an essential document for their conversation in this regard—for the conversation that otherwise is an obscure problem. With their conversation we touch on a historical question, and not just a question concerning the study of history. In what sense, then, both are Heracliteans is another question. In Tübingen, they joined with Schelling in the motto ἕν καί πᾶν [the one and whole]. This relationship among them, which stands under this common motto, later dissolved. But where does Hölderlin first name Heraclitus?

PARTICIPANT: In "Hyperion." There he speaks of ἕν διαφέϱον ἑαυτῷ [one set against itself].

HEIDEGGER: The one that in itself distinguishes itself. Hölderlin understands it as the essence of beauty. At that time, however, beauty is for him the word for being. Hegel's interpretation of the Greeks in the *Lectures on the History of Philosophy* goes in the same direction: being as beauty. With recourse to Heraclitus' word, Hölderlin names no formalistic-dialectic structure; rather, he makes a fundamental declaration. This thought has then been changed by him into a relationship of gods and humans, according to which humanity is a condition of the existence of the god . . .

FINK: . . . and humanity is nearer to the abyss than the god.

HEIDEGGER: For that reason, the relationship of gods and humans is a higher and more difficult one, a relation that is not to be determined with the terminology of customary metaphysical theology.

FINK: The relationship of humans and gods is also no *imago* relationship in so far as mortals, in their relationship to themselves, understandingly stand out into the other being of the gods, without participating in it. On one side an estrangement rules between gods and humans; on the other side, however, a clamping together also prevails in mutual understanding.

HEIDEGGER: From Hegel's viewpoint—wherein consists the affinity between him and Heraclitus? There is a well-known sentence in the *Lectures on the History of Philosophy*.

PARTICIPANT: "There is no sentence of Heraclitus' that I have not taken up in my *Logic*."

HEIDEGGER: What does this sentence mean?

PARTICIPANT: It is here a matter of Hegel's understanding of Heraclitus.

HEIDEGGER: What does the sentence say regarding the relationship of Hegel and Heraclitus?

PARTICIPANT: Heraclitus is not only taken up by Hegel; rather, he is sublated.

PARTICIPANT: Hegel sees Heraclitus dialectically from out of opposition.

HEIDEGGER: But what does "dialectical" mean? Now we can recover the answer to the question, posed in an earlier season, about the speculative with Hegel. What does "speculative" mean in Hegel?

PARTICIPANT: The presupposition of speculative thought is the identity of being and thinking.

HEIDEGGER: Where does the speculative belong for Hegel?

PARTICIPANT: The speculative is a moment of the logical.

HEIDEGGER: What is a moment?

PARTICIPANT: Moment comes from *movere, movimentum* [to set in motion, movement].

HEIDEGGER: The phase [*der Moment*] depends on "the moment" ["*das Moment*"]. When Hegel says the speculative is a moment, the phase is not meant thereby, but rather the moment. The moment is a moving something which has a share in the movement of thinking, and which gives an impetus. The moment becomes the impetus, and the impetus itself is the instant; it happens in a phase [*in einem Moment*]. Thus, the moment becomes the phase. What is the first moment of the logical?

PARTICIPANT: The abstract or intelligible.

HEIDEGGER: And the second moment?

PARTICIPANT: The dialectical.

HEIDEGGER: It is noteworthy that Hegel understands the dialectical as the second and not as the third moment. And what is the third moment?

PARTICIPANT: The speculative.

HEIDEGGER: In what connection does Hegel call the dialectical the second and not the third moment of the logical? When he speaks, at the end of the *Logic,* of the identity of matter and method, one would indeed think that the dialectical is the third moment. Hegel also calls the dialectical the negative-rational. What does the rational mean for Hegel? We need all this information for our analysis of Heraclitus, even though Hegel does not speak of Heraclitus in these pages.

PARTICIPANT: Spoken from the *Phenomenology of Mind,* reason is the sublation of the separation of subject and object.

HEIDEGGER: Where does Hegel's terminology come from?

PARTICIPANT: From Kant.

HEIDEGGER: How does Hegel characterize Kant's philosophy?

PARTICIPANT: As reflexive philosophy.

HEIDEGGER: And that means?

PARTICIPANT: As the division of two phases.

HEIDEGGER: Which phase? What does reason mean in Kant?

PARTICIPANT: For him, reason is the thinking of the ideas in distinction to understanding as the thinking of the categories. The ideas are regulative principles, in which reason thinks totality.

HEIDEGGER: Reason in Kant is thus not referred immediately to appearances but only to the rules and fundamental principles of understanding. The fundamental function of reason consists in thinking the highest unity. When Hegel says the dialectical is the negative-rational, he implies that the abstract finite determination sublates itself and goes into its opposite determination. Against that, the abstract thinking of understanding is the adherence to the determination and its distinctness vis-à-vis the other. The entire thinking, Hegel's thinking, speaks first of all in the fundamental scheme of the subject-object relationship. The abstract moment is the representation that is delivered over to the object without reference back to the subject. It is the level of immediacy. The idea is given over to the immediately given object without reference back to mediation. If now the object qua object is thought, that is, in reference back to the subject, then the unity between object and subject is thought. But why is this unity a negative one?

PARTICIPANT: Because thinking has not yet recognized the unity as unity.

HEIDEGGER: Think historically and concretely on Kant's synthetic unity of transcendental apperception. It is unity in reference to objectivity. For Hegel, however, it is only this whole itself, i.e., subject and object in their unity, which is the positive unity wherein the whole of the dialectical process is deposited. The glimpse of this unity, that is, the glimpse of the abstract and dialectical moments in their unity, is the speculative. The speculative, as the positive-rational, comprehends the unity of determinations in their opposition. When Hegel brings Heraclitus into connection with his logic, how does he then think what Heraclitus says about oppositions? How does he take up what is said by Heraclitus about oppositions in distinction to what we attempt? He takes the opposing references of Heraclitus—spoken from out of Kant—as a doctrine of categories at the level of immediacy, and thus in the sense of an immediate logic. Hegel does not see in Heraclitus the cosmological references as you understand them.

FINK: Hegel interprets the relationship of oppositions from out of mediation.

HEIDEGGER: He understands the whole of Greek philosophy as a level of immediacy, and he sees everything under the aspect of the logical.

FINK: One could also say that for Hegel the thought of becoming is of significance in Heraclitus. One could also call Heraclitus the philosopher of flux. For Hegel, the element of flux gains the character of a model for undoing oppositions.

HEIDEGGER: Becoming is movement, for which the three moments— namely, the abstract, the dialectical, and the speculative—are what gives impetus [das Ausschlaggebende]. This movement, this method, is the matter itself for Hegel after completion of the Logic. The third Heraclitean, beside Hölderlin and Hegel, is Nietzsche. But we would be going out of our way to go into this question. I have touched on all that is now said only to show you where we are at this point. Our Heraclitus interpretation has a wide perspective; it also speaks in the language of the tradition. We can speak only out of the conversation that is fundamental for thinking, and that is fundamental above all for the way on which we move.

Perhaps it would be appropriate if you, Mr. Fink, indicated the further step that you have in view for the progress of the seminar, setting out from the allusion to the reference of the mutual open-standing character of gods and humans that characterizes the phenomenon, "to live the death of another, to die the life of another." Thus the participants will see where the way leads us.

FINK: I believe that one must drive on from the doctrine of fire and the πυρὸς τροπαί to the question of the relatedness of ἕν and πάντα, for which we receive help from the fragments in which the life-death relationship is thought. The relationship of gods and humans is not to be equated with the relatedness of ἕν and πάντα. In the standing open for one another of gods and humans, we have, as it were, a brake against thinking what is said in Fr. 90 simply as a change-over of familiar kind, or as transformation of stuff into another form, or on the model of the exchange of goods. We have indicated that in χρυσός [gold], the glimmer of gold must also be thought. Here a relationship is thought between the light-character of fire and that into which it turns. We must not understand the turning bluntly in the sense of a change of stuff.

HEIDEGGER: We must think the radiant, the ornamental, and the decorative element together in κόσμος, which was for the Greeks a customary thought.

FINK: But the most beautiful κόσμος is also, when measured against the fire, a scattered junk heap. To be sure, it is in itself the most beautiful joining, but in reference to the ἕν it compares like a junk heap.

HEIDEGGER: I would still like to add something as to the relationship of gods and humans. I have called the mutual self-understanding the open-standing character. But if the gods, in their relationship to mortals represent ἕν in its relationship to πάντα, then the ἕν-character gets lost . . .

FINK: . . . and indeed because the gods, as representatives of ἕν, stand in the plural, and thus appear as foreign forms. But in his theology, which we will turn to later, Heraclitus thinks the coincidence of oppositions in the god. In order now to clarify the further course of our interpretation of Heraclitus, we must attempt to go from the fragments that treat the relationship of life and death and the intermediate phenomenon of sleep over to a fundamental discussion of all oppositions and their coincidence in the god, and finally to Zeus, with which name ἕν τὸ σοφόν is unwilling and yet willing to be named. Before this, we would also have to deal with the series of flux- and movement-fragments, then with the problem of ἁρμονία ἀφανής [hidden harmony], life and death in the lyre and bow, the intertwining of life and death proper in the double meaning of the bow, the explication of fire as φῶς [light] and as that which makes σαφές [clear], allows shining-up, and brings to light, and finally the character of σοφόν and the λόγος. The way of our Heraclitus interpretation is the relatedness of ἕν and πάντα. Our explication begins with the appearances of fire; it then goes over to the relationship of life and death, to the doctrine of the contrasts and the coincidence, to the movement-fragments, the fragment about the god, and from there to ἕν τὸ σοφὸν μοῦνον [one thing, the only wise],²⁷ and finally to the λόγος-fragments. It seems important to me first of all to gain an abundant arsenal of ideas and ways of thought. Heraclitus operates with many relationships. When he takes up a differentiation in the sleep-fragments, this is not to be conceived of in the sense of copious vocabulary, but of ways of understanding. His fundamental thoughts are indeed relatively easy to formulate, but the difficulty lies in the refraction of these thoughts into the many ways of thought and ideas with which he is concerned. The fundamental thought of Heraclitus is broken into a great number of ways...

HEIDEGGER: ... which gives an insight into τὰ πάντα.

FINK: The thinking of the one happens in a manifold manner. As with Parmenides, the ἕν is thought of in a great many σήματα [signs] so with Heraclitus the relatedness of ἕν and πάντα is thought of in a great many ways of understanding.

HEIDEGGER: Where do gods and humans belong?

FINK: In one regard in πάντα, and in another regard in ἕν.

HEIDEGGER: The other regard is precisely what is of interest.

FINK: The relatedness of ἕν and πάντα mirrors itself in the relation of gods and humans. Since ἕν is no factual unity but rather the unity of λόγος, gods and humans are those struck by the lightning of λόγος. They belong together in the λόγος-happening.

HEIDEGGER: Gods and humans in their intertwining relationship have a mirroring function in reference to ἕν and πάντα.

FINK: In Heideggerian language, we could say that humans and gods belong in one respect in what is, but in the essential respect they belong in being. This special position of gods and humans among all that is, which position does not subsume them...

HEIDEGGER: ... under all that which is...

FINK: ... is very much more difficult to grasp. Gods and humans exist as understanding of being. The godly and the human understanding of being are ways of the self-clearing of being.

HEIDEGGER: But that cannot be read in Heraclitus.

FINK: We could find the light-nature of ἕν by means of the relationship between gods and humans.

HEIDEGGER: Perhaps this is the appropriate place to make the transition to Fr. 26.

FINK: First, I would like to return once again to Fr. 88: ταὐτό τ᾽ ἔνι ζῶν καὶ τεθνηκὸς καὶ (τὸ) ἐγρηνορὸς καὶ καθεῦδον καὶ νέον καὶ γηραιόν· τάδε γὰρ μεταπεσόντα ἐκεῖνά ἐστι κακεῖνα πάλιν μεταπεσόντα ταῦτα. Diels translates, "And it is always one and the same, what dwells (?) within us: living and dead and waking and sleeping and young and old. For this is changed over to that and that changes back over to this."

Here a ταὐτό is expressed, but not a same-being [*Selbigsein*] of a same thing [*Selbigen*] lying before us, not the empty identity that belongs to everything there is; rather a same-being that is referred to distinction. It is referred to that which seems to us to be most distinguished. The distinctions named here are not such as are in constant movement, but are such as concern all living things. Being alive, being awake, and being young have a positive character for our customary ideas vis-à-vis being dead, being asleep, and being old. But the fragment that expresses same-being speaks not only against the customary opinion of the superiority of living, waking, and being young vis-à-vis the dead, the sleeping, and the old; rather, it also expresses a belonging together of the three groups. Being asleep, which stands in the middle, has a distinguished inbetween position out of which an understanding standing open is possible for being dead and being old in the sense of wasting away.

But the fragment says still more. Not only are living and dead, awake and asleep, young and old one and the same, but this is the change-over of that and that again is the change-over of this. A phenomenal change-over is only to be seen in the relationship of waking and sleep. For what goes to sleep from waking also turns again from sleep back into waking. Only the change-over from waking into sleep is reversible. Against that, the change-over of life into death and of being young into being old is not reversible in the phenomenon. But in the fragment it is said that as being awake goes over into being asleep and vice versa, so also the living changes over into the dead, the dead into the living, the young into the old, and the old into the young. It treats the distinction of waking and sleeping in the same manner as that of living and dead and of young and old. But of whom is this reversible change-over expressed? The expression, "changing over again," recalls the ἀνταμοιβή [interchange], the change of gold into goods and goods into gold. There, the relationship of the change-over is referred to the relatedness of ἕν and πάντα as well as πάντα and ἕν. The question is whether transitions, referred to the living who are named in Fr. 88, have their place within *animalia* [animals], or whether changes-over in the sense of πυρὸς τροπαί are meant by it. Is the ταὐτό said of *animalia,* or rather of πῦρ ἀείζωον, about which we hear that it always was and is and will be (ἦν ἀεὶ ἔστιν καὶ ἔσται), but which itself is no inner temporal constancy, but which rather makes possible the having been, being present, and coming to be of πάντα? Are the changes-over named in Fr. 88 to be thought as mere contentions about phenomena given and not given in the animal world, or do they concern πῦρ ἀείζωον? Let us leave this question open.

HEIDEGGER: How does ζῶν καὶ τεθνεκὸς [living and dead] in Fr. 88 relate to ζῶντες [those living] and τεθνεῶτες [those dying] in Fr. 62? How are they mentioned in the one and how in the other fragment?

FINK: In Fr. 62, ζῶντες and τεθνεῶτες are referred to ...

HEIDEGGER: ... the manner of being of immortals and mortals; in Fr. 88, on the contrary, ζῶν καὶ τεθνηκὸς is referred to what is.

FINK: Not to what is, but to being alive and being dead. ζῶν does not mean a living being, but rather the living as *terminus* [term] for being alive, just as τεθνηκός does not mean something dead, but rather the dead as *terminus* for being dead. The same also holds for the waking and sleeping and for young and old. Waking and sleeping are *termini* for being awake and being asleep, and young and old are *termini* for being young and being old.

HEIDEGGER: Is ζῶν in Fr. 88 only the singular of the plural ζῶντες in Fr. 62? Are gods and humans also meant in Fr. 88?

FINK: ζῶν καὶ τεθνηκὸς does not refer only to gods and humans, for Fr. 88 is stretched wider. But for whom are being alive and being dead, being awake and being asleep, and being young and being old the same, living beings or πῦρ ἀείζωον?

HEIDEGGER: Thus, in Fr. 88 something else is said than in Fr. 62. Fr. 62 has a wider sense.

FINK: ζῶν and τεθνηκός are to be understood like τὸ καλόν, τὸ δίκαιον. How is the article τὸ ἐγρηγορός [the waking] to be understood? Professor Heidegger has indicated that it is not a matter of relationships and counterreferences that would have a possessor. In the second sentence of the fragment, Heraclitus speaks in the plural, which does not, however, refer to facts but to the three different relationships. Of whom can ταὐτο be said at all? The coincidence thought here does not signify one such as in a distinctionless indifference. What is meant is even a mutual changeover. μεταπεσόντα [things changing around] refers to Fr. 90, in which ἀνταμοιβή is named, the exchange of gold for goods and of goods for gold. But what change over in Fr. 88 are not only things as against the gathering unity, but the harder opposition of being alive and being dead. Here a sameness is mentioned that slaps in the face and contradicts the everyday opinion that insists on the difference between life and death. On that account, the question of where the place is, the abode, of this change-over is disconcerting.

HEIDEGGER: Does being dead (τεθνηκός) mean the same as having deceased?

FINK: Yes, when τεθνηκός is said against ζῶν. It does not mean what is lifeless in the sense of the minerals ...

HEIDEGGER: . . . thus not dead nature. A stone, for example, is not dead.

FINK: In Fr. 88, life and death, which we know in phenomenon only in a specific domain, are referred to the whole relatedness of ἕν and πάντα. But let us leave this question open. For without further verification, it cannot be said what ταὐτό is. We can at first only presume that the same-being of life and death refers to ἕν. Professor Heidegger has designated the relatedness of ἕν and πάντα as state-of-affairs [Verhalt], as being- and world-state-of-affairs. When this original state-of-affairs is mentioned in the ταὐτό of Fr. 88, then we have a contradiction in the phenomenon. For nobody dead becomes alive again. Living and dead, waking and sleeping, young and old, are phenomena that in a certain manner mean all the sojourn of the living in time. Life is the whole time of a living being; death is the end of life-time. Waking and sleep form the basic rhythm during life. Being young and being old refer to being in the corrupting power of time which not only brings everything but also takes everything. The question for me is whether the relatedness of ἕν and πάντα is a relatedness of maturation.

Finally, I would like to attempt an explication of Fr. 26. It runs: ἄνθρωπος ἐν εὐφρόνῃ φάος ἅπτεται ἑαυτῷ (ἀποθανὼν) ἀποσβεσθεὶς ὄψεις, ζῶν δὲ ἅπτεται τεθνεῶτος εὕδων, (ἀποσβεσθεὶς ὄψεις) ἐγρηγορὼς ἅπτεται εὕδοντος. Diels translates: "A human touches on (kindles) a light in the night, when his eyesight is extinguished. Living, he touches on death in sleep; in waking he touches on sleeping."

This fragment clearly begins with a human. A human kindles a light in the night. Fr. 26 begins with the human and his capacity of kindling a light in the night, when his ὄψις is extinguished. Diels translates ἀποσβεσθεὶς ὄψις with "when his eyesight is extinguished." But the meaning thus suggests itself that a human sees in his dream—and that he is in a light while in darkness during the dream. I would rather translate the plural, ἀποσβεσθεὶς ὄψις, with "extinguished in his manners of seeing." A human has his uneasy place between night and light. The fragment refers to the unsteady place of a human between night and light. He is near to the light. That is indicated when he is able to lighten the night. A human is a kind of Promethean fire thief. He has the ability to make light in the night, when his manners of seeing are extinguished, i.e., not when he sleeps but when he relates to the dark. "Living, he touches on the dead in sleep; in waking, he touches on the sleeping." Life and death are here bound to one another by the in-between position of sleep. Sleeping is a manner of being alive akin with death; waking is a manner of lingering touching on death in the light in reference to the sleeping. Being alive and being awake, being asleep and being dead are not three conditions, but three possible manners of relationship of humans in which they come into proximity to the dark passing of night and to light openness.

HEIDEGGER: We must get clear what touching (ἁφή) actually means. Later, "the touching" appears as θιγεῖν with Aristotle in the *Metaphysics,* θ 10.

FINK: What we have now said concerning Fr. 26 is only a foreshadowing of the difficulty with which we must begin in the next session.

11

The "Logical" in Hegel.—
"Consciousness" and "Dasein."—
Locality of Human Beings between Light
and Night. (Correlated Fragments: 26, 10).

HEIDEGGER: First, I must make a correction regarding the last seminar session. In reference to Heraclitus' word ἕν διαφέρον ἑαντῷ, at the place in the summary where it says that Hölderlin interprets truth as beauty, I said by mistake that the same thought is to be found in Hegel in the *Lectures on the History of Philosophy*. This thought appears, rather, in the *Lectures on the Philosophy of World History*, in Volume III, "The Greek and Roman World" (Lasson edition, p. 570 ff.). "Thus, the sensory is only the appearance of spirit. It has shed finitude, and beauty consists in this unity of the sensory with spirit in and for itself" (p. 575). "The true deficiency of the Greek religion as opposed to the Christian is that in it appearance constitutes the highest form, in general, the whole of the divine, while in the Christian religion appearing obtains only as a moment of the divine" (p. 580). "But if appearing is the perennial form, so the spirit which appears in its transfigured beauty is a thither side of subjective spirit . . ." (p. 581). Here Hegel thinks the identity of appearing and beauty that is also characteristic and essential for the early Hölderlin. We cannot go into the details of Hegel's elaborations, but I recommend that you sometime reread his *Lectures on the Philosophy of World History*. Then you will gain another idea of Hegel, who had an inkling of much in Greek thought when, for example, he thinks Apollo as the knowing god, and the god of knowledge, as the eloquent, prophesying, foretelling god, as bringing everything concealed to light, as the god looking into the darkness, as the god of light, and when he thinks the light as what brings everything to appearance.

Aside from that, I have still another omission to correct. We have spoken of the three moments of the logical in Hegel in the last session, the abstract-intelligible, the dialectical, and the speculative. But what have we omitted thereby?

PARTICIPANT: We have no longer asked about what we understand by the speculative in regard to our own procedure in distinction to Hegel. For the question about the meaning of the speculative in Hegel came up when one of the participants characterized our attempt to think by starting out from Heraclitus with the expression, a speculative leap.

HEIDEGGER: We will talk about this problem later. For the moment, let us remain within Hegel's philosophy. We followed Hegel's text with the elucidation of the three moments of the logical. But what remains to be asked, if one speaks of the three moments of the logical in Hegel?

PARTICIPANT: One could perhaps say that the dialectical and the speculative moments appear as two sides of negativity.

HEIDEGGER: Let us not go into negation and negativity.

PARTICIPANT: We have forgotten to ask about the totality of the three moments.

HEIDEGGER: How do you wish to determine the course of the three moments? The abstract, dialectical, and speculative are not side by side. But what must we return to in order to find out how the three moments belong together? As I subsequently reflected on the course of our conversation, I was alarmed about our carelessness.

PARTICIPANT: We must ask where the *Logic* has its place in the system.

HEIDEGGER: We do not need to go so far, but we must ask . . .

PARTICIPANT: . . . what the logical means in Hegel.

HEIDEGGER: We have spoken about the three moments of the logical, but we have not thereby reflected on the logical itself. We have failed to ask what Hegel means by the logical. One says, for example, "that is logical." Or one can hear it said that the great coalition is logical. What does "logical" mean here?

PARTICIPANT: In the "Introduction" to the *Science of Logic,* Hegel says that the content of logic "is the depiction of God, as He is in His eternal essence before the creation of nature and of a finite spirit."

HEIDEGGER: Let us remain at first with what the "logical" means in the customary sense, i.e., for the man on the street.

PARTICIPANT: It means the same as "conclusive in itself."

HEIDEGGER: Thus, "consistent." But is that what Hegel means when he speaks of the three phases of the logical? Certainly not. Thus, we have not made clear to ourselves what we are talking about. In paragraph 19 of the *Encyclopedia of Philosophical Sciences,* Hegel says, "Logic is the science *of the pure idea,* that is, the idea in the abstract element of thinking." We do not want to dwell too long on Hegel here. I only want to make clear the gulf that separates us from Hegel, when we are dealing with Heraclitus. What does "science of the pure idea" mean with Hegel; what for him is the idea?

PARTICIPANT: The complete self-comprehension of thought.

HEIDEGGER: What does Hegel's concept of the idea presuppose? Think about Plato's ἰδέα [form]. What has happened between the Platonic idea and Hegel's idea? What has in the meantime happened when Hegel and modern times speak of the idea?

PARTICIPANT: In the meantime, Plato's ἰδέα took the road toward becoming a concept.

HEIDEGGER: You must be somewhat more cautious. With Descartes, the idea becomes *perceptio* [perception]. With that, it is seen from the representation of the subject and thus from subjectivity. The absolute idea of Hegel is then the complete self-knowledge of the absolute subject. It is the inner coherence of the three phases in the process characterizing the self-manifesting of the absolute spirit. In this absolute, Plato's thought of the idea, the self-showing, still plays a role, despite subjectivity. Why can Hegel now say that the idea is thinking? That must seem paradoxical to us at the first glance at Hegel's sentence. The sentence is only to be understood if one observes that the Platonic idea becomes *perceptio* in Descartes. Prior to that, the ideas become the thought of God, and gain significance for the notion of *creatio*. We give only this brief determination of the logical in Hegel in order to see what we are talking about when we name the three moments of the logical. The logical in Hegel is a rubric that has full importance and that hides a richness that one cannot quickly and easily comprehend. In paragraph 19 of the *Encyclopedia,* it says, among other things, "But in so far as the logical is the absolute form of truth, and even more than this, is the pure truth itself, it is something quite other than *useful.*" What is truth here? If one wants to understand Hegel's concept of truth, what must one also think? Think back to what we have already said, that the idea in Descartes becomes *clara* and *distincta perceptio* [clear and distinct perception], and this goes together with . . .

PARTICIPANT: . . . *certitudo*

HEIDEGGER: Thus, with certainty. In order to be able to understand Hegel's concept of truth, we must also think truth as certainty, as place in absolute self-knowledge. Only thus can we understand that the logical should be the pure truth by itself. This reference to the meaning of the logical in Hegel will be important, when later—though not in this semester—we come to speak about the *Logos* with Heraclitus.

Now I wish to have another clarification. You, Mr. Fink, spoke about the fact that the godly knowledge of a human's being bound by death is no mere consciousness, but an understanding relationship. Thus you contrast the understanding relationship, which we have also called standing open, to mere consciousness.

FINK: A mere consciousness of something would be given, for example, if one said that a human, as animated, knows about inanimate nature. Here one can speak of a mere knowledge relationship, although I believe that it is also a matter of more than just a consciousness of . . . Not only the understanding of being of immortal being belongs to the self-understanding of the gods, but also, as an implicit component, the understanding of being of mortal being. The godly understanding of being is not of a neutral kind; rather, it is referred back to the mortal being of humans. The gods understand their blissful being in ricochet back from the frailty of mortals.

HEIDEGGER: When you say that the reference of the gods to humans' being bound to death is no mere consciousness, then you mean that the reference is no mere human representation that humans are so and so. You said that the reference of the gods to humans is an understanding relationship, and you mean a self-understanding relationship.

FINK: The gods can have their being only in so far as they stand open for mortals. Standing open for mortals and the mortals' transient being cannot be lacking from the gods. We may not understand this, however, as Nietzsche says with Thomas Aquinas concerning the blissfulness of paradise, that the souls will view the torment of the damned, thereby suiting their blissfulness more. (*Geneology of Morals,* First Essay, 15). The immortals are undoubtedly θνητοί. They know their eternal being not only from viewing contemplation (θεωρία), but at the same time in ricochet back from the transient being of mortals. They are affected by humans' being bound to death. It is difficult to find the right term here.

HEIDEGGER: I want to get at precisely this point. Whether we find the terminologically appropriate form is another question. Standing open is not something like an open window or like a passageway. The standing open of humans to things does not mean that there is a hole through which humans see; rather, standing open for . . . is being addressed by [*Angegangensein von*] things. I speak about this in order to clarify the fundamental reference which plays a role in the understanding of what is thought with the word "Dasein" in *Being and Time.* My question now aims at the relationship of consciousness and Dasein. How is that relationship to be clarified? If you take "consciousness" as a rubric for transcendental philosophy and absolute idealism, another position is thus taken with the rubric "Dasein." This position is often overlooked or not sufficiently noticed. When one speaks of *Being and Time,* one first thinks of the "they" or of "anxiety." Let us begin with the rubric "consciousness." Is it not, strictly speaking, a curious word?

FINK: Consciousness is, strictly speaking, referred to the state of affairs. So far as the state of affairs is represented, it is a conscious being and not a knowing being. However, by consciousness we mean the fulfillment of knowing.

HEIDEGGER: Strictly speaking, it is the object of which we are conscious. Consciousness, then, means as much as objectivity, which is identical with the first principle of all synthetic judgments a priori in Kant. The conditions of the possibility of experience in general are at the same time the conditions of the possibility of objects of experience. With consciousness, we are concerned with a knowing, and knowing is thought as representation, as for example in Kant. And how does it stand now with Dasein? If we wish to proceed pedagogically, from where must we set out?

PARTICIPANT: We can set out from the word. The concept of "Da-sein" in Kant means actuality.

HEIDEGGER: The concept of actuality in Kant is a dark problem. But how does the concept of Dasein develop in the eighteenth century.

PARTICIPANT: As a translation of *existentia* [existence].

HEIDEGGER: Dasein means, then: being present now. But how is the word "Dasein" to be understood from out of the hermenuetic of Dasein in *Being and Time?*

PARTICIPANT: The hermeneutic in *Being and Time* sets out from Dasein, whereby it does not understand Dasein in the customary manner as present at hand.

HEIDEGGER: In French, Dasein is translated by *être-là* [being there], for example by Sartre. But with this, everything that was gained as a new position in *Being and Time* is lost. Are humans there like a chair is there?

PARTICIPANT: "Dasein" in *Being and Time* does not mean pure human factual being.

HEIDEGGER: Dasein does not mean being there and being here. What does the "*Da*" mean?

PARTICIPANT: It means what is cleared in itself. Human being, like Dasein's being is no pure thing present at hand, but a cleared being.

HEIDEGGER: In *Being and Time,* Dasein is described as follows: Da-sein. The *Da* is the clearing and openness of what is, as which a human stands out. Representation, the knowledge of consciousness, is something totally different. How does consciousness, knowledge as representation, relate to Dasein? In this you must not reflect, but rather see. Mr. Fink has referred to the fact that consciousness is properly the knowledge of the object. In what is objectivity, and that which is represented, grounded?

PARTICIPANT: In representation.

HEIDEGGER: Kant, and with him the absolute idealism of the absolute idea, was content with this answer. But what is thereby suppressed?

FINK: That wherein consciousness and object play.

HEIDEGGER: Thus, the clearing in which something present comes to meet something else present. Being opposite to . . . presupposes the clearing in which what is present meets a human. Consciousness is only possible on the ground of the *Da,* as a derivative mode of it. From here one must understand the historical step that is taken in *Being and Time,* which sets out from Dasein as opposed to consciousness. That is a matter that one must see. I have alluded to this because this relationship will still play a role for us along side the other relatedness of ἕν and πάντα. Both belong together. With Heraclitus, ἀλήθεια, nonconcealment, stands in the background, even if it is not mentioned directly. He speaks on this ground, although it is not further pursued by him. What I said in the last session is also to be understood from out of this: ἕν is the re-latedness [*Ver-hältnis*] of πάντα.²⁸ Re-lating [*Ver-halten*] and holding mean first of all tending, keeping, and yielding in the widest sense. The content of this holding is fulfilled for us in the course of time, that is, in passage through the fragments of Heraclitus. Mr. Fink has repeatedly alluded to the fact that the determinations of ἕν, as lightning, sun, seasons, and fire are no images, but rather characteristics that characterize the holding and the way and manner that τὰ πάντα are for ἕν, and which characterize ἕν itself as the unifying, gathering . . .

FINK: . . . and discharging. We must contrast this relatedness of ἕν and πάντα against the naïve conception according to which ἕν is thought like a depository, like a pot in which all πάντα are. One cannot apply this ontically familiar encompassing relation to the reference of ἕν and πάντα.

HEIDEGGER: In Southern German, *Topf* [pot] means *Hafen* [port]. That is the same word as ἅπτεσθαι [to be brought together]. The word "hawk" [*Habicht*] also belongs here, that is, the bird which grasps. Language is much more thoughtful and open than we are. But probably this will be forgotten in the next centuries. Nobody knows whether one will ever come back to this again.

FINK: In the last session, we began to consider Fr. 26, and to emphasize some elements, namely the peculiar situation of humans as fire kindling beings placed between night and light.

HEIDEGGER: For me, the way in which the fragment is quoted by Clement already creates a difficulty. When I read the context of Clement, it is unclear to me in which connection and out of which motive he cites Fr. 26. There it says: ὅσα δ᾽ αὖ περὶ ὕπνου λέγουσι, τὰ αὐτὰ χρὴ καὶ περὶ θανάτου ἐξακούειν. ἑκάτερος γὰρ δηλοῖ τὴν ἀπόστασιν τῆς ψυχῆς, ὅ μὲν μᾶλλον, ὅ δὲ ἧττον, ὅπερ ἐστὶ καὶ παρὰ Ἡρακλείτου λαβεῖν.²⁹ The first sentence says in translation, "One must also hear the same about death as what is said about sleep." How this text should be connected with Fr. 26 is incomprehensible to me. I myself can find no connection. Clement's text is unintelligible to me in connection with Fr. 26 because nothing is to be found in the fragment about ἀπόστασις τῆς ψυχῆς [departure of the soul]. Clement's text is a completely different one than that of the fragment. Another difficulty for me is the following. Heraclitus says that humans kindle a light in the night when eyesight is extinguished. Is that only to be thought in such a way that a human kindles a light in the dark, either with a match or by pressing a button?

FINK: I would suppose that the basic situation, mentioned in the fragment, is the human situation between night and light. A human is not just like other living beings between night and light; rather, he is a living being who stands in a relationship to night and light and who is not overcome by night and the dark. When his ὄψις is extinguished, he has the capacity, as the being with an affinity to fire, to bring forth fire and light. A human relates himself to night and day.

HEIDEGGER: Let us stay at first with night and day.

FINK: The human situation is different from that of living beings which are exposed to night and day. When it is night for a human, then light is extinguished. Indeed, there is a seeing of the dark. ὄψις does not mean here the capacity of seeing, but the capacity of seeing *in actu* [in actuality]. When his ὄψις is extinguished it means, therefore, when his capacity of seeing is no longer *in actu*. The capacity of seeing as such is not extinguished with the breaking in of darkness. We also do not say that a human only hears when he hears sounds. For he also hears silence.

HEIDEGGER: A human sees nothing in the dark.

FINK: Nevertheless everyone sees something in the dark.

HEIDEGGER: I am aiming at precisely what extinguishing means.

FINK: Extinguishing can have two-fold meaning: first, it refers to not seeing in the dark; second, to not seeing in sleep.

HEIDEGGER: Let us leave sleep aside. In the phenomenon, we must distinguish between "not seeing anything in the dark" and "not seeing." If we speak now of the extinguishing of sight, that is still not clear enough to me. Not seeing means . . .

FINK: . . . that the ability to see is closed. With the open ability to see, we see nothing determinate in the dark. But that is still a seeing.

HEIDEGGER: It concerns me now to determine what is negated by the extinguishing of ὄψις.

FINK: One can read Fr. 26 such that a human kindles a light in the dream. Still, this way of reading appears questionable to me. When we say that a human is extinguished in reference to ὄψις, it can mean either a closing of the ability to see or a failing to find the visible on account of the darkness. The latter means that the ability to see is open, but we cannot make out anything specific in the darkness.

HEIDEGGER: In the dark I see nothing, and nevertheless I see.

FINK: This is similar with hearing. A sentry, for instance, listens intensely into the silence without hearing something determinate. When he hears no determinate sound, still he hears. His harkening is the most intense wakefulness of wanting to hear. Harkening is the condition of possibility for hearing. It is being open to the space of the hearable, whereas hearing is meeting the specifically hearable.

HEIDEGGER: If we think through what is said about "seeing nothing" and "not seeing" in the situation in which a human concerns himself with a light, for example with a candle, then how is ἑαυτῷ [for himself] out of Fr. 26 to be understood? I am concerned to preserve the ἑαυτῷ.

FINK: I do not regard it as pleonastic. A human has the capacity, akin to the day, to clear, even though in a weak manner in comparison to day. The human power to clear is something other than the light that comes with the daylight. The light kindled by the human is the little light in the great dark of night.

HEIDEGGER: When he kindles a little light in the night, he does it so that something is still given to him in the darkness by the light.

FINK: The little light stands in opposition to the rhythmic, great light of day that befalls us and that has nothing dark about it. The human is the light-related being who, it is true, can kindle light, but never such as would be able to completely annihilate the night. The light started by him is only an island in the dark of night on account of which his place is clearly characterized between day and night.

HEIDEGGER: You emphasize night, and understand it speculatively. But let us remain at first with the dark: in the dark, in twilight, a human kindles a light. Doesn't this darkness in which he kindles a light go together with the light of which you speak?

FINK: This light that a human kindles is already an offspring. All fires on earth, and that which is started by the fire kindling being, are offsprings, as in Plato. The gods do not comport themselves in the same way as humans toward light and night. A human has a Janus-like face; he is turned as much to the day as to the night.

HEIDEGGER: A human, who extinguishes in reference to the possibility of seeing, kindles a light. Now ἀποσβεσθεὶς ὄψις becomes clearer. It thus means "when he cannot see because of darkness" but not "when he cannot see."

FINK: I translate ὄψις with possibility of sight.

HEIDEGGER: I don't quite understand that.

FINK: A human kindles a little light in the dark measured by the great light.

HEIDEGGER: I would still like to stay with the little light; thereby we clarify and preserve the ἑαυτῷ.

FINK: I translate ἑαυτῷ with "for himself."

HEIDEGGER: But what does "for himself" mean?

PARTICIPANT: It means that the little light is a private light . . .

FINK: . . . as against the great one.

HEIDEGGER: ἅπτεται ἑαυτῷ [touches on himself]: why do I kindle a candle for myself? To be sure, because the candle shows something to me. This dimension must also be included.

FINK: I would like to accentuate the island-character of the little light in which something still shows itself to me. The little light in the dark of night is a fragmentary, insular light. Because a human does not dwell in the great light, he resembles the night owl (νυκτερίδες), that is, he finds himself on the boarder of day and night. He is distinguished as a being akin to light, but who stands at the same time in relationship to night.

HEIDEGGER: What indicates the relationship to night?

FINK: At the beginning it says that a human kindles a light in the night. Then it says further that in sleep he touches on the dead, and in waking he touches on the sleeping. Sleep is the twilight of life. A human does not exist in the full richness of life in so far as he touches on the dead through sleep. The dead stand in a reference to night.

HEIDEGGER: What does "to touch on" mean?

FINK: To touch on here does not mean to touch, but aims at a relationship of adjoining. And it is also important to notice here that it is not a question of simple boardering, but of a relationship of adjoining.

HEIDEGGER: Here at the table, when I lay the chalk by the glass, we speak of a simple adjoining of both things on one another.

FINK: But when a human touches on the dead through sleep, he does not adjoin the dead like the chalk on the glass. In sleep, he touches relatedly on the dark.

HEIDEGGER: Thus it is a question of an open-standing touching on. That goes with the fact that the kindled light also grants an open-standing quality to the little orbit of the room that is illuminated by the candle. I prefer that Fr. 26, and above all the ἅπτεται ἑαυτῷ, come into the dimension of open-standing reference. To me, you go much too fast into the speculative dimension.

FINK: In that a human relates himself to the boardered space of light, he relates himself at the same time to that which repels the quality of standing open. One must find a word in order to be able linguistically to comprehend the reference of the human not only to the open but also to the night that surrounds the open.

HEIDEGGER: The dark is in a certain sense also the openness, if a light is kindled in it. This dark openness is only possible in the clearing in the sense of the *Da*.

FINK: I would suppose that we may think the concealment of the dark not only out of the relationship of clearing of the *Da*. There is the danger that one understands the dark only as boundary of what stands open, as the exterior walling of the open. I would like above all to indicate that a human relates himself at the same time to the open and to the concealing darkness.

HEIDEGGER: What you say may be true, but it is not directly mentioned in the fragment. I will not contest the dimension you have in view.

FINK: Let us start from the situation of light in the night. Somebody kindles a torch in the night. It casts its shine on the way, so that one can orient oneself on the way. In that he moves in brightness, and relates himself to it, he relates himself at the same time to the menacing darkness, for which he is understandingly open even though not in the manner of standing open. The clearing in the concealing darkness has its limitation. ἀλήθεια [nonconcealment] is surrounded by λήθη [conceal-ment].

HEIDEGGER: In Fr. 26, I lay importance on precisely the relation-ship of standing open.

FINK: The fragment does not speak of brightness, but of light in the night. It speaks of the curious human place between light and night which is open to death and referred to death through sleep. The refer-ence to death also belongs to the understanding of those who are awake. For those who are awake touch on the sleeping and the sleeping touch on the dead.

HEIDEGGER: I am still with the light in the night. ἀποθανών [dying] is stricken by Wilamowitz as an annotation.

PARTICIPANT: If one retains αποθανών, the fragment moves into the neighborhood of meaning of the orphic-eleusinian world outlook. Then the meaning of εὐφρόνη [in the night] also changes.

HEIDEGGER: How do you understand ζῶν [living]? Doesn't one have to strike out ἀποθανών on the basis of ζῶν δὲ [and living]?

PARTICIPANT: ἀποθανών is an annotation to ἀποσβεσθεὶς ὄψις [when his eyesight is extinguished].

HEIDEGGER: Referred to ἀποθανών, ἀποσβεσθεὶς ὄψις then means: after the possibility of seeing is deprived.

FINK: But then the fragment moves into the domain of a mystic assertion that I cannot follow.

HEIDEGGER: Everything that follows ἑαυτῷ is puzzling to me. I do not see the thrust of the fragment. What is treated in this text? ἅπτεται [touch on] is mentioned three times, and each time in another reference. First, it says that a human touches on (kindles) a light in the night. Then it says that while living, he touches in sleep on the dead, and in waking he touches on the sleeping. How does ἅπτεται fit in here?

FINK: First, Heraclitus speaks of ἅπτεται in reference to φάος [light of the kindled fire]. Touching on is also meant in fire-kindling. If a human is the in-between being, between night and light, then he is also the in-between being between life and death, the being who is already near to death in life. In life, he touches on death while sleeping; in waking, he touches on the sleeping. ἅπτομαι [reciprocal touching] means a more intimate manner than just the abstract representation. Sleep is the mean between life and death. The sleeping have the inactivity of the dead and the breathing of the living.

HEIDEGGER: What does "awake" mean?

FINK: The wakeful one is he who stands fully open.

HEIDEGGER: Awake is connected with "to awaken."

PARTICIPANT: In waking up, one touches on sleep. Waking up is the counterpart of falling asleep.

HEIDEGGER: Do you thus mean that in waking up we are at the edge of sleep? But in the fragment it is a matter of an essential reference of waking and sleep and of sleep and death...

FINK: ... and it is not a matter of what is accidentally given. Here it is a matter of the human as the one who is between-night-and-day.

HEIDEGGER: For me, the in-between is still not the *da*. Also, we sometimes call a wakeful human a bright, lively one. His attention is directed toward something. He exists in that his bearings are directed toward something.

FINK: The relationship between waking and sleep is similar to that between gods and humans. Comportment toward the sleep that permeates all wakefulness belongs to the self-understanding of being awake.

HEIDEGGER: Being waked up includes in itself the reference to sleepiness. Naturally, that is not meant in Fr. 26. It is not a question here of external relationships but of inner references. As understanding comportment toward the mortal being of humans belongs to the self-understanding of the gods, so also the understanding reference to sleep belongs to the self-understanding of those who are awake. Something of the meaning of sleep in the life of humans shows itself here.

FINK: The countertension to sleep belongs to being awake. But the sleeper touches on death. Sleep is the way of being engulfed and being untied from all that is many and structured. Thus seen, the sleeper comes into the neighborhood of the dead, who have lost the domain of the distinctions of πάντα.

HEIDEGGER: For the Hindu, sleep is the highest life.

FINK: That may be a Hindu experience. Sleeping is a manner of being alive, as waking is the concentrated and proper manner of being alive. Those who are awake do not immediately touch on the dead, but only indirectly through sleep. Sleep is the middle part between waking and being dead. Being dead is viewed from sleep.

HEIDEGGER: Do you say that the experience of sleep is the condition of possibility of the experience of death?

FINK: That would be saying too much. Sleep is a way of being similar to being dead, but a way that does not occur only in an objective biological sense. For in the understanding of sleep we have a twilight understanding of being dead. In a certain manner it is true that like is cognized through like and unlike through unlike.

HEIDEGGER: Isn't the correspondence of sleep and death a rather external view? Can one experience sleep as sleep?

FINK: I would like to answer this question positively in the same way that one says that one can encounter death internally. There are dark ways of understanding in which a human knows himself to be familiar with uncleared being. We know of sleep not only in the moment of waking up. We sleep through time.

HEIDEGGER: According to Aristotle, we know nothing of sleep.

FINK: I would like to contest that. What Aristotle says in this way about sleep does not spring from a phenomenological analysis of sleep, which—as I believe—is still undone today.

HEIDEGGER: I don't contest the possibility of experiencing sleep as sleep, but I see no access.

FINK: When Heraclitus speaks of the ἅπτεσθαι of those who are awake in reference to those who are asleep, that cannot mean the exterior appearance. Touching on ... is a coming into nearness (ἀν-χιβασίη), a form of approach that does not happen only objectively, but which includes a dark mode of understanding.

HEIDEGGER: If we now summarize the whole, we can say that you have already foreshadowed where you place ἅπτεσθαι. The three manners of ἅπτεσθαι are relationships that a human encounters...

FINK: ... but a human as distinctive elucidation of the basic reference. As the counterreference of gods and humans was thematic before, now a human becomes thematic in the midst of oppositions. A human is the twilight, fire-kindling being in the counterplay of day and night. It is the basic situation of humans to be placed in an extraordinary manner in the counterplay of day and night. A human does not come forth like the other living beings in this counterplay; rather, he comports himself toward it, is near fire and related to σοφόν. What is said in Fr. 26 about references, belongs in discussion of the counterplay of opposites. What ἕν holds apart and together is thought in the image of the god, in the image of bow and lyre and in ἁρμονία αφανής. There the counterturning is taken in view. But here in Fr. 26, it is not a matter of counterturning, but of what is opposed ...

HEIDEGGER: ... which belongs together.

FINK: A human is not only exposed to the counterplay of day and night; rather, he can understand it in a special manner. But the many do not understand it; rather, only he who understands the relatedness of ἕν and πάντα.

HEIDEGGER: With the difficulty that Fr. 26 creates for me, I could—above all in order to clarify ἅπτεται—solve the difficulty only when I took Fr. 10 into consideration: συνάψιες ὅλα καὶ οὐχ ὅλα συμ-φερόμενον διαφερόμενον, συνᾷδον διᾷδον, καὶ ἐκ πάντων ἕν καὶ ἐξ ἑνὸς πάντα.[30] The decisive word here is συνάψιες [connections]. It is the same word as ἅπτω [to fasten], but sharpened by the σύν [together]. Our German word haften [to fasten], Haft [arrest], is connected with ἅπτω. We can place a semicolon behind συνάψιες. I do not translate it with "fastened-together," but with "letting-belong-together." In the fragment, it is not said what determined the συνάψιες. It simply stands there.

FINK: I would say that the first two illustrations of συνάψιες, ὅλα καὶ οὐχ ὅλα [wholes and not wholes], prevent the σύν from being understood in the sense of a familiar wholeness. The usual idea of wholeness is oriented toward joining together. But in the fragment it says: wholes and not wholes. Thus, it is a matter of συνάψιες, not only of simple moments into a whole, but of wholes and not wholes, as well as of harmonies and not harmonies.

HEIDEGGER: We can bracket the καὶ between ὅλα and οὐχ ὅλα.

FINK: The fragment then says further: ἐκ πάντων ἓν καὶ ἐξ ἑνός πάντα [out of everything one and out of one everything].

HEIDEGGER: What is surprising is that πάντα and ὅλα occur at the same time.

FINK: ὅλα are in πάντα.

HEIDEGGER: Thus, τὸ ὅλον does not mean the world.

FINK: The fragment speaks in the plural of wholes ...

HEIDEGGER: ... that are not to be understood, however, in the sense of things.

FINK: At first, one thinks it is a matter here of oppositions on the same level. But at the close of the fragment it is said that it is not a matter of the union of opposites; rather, everything can be thought only from out of the relatedness of ἕν and πάντα.

HEIDEGGER: How do you understand the ἐκ [out of]?

FINK: From out of συνάψιες. That is a form.

HEIDEGGER: Do you mean a form or the form?

FINK: The form. You have interpreted the relatedness of ἕν and πάντα as state of affairs.

HEIDEGGER: Is ἐκ πάντων [out of everything] the same as ἐξ ἑνός [out of one]?

FINK: Here the συνάψιες is taken in view from both sides, the one time as relatedness of πάντα and ἕν, the other time as relatedness of ἕν and πάντα.

HEIDEGGER: But we must determine that more precisely, because the basic relatedness of ἕν and πάντα lies at the basis of Fr. 26 on a smaller scale.

FINK: I cannot see it there.

HEIDEGGER: When one reads ἐκ πάντων ἕν at first reading, just as it stands there, then it says that the one is put together out of everything.

FINK: That would be, then, an ontic process—which, however, is not meant in the fragment.

HEIDEGGER: But what is the meaning of ἐκ and then ἐξ? ἕν is indeed the re-latedness of πάντα, but πάντα are not on their part the re-latedness of ἕν.

FINK: The ἐκ must in each case be thought differently. The πάντα are in συνάψιες in reference to the ἕν. They are held from out of ἕν; they are συναπτόμενα [fastened].

HEIDEGGER: Out of their being fastened is the holding ...

FINK: ... of what holds ...

HEIDEGGER: ... visible. The fragment does not say that one develops out of everything combined, but that the unifying ἕν becomes visible in the allness, from out of the allness. Is it a question here only of the *ratio cognoscendi* [order of knowledge] or the *ratio essendi* [order of being]?

FINK: Of the *ratio essendi*.

HEIDEGGER: But how? We understand the ἐξ ἑνὸς πάντα, but the ἐκ παντων ἕν has not occurred up till now.

FINK: We already came across ἐκ πάντων ἕν in the relationship of goods and gold. The πάντα as the many in entirety, which stand fastened by ἕν, refer to the one. All ὄντα are already from the beginning held in the care, in the guard, of ἕν.

HEIDEGGER: I cannot follow that through sufficiently.

FINK: The words συμφερόμενον διαφερόμενον [concord and discord] sound very hard. The phrase brings us up short, which is its express intention. But at the same time, it is taken back in the συνάψιες.

HEIDEGGER: The reference of πάντα and ἕν must be specified differently than the reference of ἕν and πάντα. To be sure, both references belong together, but as distinguished. The ἐξ ἑνος πάντα is not equal to ἐκ πάντων ἕν, but it is the same in the sense of belonging together. The difficulty that has shown itself again and again in the course of the seminar lies in the methodological starting point, the justification of which I certainly do not want to contest. So long as one does not have λόγος in view, it is hard to get through the text, and Heraclitus reads with difficulty. For that reason, it seems to me that one must take Fr. 1, which is regarded as the beginning of Heraclitus' writing, as also the basis for the beginning of the explication of Heraclitus. With the phrase ἐκ πάντων ἕν, the question we have posed in reference to the relatedness of ἕν and πάντα comes into play again, namely, how the relatedness is to be determined, if it is neither a matter of a making nor of a casting of light. What is the basic character of πάντα as πάντα in ἕν, πάντα as reined in by ἕν? Only when one sees this aspect can one determine the ἐκ πάντων ἕν. συνάψιες is probably the key to understanding this.

PARTICIPANT: If we may also consider the context of Fr. 10, we find the word συνῆψεν [concord] in it.

HEIDEGGER: There it says that nature brought about the first concord by the union of opposites. The fragment does not, however, say that the ἕν occurs out of the many.

FINK: I would understand συνάψιες verbally.

HEIDEGGER: I lay great importance on the word συνάψιες in reference to Fr. 26. Here, everything is still dark. I am concerned only to see what is questionable in the matter, if one avoids operating from the beginning on the level of things.

PARTICIPANT: The word συνάψιες has, among others, also been contested.

PARTICIPANT: Instead of συνάψιες, συλλάψιες [taking together] is a possible rendition, which is to be understood from συλλαβή [what holds or is held together].

HEIDEGGER: συλλαμβάνειν [to gather together] and συνάπτειν [to join together] are not so far from one another.

PARTICIPANT: συλλάψιες would be simpler to understand, and means taking-together. The context gives examples of it.

HEIDEGGER: What is puzzling is the σύν, whether we now remain with συνάψιες or συλλάψιες. The σύν comes first before συμφερόμενον διαφερόμενον. συνάψιες means the belonging-together of συμφερόμενον and διαφερόμενον.

FINK: συνάψιες means no simple clasping together, but the clasping-together of what is clasped-together and what is not clasped-together. That allows itself to be understood, however, first from the relatedness, of ἕν-πάντα. συνάψιες, thought verbally, means not only the condition of what is clasped-together, but a happening, a constant counterplay . . .

HEIDEGGER: . . . a continuous bringing-toward-one-another. Thinking in Greek, we can say that everything plays here in nonconcealment and concealing. We must also see that from the beginning, because otherwise everything becomes opaque.

12

Sleep and Dream—Ambiguity of ἄπτεσθαι
(Correlated Fragments: 26, 99, 55).

FINK: We move into a metaphorical manner of speaking, when we speak of sleep as the brother of death. Someone who wakes up out of a deep sleep and reflects on sleep says, "I have slept like a dead man." This metaphorical interpretation is doubtful.

HEIDEGGER: A second difficulty is expressed with the question whether all sleeping is also dreaming. Is sleeping to be identified with dreaming? Today, psychology maintains that all sleeping is also dreaming.

FINK: In dreaming, we must distinguish the one who dreams and the dreamed I. When we speak of a light in the dream, this light is not for the dreamer, but rather for the dreamed I of the dream world. The sleeper, or the sleeping I, is also the dreaming I, who is not the I of the dream world who is awake and sees in the dreams. In the dream world, the I of the dream world behaves similarly to the wakeful I. While the dreaming I sleeps, the dreamed I of the dream world finds itself in a condition of wakefulness. What is important, however, is that the light of the dream world is a light not for the dreaming or sleeping I, but for the dreamed I. The I of the dream world can have different roles and vary in its self-relatedness. A phenomenological analysis of the dream indicates that not the sleeping, but the dreamed I kindles a light. Although the sleeper does not see, still, as a dreamer, he has a dreamed I that has encounters.

HEIDEGGER: Thus one cannot identify sleeping and dreaming.

FINK: Sleeping is a vivid form of human absorption. Dreaming is a mode of the real I, while being awake in the dream world is the mode of an intentional I. The relationship of the sleeping I to the dreamed I, or of the real I to the intentional I, one can compare with recollection. The recollector is not the subject of the recollected world. We must also distinguish here between the recollecting and the recollected I. While the recollecting I belongs in the actual surroundings, the recollected I, or the I of the recollected world, is referred to the recollected world. Only because we customarily do not make the distinction between the sleeping-dreaming I and the I of the dream world, can one say that the sleeper kindles a light in the dream. Seen phenomenologically, however, that is not correct. The I of the dream world, and not the sleeping I, kindles a light. If one wishes to interpret fire-kindling as a dreamy fire making, then on the one hand the phenomenological distinction between the sleeping and the dreamed I will be overlooked and, on the other hand, the human situation, aimed at (in my opinion) in the fragment, of standing between light and night gets lost. Dreaming is not the essential distinction of humans vis-à-vis animals. Animals also dream, for example, the hunting dog, when they make noises in their sleep. There is also something like a dreamed dog-world. I myself reject the interpretation according to which the human position between night and light is a matter of dreaming. Indeed, it is a possibility of interpretation, but one must ask what philosophical relevance such an interpretation has in the whole context of the fragments.

HEIDEGGER: We must notice that the thesis "no sleep without dream" is an ontic discovery that suppresses the existential distinction of the sleeping and the dreamed I and only claims that all sleeping is also dreaming.

FINK: The same thesis also levels down the distinction between waking in reality and the dreamed waking in the dream world.

HEIDEGGER: The phenomenological distinction between sleeping and dreaming is lacking in that thesis which identifies sleeping with dreaming. It is always an advantage to save the unity of the text, which is philologically always a principle to be positively valued. There are phases in philology in which everything is dropped and cancelled, and then again, phases in which one tries to save everything. When I came to Marburg in 1923, my friend Bultmann had stricken so much out of the New Testament that scarcely anything remained. In the meantime, that has changed again.

The whole of Fr. 26 is difficult, especially because of ἅπτεται. Perhaps more clarity in this regard will come if we now proceed.

FINK: I would like to say at the outset that the entire interpretation that I now give of Fr. 26 is only an attempt at interpretation. When we proceed from the fact that a human kindles a light in the night, he is spoken of as the fire kindler, that is, as the one who holds sway over the ποίησις of fire-kindling. We must recall that it was a decisive step in human cultural development to gain power over fire—which otherwise was perceived only, for example, as lightning—to get command and use of fire. A human is distinguished from all animals by the heritage of Prometheus. No animal kindles fire. Only a human kindles a light in the night. Nevertheless he is not able, like Helios, to kindle a world-fire that never goes out, that drives out the night. Fr. 99 said that if Helios were not, it would be night despite the remaining stars. The moon and stars are lights in the night. Helios alone drives out the night. Helios is no island in the night, but has overcome the insular nature. A human is not able to kindle a τὰ πάντα-illuminating fire like Helios. In the night, his possibilities of sight are extinguished, in so far as the dark makes seeing impossible despite open ὄψις. When a human, in the situation of wanting to see and not being able to see in the night, employs his power of kindling fire, he touches on the power of light. Kindling fire is also a touching on. Touching on the power of light is a kindling. In contrast, touching on the night has another character. Human fire kindling is a projection of a light brightness in which many, that is, the multiplicity of πολλά are lit up. I intentionally speak of πολλά now and not of πάντα. The finite, small light-shine of human fire is also a ἕν in the sense of a brightness in which many things show up. Here the relatedness of ἕν and πάντα repeats itself in reduced manner as the relationship of ἕν (in the sense of the brightness of the fire kindled by a human) and πολλά (that is, the things that show up in each bounded brightness).

HEIDEGGER: When you speak about kindling fire, do you mean fire only in the sense of brightness and not also in regard to warmth?

FINK: Helios brings forth the seasons, which bring everything (πάντα). The structure of ἕν, as the brightness of the sun, and πάντα, as the many in entirety which come forth to appearance in the sun's brightness, has a moment of repetition in reduced manner in the relationship of ἕν as the brightness of the fire kindled by a human and πολλά which show up in this finite brightness. Human fire cannot illuminate everything (πάντα), but only many things (πολλά). On the contrary, the brightness of the sun-fire surrounds everything (πάντα).

HEIDEGGER: Does the distinction between the brightness of fire projected by humans and the brightness of Helios consist in the fact that one is restricted, while the latter is referred to all?

FINK: Yes.

HEIDEGGER: Is there brightness of fire without the light of Helios?

FINK: No. Rather, the brightness of fire projected by humans is derivative from the sun's brightness.

HEIDEGGER: We must also emphasize that the candlelight does not show anything for itself, and that a human is not a seer for himself alone. The candlelight only shows something, and a human sees what is self-showing in the light-shine of the candle only in so far as he stands always and already in what is cleared. Openness for the light in general is the condition for his seeing something in the candlelight.

FINK: The candlelight is an insular light in the night, such that we can distinguish between brightness and darkness. The brightness of the candlelight disperses itself in the dark, while the brightness of Helios is no longer experienced as brightness in the night. The brightness of the sun in general makes possible and supports human seeing and the visual ability to relate to what shows itself. In the brightness that a human brings forth, in the light-shine kindled by him, there emerges a relationship of grasping human to grasped state of affairs in his surroundings that has the character of distantiality. Seeing is a distantial being with things. As a distance sense, seeing needs an optimal nearness to what is seen. There is a constitutive distance between seeing and what is seen in the unity of the overarching light that illuminates and makes visible.

HEIDEGGER: Here we can draw on Fr. 55: ὅσων ὄψις ἀκοὴ μάθησις, ταῦτα ἐγὼ προτιμέω.

FINK: ὄψις and ἀκοή, sight and hearing, are both distance senses. The one is a relationship to the light-space, the other a relationship to the space of sound.

HEIDEGGER: The Diels translation, "Everything of which there is sight, hearing, learning, that do I prefer," is inverted if you equate ὄψις, ἀκοή, and μάθησις [learning], and do not understand ὄψις and ἀκοή as μάθησις. From this we must say: "Everything of which there is learning from sight and hearing, that do I prefer. What one can see and hear, that gives learning."

FINK: It is thus a matter of μανθάνειν through seeing and hearing. Every other sense also gives learning. However, the learning that sight and hearing give is preferred. Sight as well as hearing are distance senses and as such are characterized by the distantial relationship of grasping and grasped.

HEIDEGGER: ὄψις and ἀκοή have an advantage that can be seen from Fr. 55.

FINK: Seeing is a grasping in visual space, hearing a grasping into auditory space. With hearing, we do not so easily see a ζυγόν [yoke] that spans hearing and what is heard, like light, with seeing, spans the eye and what is seen. And nevertheless—so I would think—there is also something here like a ζυγόν. One would have to form here the concept of an original silence that is the same as light with seeing. Every sound breaks the silence and must be understood as silence-breaking. There is also the silence into which we harken, without hearing something determinate. The original silence is a constitutive element forming the distance of the auditory space of hearing.

HEIDEGGER: Perhaps the silence reaches still further into the direction of collection and gathering.

FINK: You are thinking of the ringing of silence.

HEIDEGGER: I believe that we can draw upon Fr. 55 as evidence for your emphasis on the distance sense.

FINK: In contrast to the relationship, determined by distance, of grasping and grasped in the light, or in the brightness, there is another touching on which shows itself in feeling [Tasten]. Here there is an immediate proximity between feeling and what is felt. This proximity is not transmitted through the medium of distance in which the seer and what is seen, or the hearer and what is heard, are set apart from one another. In seeing, the grasping in light is separated from what is grasped. In the unity of the light that surrounds the one who grasps and the grasped, the manifold of πολλά shows up. A distantial distance holds sway be-

tween the one who grasps by seeing and what is grasped. This distantial
distance is a fundamental way of understanding. Contrary to that would
be an understanding grounded in a being-in-the-proximity in the sense
of immediate touching on. Touching on is an understanding that does
not come out of the survey, out of the expanse, or out of the region
toward what is grasped.

HEIDEGGER: But what about when I now give you my hand?

FINK: That is an immediate touching of hands. In περὶ ψυχῆς [*On
the Soul*], Aristotle calls flesh the medium of the sense of touch. But a
phenomenological objection must be made here, because flesh is not the
medium in the proper sense for touching and what is touched. Seeing is
referred to a visible thing, to a visible object, which, however, meets us
out of a region. Encounter out of the open ambit, which is cleared by the
brightness, is distinctive of the special kind of grasping that consists in
the distance between the one who grasps and what is grasped.

HEIDEGGER: And how does it relate with the reaching of hands?

FINK: The reaching of hands is a coming up to one another of
touching hands. Between the touching hands there is an immediate
proximity. But at the same time, the hands can also be seen by us.
Touching ourselves is also a special phenomenon. A minimum of distance holds sway between what touches itself. Feeling and touching are
proximity senses, and as such they are the way of an immediate standing
at and lying near to an immediate neighborhood. One must understand
the relationship of the waking to the sleeping, and of the sleeping to the
dead, from the immediacy of the neighborhood of touching on.

PARTICIPANT: In a phenomenological analysis of seeing and hearing as the two distance senses, you have worked out the phenomenological structure of the region that is identical with the space of seeing and
hearing, or with the field of seeing and hearing. You have then further
indicated that, in distinction to the two distance senses, feeling and
touching as proximity senses are due not to the phenomenological structure of the region but to immediate proximity. Now it only concerns me
to indicate that the phenomenologically obtained structure of region in
the domain of both distance senses is not synonymous with the ontologically understood region in the sense of the openness and the clearing in
which something present meets a human being. For not only what is seen
and heard, but also what is felt, is encountered out of the ontologically
understood region. If I have understood you correctly, you have em-
ployed the phenomenological distinction between distance sense and
proximity sense, that is, between the region out of which the seer encounters the seen and the hearer encounters the heard, and the immediate proximity of feeling and felt, as springboard for a speculative
thought according to which two different ways of understanding being
are distinguished. Setting out from the immediate touching of feeling

and what is felt, you go over to the touching of the waking on the sleeping and the touching of the sleeping on the dead.

FINK: I must make a slight correction of that. I am not so much starting out from a phenomenological investigation of seeing but more in reference to the structure of brightness. A small, finite fire is also a unity that is not alongside things. The brightness of the fire kindled by humans is not only the radiance on things, but the space-and-time-filling light in which not only many things but many kinds of things show up. The way that the one who grasps is in the brightness is the way of distantial perception. If ἅπτεται ἑαυτῷ is pleonastic when seen linguistically, I would not reject the pleonism. For one can say that a human kindles a fire that is for him in contrast to the fire that is for all and in which, from the beginning, all humans reside as in the brightness of the day-star. A human kindles for himself a light that illuminates him as the one who is off the track and helpless. I started out from this phenomenon, and I have then characterized not only the relationship of ἕν (in the sense of the brightness cast by a human) to πολλά, but also the human dwelling in brightness as a distantial reference. Fire kindling cancels the moment of immediacy of touching because the fire in itself is cast over a distance.

HEIDEGGER: Somebody kindles a candle or a torch. What is produced with the kindling of the torch, the flame, is a kind of thing...

FINK: ... that has the peculiarity that it shines...

HEIDEGGER: ... not only shines, but also allows seeing.

FINK: It makes a shine, casts out brightness and lets what shows itself be seen therein.

HEIDEGGER: This thing at the same time has the character that it fits itself into the openness in which humans stand. The relationship of light and clearing is difficult to comprehend.

FINK: The source of light is first seen in its own light. What is noteworthy is that the torch makes possible its own being seen.

HEIDEGGER: Here we come up against the ambiguity of shine. We say, for example, the sun shines.

FINK: If we think in terms of physics, we speak of the sun as light source and of the emission of its rays. We then determine the relationship of clearing to light such that the clearing, in which the sun itself is seen, is derivative from the light as the sun. We must put precisely this derivative relationship into question. The light of the clearing does not precede but, the other way around, the clearing precedes the light. A light is only possible as an individual because it is given individually in the clearing. The sun is seen in its own light, so that the clearing is the more original. If we trace the brightness back only to the source of light, we skip over the fundamental character of the clearing.

HEIDEGGER: So long as one thinks in terms of physics, the fundamental character of the clearing, that it is prior to the light, will not be seen.

FINK: A human, as the heir of the fire thief, has the possibility of bringing forth light in a certain sense, but only because there is a clearing...

HEIDEGGER: ... because a human stands in the clearing...

FINK: ... and indeed by nature. Not only does the occurrence of things belong to standing within the clearing, but also the grasping occurrence of the human who, however, is for the most part simply installed among things, and who does not think the light in which things are grasped. Grasping indeed stands in the light, but it does not properly grasp the light; rather, it remains turned only toward the grasped things. The task of thinking, therefore, is to think that which itself makes shining up and grasping possible...

HEIDEGGER: ... and also the kind of belongingness of the light to the clearing, and how the light is a distinctive thing.

FINK: No better analogy shows itself for the special position of humans in the midst of τὰ πάντα than that they, different from all other living beings, are light-nigh. Touching on the power of fire is the way of fire kindling. One can now interpret the phenomenal features mentioned ontologically in that one understands the light not only as the light perceptible by the senses, but as the light or as the light-nature of σοφόν, which makes all σαφές. The human comportment toward σοφόν is human standing within the original clearing, a touching being-nigh σοφόν in the manner of an understanding explication of things in their essence. The danger here is that the clearing or brightness itself is not thought. In the brightness many and various things show up. There is no brightness in which there is only one thing. In the brightness, many things set themselves off. In the light, their boundedness is outlined, and they have boundaries against one another. The seer sees himself distinguished from the ground on which he stands, and from the other things on the ground and round about him. But there is also no brightness in which only one kind of thing would be given. In the brightness, not only a great number show up, but also many and various kinds, for example, stone, plant, animal, fellow-human, and alongside natural things also artificially made things, etc. We do not see only things of the same kind, but also different kinds of things. A human, in the brightness brought about by him, is as the finite reflection of σοφόν in the midst of the entirety that is the articulated joining. Human understanding in the light happens as an understanding of πολλά, and this understanding is at the same time variously articulated according to kind and species. πολλά are not only a multiplicity of number but also a multiplicity according to kind. In contrast to this articulated understanding in the brightness, there is perhaps a manner of dark understanding that is not articulated and that does not happen in the shine of brightness that sets apart and joins together. The dark understanding is a kind of nightly touching on, which can be characterized as the neighborhood of ontic relation. In the position of *Being and Time,* a human is regarded as the entity that is unique in the constitution of its being. Although he is ontically distinguished from all of what is, and customarily understands himself estranged from other entities, he has the understanding of the manner of being of all domains of things . . .

HEIDEGGER: . . . and indeed precisely on the ground of the ontic distinctness.

FINK: The ontic distinctness of nonhuman entities is no barrier for human understanding of the manner of being, but precisely goes together with it. But a human is not only a cleared being; he is also a natural being and as such he is implanted in a dark manner in nature. There is now also a dark understanding that presupposes not the ontic difference, but precisely the ontic proximity, an understanding, however, that lacks clarity and historical investigation. One such dark understanding of the nightly ground is also meant with the ἅπτεται in reference to εὐφρόνη, and in the manner that the waking touch on the sleeping and the sleeping touch on the dead. This dark understanding is no kind of distantial understanding, but an understanding that stands in, that rests on, the ontic proximity, but that exhibits no ontological abundance. A human is predominantly a light kindler, he who is delivered over to the nature of light. At the same time, however, he also rests on the nightly ground that we can only speak of as closed. The sleeping and the dead are figures indicated by human belonging in living and dead nature.

HEIDEGGER: The concept of ontic proximity is difficult. There is also an ontic proximity between the glass and the book here on the table.

FINK: Between the glass and the book there is a spatial proximity, but not a proximity in the manner of being.

HEIDEGGER: You indeed mean an ontological and not an ontic proximity.

FINK: No, here it is precisely a matter of an ontic proximity. We can make clear what the ontic proximity implies on the opposite structure. As Dasein, a human is distinguished from the rest of what is, but at the same time he has the ontological understanding of all of what is. Aristotle says: ἡ ψυχὴ τὰ ὄντα πώς ἐστι πάντα. The soul is in a certain sense all things (περὶ ψυχῆς, Γ 8, 431 b 21). That is the manner in which a human comes nigh to σοφόν, to λόγος, to the articulated joining of the κόσμος. Because he himself belongs in the clearing, he has a limited lighting capacity. As the one who can kindle fire, he is nigh to the sunlike and the *sophon*-like.

HEIDEGGER: But what do you understand by the ontic proximity? When you say proximity, do you not then mean a small distance?

FINK: The ancients knew two principles of understanding; like cognized through like and unlike cognized through unlike. A human is distinguished from all of what is. Nevertheless, that does not preclude him from understanding and determining all the rest of what is in its being. Here the principle functions that unlike is cognized by unlike. But in so far as a human is a living being, he also has still another character of being with which he reaches into the nightly ground. He has the double character: on the one hand, he is the one who places himself in the clearing, and on the other, he is the one who is tied to the underground of all clearing.

HEIDEGGER: This would become intelligible first of all through the phenomenon of the body . . .

FINK: . . . as, for example, in the understanding of Eros.

HEIDEGGER: Body is not meant ontically here . . .

FINK: . . . and also not in the Husserlian sense, . . .

HEIDEGGER: . . . but rather as Nietzsche thought the body, even though it is obscure what he actually meant by it.

FINK: In the section "Of the Despisers of the Body," Zarathustra says, "Body am I entirely, and nothing else; . . ." Through the body and the senses a human is nigh to the earth.

HEIDEGGER: But what is ontic proximity?

FINK: Human lack of ontological affinity with other entities belongs together with the ontological understanding of his manner of being. But if a human exists between light and night, he relates himself to night differently than to light and the open, which has the distinguishing, joining together structure. He relates himself to night or to the nightly ground in so far as he belongs bodily to the earth and to the flowing of life. The dark understanding rests as it were on the other principle of understanding according to which like is cognized through like.

HEIDEGGER: Can one isolate the dark understanding, which the bodily belonging to the earth determines, from being placed in the clearing?

FINK: True, the dark understanding can be addressed from the clearing, but it doesn't let itself be brought further to language in the manner of the articulated joining.

HEIDEGGER: When you say ontic proximity, then no small distance is meant in what you call proximity, but a kind of openness . . .

FINK: . . . but a twilight, dark, reduced openness that has no history of concepts behind it, to which we may have to come sometime. A human has his place between heaven and earth, between the openness of ἀλήθεια and the closedness of λήθη. Nevertheless, we must say that all comportment toward the dark ground is to be experienced as comportment when a residue of clearing remains, because in the absolute night not only all cows are black, but also all understanding is obliterated.

HEIDEGGER: A human is embodied [leibt] only when he lives [lebt]. The body in your sense is to be understood thus. Thereby, "to live" is meant in the existential sense. Ontic proximity means no spatial proximity between two things, but a reduced openness, thus a human ontological moment. And nevertheless, you speak of an ontic proximity.

FINK: You have, one time when you came to Freiburg, said in a lecture that the animal is world-poor. At that time, you were underway toward the affinity of the human with nature.

HEIDEGGER: The body phenomenon is the most difficult problem. The adequate constitution of the sound of speech also belongs here. Phonetics thinks too physicalistically, when it does not see φωνή [speech] as voice in the correct manner.

PARTICIPANT: Wittgenstein says an astounding thing in the Tractatus. Language is the extension of the organism.

FINK: The only question is how "organism" is to be understood here, whether biologically or in the manner that human dwelling in the midst of what is is essentially determined by bodiliness.

HEIDEGGER: One can understand organism in the sense of Uexkülls or also as the functioning of a living system. In my lecture, which you mentioned, I have said that the stone is worldless, the animal world-poor, and the human world-forming.

FINK: It is thereby a question whether the world-poverty of the animal is a deficient mode of world-forming transcendence. It is questionable whether the animal in the human can be understood at all when we see it from the animal's viewpoint, or whether it is not a proper way that the human relates to the dark ground.

HEIDEGGER: The bodily in the human is not something animalistic. The manner of understanding that accompanies it is something that metaphysics up till now has not touched on. Ontic proximity holds of many phenomena from which you want to comprehend ἅπτεται.

FINK: ἅπτεται appears at first to be spoken from a clinging to and touching on, from the sense of touch. In touching on the dark power, a neighborhood of proximity holds sway; while touching on the light is a standing in the light. What is in the light has in itself the moment of distantiality, against which, however, it is no objection that a human also touches on the power of light of σοφόν.

HEIDEGGER: How do you now understand "touching on"?

FINK: Touching on the power of light of σοφόν is a distanced touching on. To the contrary, touching on the dark power is a distanceless touching on. Such a distanceless touching on is the awake one's touching on the sleeper and the sleeper's touching on the dead. How is the relationship of the wakeful to the sleeping to be determined? The wakeful one has a knowledge of sleep that is more than simply a memory of having slept, falling asleep, and waking up. The knowledge of the wakeful concerning sleep is a manner of the dark flux of life where the I is extinguished for itself in a reduced manner. The living touch in sleep on the manner of uncleared dwelling. A human, who belongs to the domain of light and harkens to it, has in sleep a kind of experience with being returned to the dark ground, not in the state of unconsciousness but in nondistinctness. While ἕν καὶ πάντα stands for a thinking mandate for the relationship in the domain of light, the experience of the dark ground of life is the experience of ἕν καὶ πᾶν. In ἕν καὶ πᾶν we must think the coincidence of all distinctions. The experience of ἕν καὶ πᾶν is the relationship of the human, who stands in individuation, to the nonindividuated but individuating ground. But the danger here is that we speak all too easily about metaphysical entities.

HEIDEGGER: When you speak of the uncleared, is that to be understood as privation or as negation?

FINK: The uncleared is not privative in regard to the cleared. To be sure, we understand the uncleared from out of the cleared. But we are concerned here with an original relationship to λήθη. Out of the situation of an essence determined by ἀλήθεια, the human has at the same time a relationship to λήθη. He does not always stand in ἀλήθεια; rather, he stands in rhythmic oscillation between waking and sleeping. The night, which he touches on in sleep, is not only to be understood privatively, but is to be understood as an autonomous moment alongside the moment of day or of the brightness to which he relates in waking. As φιλόσοφος [lover of wisdom], a human is not only a φίλος of σοφόν, but also of λήθη.

HEIDEGGER: Is λήθη to be identified with night?

FINK: Night is a kind of λήθη.

HEIDEGGER: How do you understand the uncleared? When you speak of reduced openness, that sounds like στέρησις [privation].

FINK: Being awake is, in its tautness, suffused by the possibility of the sinking away of tension and the extinguishing of all interest. Sleep is a way in which we come into the proximity of being dead, and is not merely a metaphor for death. Perhaps one must also treat phenomena like dying ontologically sometimes.

PARTICIPANT: I believe that we must distinguish between the reduced clearedness of the dark understanding, for example, of the understanding of the dark ground in sleep, and the dark ground itself, which is uncleared pure and simple. The understanding of the dark ground, and not the dark ground itself, is half cleared.

FINK: A human as a torch in the night implies that he is allied to the light-brightness of day and to the night which extinguishes all distinctions and the possibility of sight.

HEIDEGGER: The experience of sleep does not imply a mere remembering that I was falling asleep. The experience does not refer to sleep as a mere occurrence . . .

FINK: . . . in conscious life, . . .

HEIDEGGER: . . . but signifies a manner of my being in which I am implicated . . .

FINK: . . . and that still determines me in being awake. The brightness of being awake always stands upon the dark underground.

HEIDEGGER: Do you mean that in the actual [*aktuellen*] sense?

FINK: Similarly to the way the gods relate understandingly in their own life, by relating at the same time to the transient being of mortals, so we relate ourselves wakefully to the manifold, ordered cosmos which is a joining. Thereby, we know at the same time in a dark manner about the ability to be extinguished in sleep.

HEIDEGGER: But this knowledge is not necessarily actual [*aktuell*].

FINK: No. Perhaps this knowledge may be characterized from the problem of thrownness as being abandoned to that which a human has to be, and which does not belong to reason. As soon as one speaks of understanding of the dark ground as a relationship, one already means a distantial understanding.

HEIDEGGER: When we speak of the relationship to sleep, that is an inadequate manner of speaking. Is sleep the genuine understanding of the dark ground?

FINK: Not the sleeper, but the awake one relates himself to sleep.

HEIDEGGER: Concerning this reference, is there still another ontological possibility?

FINK: If being awake is the intensity of the process of life, the tautness is supported by the possibility of being able to let loose the tension of all fixation, of distinction and contrast in relationship to things and to the brightness. Someone could say that we are dealing here with an observation to the effect that life relates to death like waking to sleep, or like sleep to being dead, and that these analogical relationships would be spoken externally. But with that, one misses our real problem, which concerns the manner in which the awake one touches on sleep and the living sleeper touches on the dead. Touching on is our problem, and not the everyday observation or everyday philosophy according to which sleep is the brother of death, and life and death are regarded as mediated through the link of sleep. In Leibniz, we find the philosophical tendency to attempt to understand the being of the lower monads through dreamless sleep, impotence, and death, which is no death for him in the strict sense. The three phenomena mentioned are for him grades of receding differentiation of understanding. For Leibniz, being dead is still a manner of life, that is, of undifferentiated representation, since, strictly speaking, the monads cannot die. Thereby, he interprets the seriousness of death in terms of an extreme weakness of consciousness. He interprets sleep, impotence, and death in reference to a scale of regression of differentiation of living representation of the lower monads.

Heraclitus' Fr. 26, however, is not concerned with an observation concerning life and death and their mediation through waking and sleep, but with a statement on the essence of humanity. A human, as the one who is able to kindle fire and as the one who is able to touch on the power of light, is at the same time also the one who is able to touch on the dark in sleep and in death. But what is the meaning of touching on the dark which does not have the distantiality of one who grasps and what is grasped within the brightness? Here we cling to the troublesome expression of ontic proximity. We are concerned with the philosophical problem of the double relationship of the human with the relationship to light and to fire, which is a distantial understanding of one who grasps in reference to what he grasps, and with the understanding which is oriented to the immediacy of ἅψις [touching] in which the distinctions between grasping and grasped escape us. We have here only the modes of escape and absorption, and we cannot say more because otherwise we easily decline into a speculative mysticism.

HEIDEGGER: The relationship to death includes the question about the phenomenon of life and sleep. We cannot circumvent the problem of death, because death occurs in the fragment itself. We cannot come to grips with the problem independently on the basis of sleep alone.

13

Reference to Death, Awaiting - Hoping
(Correlated Fragments: 27, 28).—
The "Contraries" and their "Transition"
(Correlated Fragments: 111, 126, 8, 48, 51).—
Closing Question: The Greeks as a Challenge.

FINK: Till now, we have come across humans only in relationship to the gods (Fr. 62). Fr. 26 deals with the human being alone, but without ignoring the other references. ἅπτεται is the fundamental word of the fragment. There is, however, a difference between ἅπτεται in reference to the light, and ἅπτεται as the touching of those who are awake on the sleeping and the sleeping on the dead. In Fr. 26, no narrative is told, no passing event is reported; rather, the basic relationships of a human are seen, on the one hand to the power of light, and on the other, to the power of what is closed, which he touches in a different manner. ἅπτεται is first referred to the light, then to the darkness of those who sleep and to the greater darkness of the dead. ἅπτεται is common to all three references. If we do not take fire as an element, but as that which casts a shine, and makes possible the distantiality of the one who grasps and what is grasped in the shine, then too little is said with the possible translation of fire-kindling as "contact." We must ask in what reference the contact must be specified. On the one hand, it is a matter of contact with the fire that makes a clearing, and not just burning and warming fire; on the other hand it is a matter of contact with, or a touching on, that which does not shine up, but which closingly withdraws itself from a human.

HEIDEGGER: What closingly withdraws itself is not at first open, in order then to close itself. It does not close itself, because it is also not open.

FINK: Self-closing does not mean being locked up. Touching on is, here, a seizing of what cannot be seized, a touching on what is untouchable. In the dark of sleep, a human touches on death, on a possibility of his own. But that does not mean that he becomes dead. For it says: ζῶν δὲ ἅπτεται τεθνεῶτος.

HEIDEGGER: In my opinion, the distress of the whole Heraclitus interpretation is to be seen in the fact that what we call fragments are not fragments, but citations from a text in which they do not belong. It is a matter of citations out of different passages . . .

FINK: . . . that are not elucidated by the context.

HEIDEGGER: Mr. Fink will now give us a preview of the further way of the attempted explication, and I will in closing make an observation on what has transpired thus far.

FINK: I go to Fr. 27, which I would like to relate to Fr. 26. The text runs: ἀνθρώπους μένει ἀποθανόντας ἅσσα οὐκ ἔλπονται οὐδὲ δοκέουσιν. Diels translates: "When they are dead, what awaits people is not what they hope or imagine."

We can start the explication with the question of what ἐλπίζω [to hope] or ἐλπίς [expectation] means. People are not related only to what is immediately present, to what lies before them in their grasping apprehension. They are not dependent only upon what they can get hold of in the perceptible environment; rather, people are, as active beings in the encounter with what is present, projected into an anticipation of the future. This projection happens, among other instances, in hope. In Νόμοι [The Laws] (I 644 c 10—644 d 1) Plato distinguishes two forms of ἐλπίς: fear (φόβος) and confidence (θάρρος). He specifies fear as anticipation of what is painful (φόβος μὲν ἡ πρό λύπης ἐλπίς), and confidence as anticipation of the opposite (θάρρος δὲ ἡ πρὸ τοῦ ἐναντίου). A human behaves confidently toward the future in anticipation of future joy and fearfully in anticipation of the approach of what threatens. Beyond that, a human not only touches on the dead; he also comports himself toward death. So long as he so projects himself into the future, he stands in his ways of comportment in the project of the future, which is formed and mastered in part by him, but which is for the greater part determined by fate.

HEIDEGGER: How is the relationship of awaiting and hoping to be specified?

FINK: In hope, I hear the anticipation of something positive; in fear, on the contrary, the anticipation of something negative. The individual human lives beyond the immediate present in anticipation of what is outstanding in the formable future. Thus the Athenians, for example, stocked up in preview of the possible event that they should begin war with Sparta. A human also has this relationship to the future beyond the threshold of death. He comports himself not only toward the future of his coming life, but also beyond his future life toward his death. All people attempt in thought to populate and settle the land behind Acheron. They approach death with a hesitant hope.

HEIDEGGER: The realtionship of hope and expectation is still not clear to me. In hope there always lies a reckoning on something. In awaiting, on the contrary—in the proper sense of the word—there lies the attitude of adjoining what is coming.

FINK: To be sure, one can specify hope and awaiting in this manner, but hope does not need to be reckoning on something. When people set up hope at the grave of the dead, they believe themselves able in a certain sense to anticipate the sphere of what cannot be anticipated.

HEIDEGGER: Hope means "to concern oneself with something very intensely," while there is an adjoining with what is to come in awaiting. Hope at the same time includes an aggressive moment; awaiting, on the contrary, includes the moment of restraint. It is in this that I see the distinction of the two phenomena.

FINK: In Greek, ἐλπίς encompasses both. In Νόμοι, a human is determined by λύπη [pain] and ἡδονή [pleasure]. Expectation (ἐλπίς) of λύπη is φόβος; expectation (ἐλπίς) of ἡδονή is θάρρος.

HEIDEGGER: Both attitudes fix themselves on that to which they refer. But expectation is the attitude of restraint and of adjoining oneself to what is coming.

FINK: Expectation is the philosophical attitude. A human does not relate himself only to the future of his life, but he also reaches hopefully beyond the threshold of death. But death is what is closed, indeterminate, and incomprehensible. Therefore, the question is whether there is a land behind Acheron or a no man's land.

HEIDEGGER: Mozart said a quarter of a century before his death, "The grim reaper speaks to me."

FINK: The grim reaper also commissioned his Requiem. Rilke's epitaph also belongs here. "Rose, O pure contradiction, desire, / to be no one's sleep among so many / lids." The rose is the simile of the poet who in many songs, or under his lids, is no more he who wrote songs, but who has lost himself in the sleep of no one. An expectant attitude lies in the characterization of death as no one's sleep, a refusal to project what lies behind Acheron. In ἐλπίς, human comportment is determined by a preview, and indeed either in preview of the future of life or of the threshold of death in reference to a postmortal life. Heraclitus says, however, that when they are dead, something awaits people that they do not hope for. Diels translates δοκέουσιν with "imagine." A derogatory connotation of false opinion lies in imagining. But I believe that δοκεῖν does not mean imagine here, but means "grasp." When they are dead, such things await people as they do not arrive at through anticipatory hope, such things as they do not grasp. The realm of death repels from itself every premature occupation and cognition.

HEIDEGGER: We must elucidate δοκεῖν still more closely.

PARTICIPANT: δέχομαι means to accept.

HEIDEGGER: "To accept," however, is not to be understood here in the sense of a supposition, as when we say "I suppose it will rain this morning." "To accept" here means, I tolerate. I accept what will be given to me. We are dealing here with the moment of toleration, because otherwise δοκεῖν means an incorrectly held opinion. We must therefore translate δοκέουσιν as to accept and to grasp. Accepting does not mean here supposition, for example, the supposition that is made thematic by

Meinong and with which Husserl struggled. δοκεῖν is here not mere imagining, but an accepting grasp.

FINK: Later on, in Plato, δόξα has predominantly the sense of opinion. But ὀρθὴ δόξα [correct opinion], which has no negative sense, is also found in Plato.

HEIDEGGER: We also come across δοκεῖν, in the significance which we have drawn upon for Fr. 27, in Parmenides, when he speaks of δοκοῦντα.

FINK: Thus, in conclusion, we can translate Fr. 27: "When they are dead, something waits for people that they do not arrive at through hope and accepting grasping." That means that a human is repelled by the inaccessibility of the domain of death.

Finally, we go to Fr. 28: δοκέοντα γὰρ ὁ δοκιμώτατος γινώσκει, φυλάσσει · καὶ μέντοι καὶ Δίκη καταλήψεται ψευδῶν τέκτονας καὶ μάρτυρας. Here again, we must not understand δοκέοντα in the negative sense of imagining.

HEIDEGGER: Snell understands δοκέοντα as that which is only a view. I cannot connect this translation with the fragment in any sense.

FINK: I would like to suggest an interpretation as a kind of support for the nonimaginary δοκεῖν of Fr. 27. The δοκιμώτατος is he who grasps most, the one who has the greatest power of grasping.

PARTICIPANT: The δοκιμώτατος is also the one most tested. Perhaps we must view both meanings together.

HEIDEGGER: How does Diels translate Fr. 28?

FINK: "(For) what the most credible witness cognizes, retains, is what is only believable. But certainly Dike will know and also seize the fabricators of lies and witnesses." Instead of "what is believable" one would rather expect "what is unbelievable." I am not of the opinion that δοκέοντα has the sense of what is merely posited and not verified. δόξα in Greek by no means signifies only mere opinion. There is also the δόξα of a hero and of the commander. Here δόξα means the manner of standing in sight of something and not, for example, having an illusion.

PARTICIPANT: δοκιμώτατος is also the one of highest repute...

FINK: ... but not with the many; rather, with regard to the thinker. The δοκιμώτατος grasped the δοκέοντα, that is, the πάντα as the many entities that shine up, appear, and become graspable in the appearing. The one who grasps the most grasps things in their shining up. I translate φυλάσσει not as "retains them," but as "joins them." The one who grasps the most receives the many entities and joins them. The πολλοί are also related to δοκέοντα in grasping, but they are given over to δοκέοντα and lost in them. They are not able to see the unification, the light, in which the δοκέοντα shine up. The δοκιμώτατος is referred to the appearing things, and he holds them together. He watches over the δοκέοντα in that he refers them to the ἕν. He is not only oriented to the many that show themselves in the shine of light, but at the same time he, as light related, has the power to join them, and he sees what makes the δοκέοντα possible.

HEIDEGGER: Thus, you interpret φυλάσσειν as holding together.

FINK: That is, the holding together of things on what holds them together; re-latedness, as you have said. The one who grasps most grasps what shines up in a joining relatedness. The δοκιμώτατος is, among common people, similar to the light itself. The second sentence of the fragment runs in translation: But surely Dike will know and also seize the fabricators of lies and witnesses. The fabricators of lies are the ones who have taken the δοκέοντα out of the joint of the gathering unity, and have grasped δοκέοντα only as such, but do not grasp the appearing in the light of ἕν. Dike watches over the right grasping attitude, over the guardianship of the δοκιμώτατος, who hold δοκέοντα together.

HEIDEGGER: καταλαμβάνω also means to take in.

FINK: Here in the fragment, however, still more is meant. Dike will find guilty those who lie. She is the watching power who behaves in accord with the δοκιμώτατος when the latter hold ὄντα together as the many in the one. The counterconcept to the δοκιμώτατος is the πολλοί, who are merely lost in the many, and do not see the joining power of light. To be sure, they see the shining up in light, but not the unity of light. In so far as they miss a fundamental human possibility, they are fabricators of lies. Their lies or their falsehood consists in their mere reference to δοκέοντα, without grasping this in reference to the unifying one. Dike is the inspiring power to the thinker who watches over the unity of πάντα gathered in ἕν. Whether one can still refer μάρτυρας [witnesses] also to ψευδῶν [false] is a philological question. The μάρτυρας are witnesses who perceive the δοκέοντα, but only these, and not also the brightness of the fire itself.

HEIDEGGER: This explanation is philologically more elegant.

FINK: By witnesses would be meant those who appeal to what they immediately see and grasp. What those who are estranged from the unity of ἕν take notice of with regard to their grasping things is not false in the sense that it turns out to be imaginary. They are witnesses of actual things, but they do not refer the δοκέοντα back to the collecting joint like the δοκιμώτατος does. I have drawn upon Fr. 28 in support of Fr. 27. δοκεῖν is here meant not in the sense of a derogatory imagining. We also have illusory and false comprehensions regarding what surrounds us. It would be nothing special if Heraclitus were only to say that we do not comport ourselves imaginatively in the face of what awaits us in death. But when he speaks of a οὐκ ἔλπονται οὐδὲ δοκέουσιν [neither what they hope nor imagine] in reference to the realm of death, which is withdrawn from us, and if δοκεῖν does not here have the significance of imagining, then the assertion has a harder specification. Also in this world, grasping does not suffice. We always move in a correct and incorrect grasping. There is error and illusion in life. Heraclitus, however, says that the grasping that we are acquainted with and place in the service of our life conduct is not sufficient for the postmortal domain. There is no grasping capable of penetrating into the no man's land.

I go to Fr. 111: νοῦσος ὑγιείην ἐποίησεν ἡδὺ καὶ ἀγαθόν, λιμὸς κόρον, κάματος ἀνάπαυσιν. Diels translates: "Sickness makes health pleasant and good, hunger satiety, toil rest." This fragment appears to be simple. One could wonder that such an everyday experience turns up formulated among the sayings of Heraclitus. We could, however, take it as an entry in the fragments that think the contraries in an unusual manner. When it is said that sickness makes health pleasant, is it then as simple as when Socrates says in the *Phaedo* that, after he is freed from the painful shackle, he now feels the pleasant sensation of scratching? Here the pleasant feeling comes out of the past discomfort. Heraclitus says that sickness makes health good and sweet. Either the past or the following health can be meant thereby. Sickness–health is no distinction of a fixed and opposing kind, but a phenomenon of contrast of such a kind that health can develop out of sickness. The same holds for hunger and satiety, and for toil and rest. It is a matter of a procedure of opposites going over into their counterpart, of the phenomenal yoking of contrasts in transition. ἡδύ [pleasant] and ἀγαθόν [good] are not specified as qualities in themselves, but are specified as coming out of a negative state from their counterpart, which is left behind and abandoned. Past riches make the following poverty bitter and, conversely, past poverty makes the following riches pleasant. These relationships of opposites are familiar to us. What is important here is only that ἀγαθόν and ἡδύ are specified only out of the contrast.

With this, I go to Fr. 126: τὰ ψυχρὰ θέρεται, θερμὸν ψύχεται, ὑγρὸν αὐαίνεται, καρφαλέον νοτίζεται. Diels' translation runs: "Cold things become warm, the warm cools, the wet dries, the arid is moistened." Diels translates ψυχρά, θερμόν, ὑγρόν, καρφαλέον by cold, warm, wet, arid. But what is meant thereby? It is a matter of neutral words that are problematic because, on the one hand, they express a specific state of something and, on the other hand, they can mean simply being cold, being warm, being wet, and being arid. If a specific state of something is meant, then we say that the cold thing that warms up goes out of the state of being cold into the state of being warm. The going over of a thing from a state into an opposite one is something different from the going over of being cold into being warm as such. The going over of being cold into being warm is a familiar phenomenal movement of change. Therewith, less is said than with the πυρὸς τροπαί. For here we are concerned with the transmutation of fire itself into something else. It is noteworthy that Heraclitus speaks once in the plural (τὰ ψυχρά) and three times in the singular (θερμόν, ὑγρόν, καρφαλέον). We must make clear to ourselves the distinction that lies between the going over of something out of being cold into being warm and the going over of being cold as such into being warm as such. If it were said that a human's being alive can go over into being dead, that wouldn't be an exciting thing to say. But the assertion that life itself goes over into death, and conversely, that death goes into life, would be more problematic, and a more trying proposition. That would be similar to the going over of being cold into being warm and of being warm into being cold.

HEIDEGGER: Are τὰ ψυχρά cold things?

FINK: That is precisely the question, whether cold things, or simply being cold is meant. Concerning things, there are such as are cold by nature, such as ice, and there are such as are occasionally cold, like water, which can be cold but also warm. But water can also go from the liquid state over to the form of steam. There are, therefore, temporal and essential transitions. A more difficult problem, however, is the relationship of being cold and being warm as such. If τὰ ψυχρά are τὰ ὄντα, then are τὰ ὄντα things that are in the state of being, and that can go over into the state of not-being? Does τὸ ὄν mean the temporal state of something which lies at the basis like a substrate? Or is no thing and no matter meant with τὸ ὄν, but rather the being of what is? For Hegel, being goes over into nothing, and nothing goes over into being. Being and nothing are the same for him. But in that, as in this sameness, there is an ambiguity. Is the relationship of the being of what is and not-being a relationship analogous to that between cold and warm? When he speaks of cold and warm, does Heraclitus mean only cold and warm things? That cold things can warm up and vice versa is a banal assertion. But it could still be that the fragment includes a problematic that goes beyond this banality, if the fragment indeed would have it that being cold and being warm, as fixed contraries, themselves go over into one another.

PARTICIPANT: We must understand the opposition between cold and warm such that warming up is already included in the cold.

FINK: With that, you fall back again on the easier rendition of the fragment. The cold is then the cold thing that warms up. However, that is no transition of being cold as such into being warm as such, but only the transition of thermal conditions in a thing. This thought creates no difficulty. But a more difficult problem is given, if the cold and the warm are not cold and warm things, but being cold and being warm as such, of which it is then said that they go over into one another. We must attempt to read θερμόν or ὑγρόν such as τὸ καλόν, τὸ δίκαιον, are to be understood in Plato. τὸ καλόν is not that which is beautiful, but what brings the καλά to beauty. For us, the question is whether only the everyday, familiar phenomenon is meant with the yoking of contrasting contraries, or whether a background lies therein, such that a phenomenally unfamiliar transition and flowing-into-one-another of otherwise fixed contraries is seen. Fr. 126 is ambiguous. On the one hand, it has a banal sense, and on the other hand, a problematic sense, which concerns not the relationship of cold and warm things, but rather the mutual going over of being cold as such into being warm as such and vice versa. The going over of being cold into being warm behaves like the going over of life into death and of death into life. A human life, which goes over into being dead, is not now meant in this going over. The real challenge of the fragment is to be seen in the gradual equation of opposites, and not in the going over of states of a thing.

HEIDEGGER: The challenge lies in going over as such...

FINK: ... in the going over of what otherwise stand as contrary. Perhaps the contrariness of life and death is also fixed like that of being cold and being warm. In the domain of reference of this contrariness, a movement of things can happen such that something which is first cold then becomes warm, and vice versa. But the question before us is whether more is said in the fragment than the banal conception, whether the provocative thesis also lies in it according to which the fixed contraries go over into one another.

PARTICIPANT: The relationship of being warm and being cold is a going-into-one-another.

HEIDEGGER: You are thinking about Aristotle's ἀλλοίωσις.

FINK: ἀλλοίωσις presupposes a ὑπομένον [what is underlying] on which the μεταβολή [change] is carried out. Then we have a going over into one another of opposed states on a thing. A conductor can first be found in the state of zero degrees temperature, and then warm up in increasing degrees. We can thereby ask where the coldness goes to and from where the warmth comes. So long as we refer such phenomena of going over to an underlying substance, these goings over are not problematic.

HEIDEGGER: But is ἀλλοίωσις still a philosophical problem?

FINK: I agree with that. It is above all problematic because Aristotle ultimately also interprets coming to be and passing away from out of ἀλλοίωσις.

HEIDEGGER: His philosophy of movement belongs to a specific domain. We must thus distinguish three things: first, how a cold thing becomes warm; second, we must interpret this becoming as ἀλλοίωσις, which is already an ontological problem because the being of what is becomes specified; and third, ...

FINK: ... the going over of being cold in general into being warm in general. Therewith, the distinction of being cold and being warm gets sublated in thought. The going over of a thing out of the state of being cold into being warm is only a movement of a thingly substrate. The problematical coincidence of being cold with being warm is something else. A still more difficult problem is the sameness of Hades and Dionysus (ὠυτὸς δὲ ᾿Αίδης καὶ Διόνυσος).

HEIDEGGER: Can one bring the distinction of cold and warm into relation to the distinction of life and death?

FINK: Life and death is a much harder distinction . . .

HEIDEGGER: . . . with which there is no comparison.

FINK: The distinction between being cold and being warm is a distinction which resides only in life.

HEIDEGGER: The distinction of cold and warm belongs in the domain of thermodynamics, . . .

FINK: . . . while the distinction of life and death does not allow itself to be grasped in a going over such as from cold into warm. The cold and the warm are substantivized qualities. The cold can mean at once the cold thing or being cold as such. The matter stands in a similar fashion with τὸ ὄν. On the one hand, it means what is, what comes to being, and on the other, the being of what is. The ambiguity holds for the cold, the warm, the wet, the dry. If one reads Fr. 126 without seeking a deeper sense, then it is a matter only of thermodynamic phenomena, which concern the going of cold things over into warm things and vice versa. One runs into the problem of ἀλλοίωσις, but it apparently contains no provocative meaning, which we otherwise know of in the Heraclitean disturbance of the standing opposites. If we read the fragment in the sense that it brings to view a going over of being cold as such into being warm as such, then it brings the contrary, which otherwise remains as the fixed structure of the phenomenal world with all change of things, not indeed into ἁρμονίη φανερή [visible harmony], but into the ἁρμονίη ἀφανής [hidden harmony].

HEIDEGGER: I see the difficulty in the fact that one does not know in which Heraclitean context Fr. 126 is found. Thus you do not mean the going over, familiar to us, of a cold entity into a warm entity, and you also do not mean the determination of the character of being of this going over, but . . .

FINK: . . . the sameness of being cold and being warm which we termed provocative.

HEIDEGGER: Can one approach this sameness from the distinction of being cold and being warm, and not just from the contrariness of life and death?

FINK: I would still like to go into Fr. 8: τὸ ἀντίξουν συμφέρον καὶ ἐκ τῶν διαφερόντων καλλίστην ἁρμονίαν. Diels translates: "What struggle against each other harmonizing; out of what goes apart, the most beautiful joining." τὸ ἀντίξουν [what struggle against each other] is a neuter noun.

HEIDEGGER: This word occurs only once in Heraclitus. I have never understood correctly what is meant, strictly speaking, by τὸ ἀντίξουν. Rather, the word is to be understood backwards, from συμφέρον [harmonizing].

FINK: τὸ ἀντίξουν means what struggle apart, what struggle against each other, but not like two living beings; rather, like something rebellious that resists power. What struggle against each other is rebellious self-confrontation. What struggle apart are at the same time what collect themselves and bring themselves together. If we start with the second half of the fragment, the first half becomes readable. The most beautiful harmony proceeds out of what is born apart. Contrary to the customary opinion that struggling apart is something negative, what struggle here in opposition are at the same time what bring together. What struggle against each other harmonize in a manner such that out of them, as what is born apart, as the counterstruggling division, the most beautiful harmony grows. With that, Heraclitus thinks programmatically beyond what we previously encountered in Fr. 111, namely, the fact that cold things can become warm and vice versa.

HEIDEGGER: But where does the "most beautiful harmony" belong? Is it the visible or the invisible harmony?

FINK: That does not allow of saying right off the bat. Fr. 48 also belongs in the group of fragments which deal with the contraries: τῷ οὖν τόξῳ ὄνομα βίος, ἔργον δὲ θάνατος. "The name of the bow is life, but its work is death." This fragment refers not only to the absurd idea that there is a misrelation between matter and name.

PARTICIPANT: Fr. 51 also belongs in this context. "They do not understand how what is born apart agrees with itself: struggling union, like that of the bow and the lyre."

FINK: In order to be able to explicate this fragment, one must first have read Fr. 48. The bow unites in itself the contrariness of the striving and the domain of death. The lyre is the instrument which celebrates the festival. It is also a unifying of what is at first struggling in opposition. It unifies the community of the festival. Fr. 51 views not only the relationship of the lyre and the community festival, but also the relationship of the dead. The work of the bow is death, a fundamental situation distinguished from the festival. Death and the festival are linked together, but not only as the bow ends are tautened by the string, but in the manner of manifold counterrelationships. Still, we must break off here, because these fragments require a fundamental consideration.

HEIDEGGER: In conclusion, I don't want to make a speech, but I would like to ask a question. You, Mr. Fink, said at the beginning of the first session that "the Greeks signify for us an enormous challenge." To what extent, I ask? You said further that it is, therefore, a question of "advancing toward the matter itself, that is, to the matter" that must have stood "before the spiritual view of Heraclitus."

FINK: The question is whether, out of our historical situation, freighted with twenty-five hundred years of further thinking, we have generally removed ourselves from the Greeks and their understanding of being and world; and whether, nevertheless, we remain inheritors of the Greek ontology in all connections.

HEIDEGGER: When you speak of the challenge of the Greeks, you mean a challenge in thought. But what is it that challenges?

FINK: We are challenged to turn about the entire direction of our thinking. This does not imply the mending of a historical tradition.

HEIDEGGER: Aren't the ancients also a challenge for Hegel?

FINK: Only in the sense of the sublation and further thinking of the thoughts of the Greeks. The question, however, is whether we are only the extension of the Greeks, and whether we have come to new problems and must give an account of three thousand years, or whether we have lost, in an ominous manner, knowledge of how the Greeks dwelled in the truth.

HEIDEGGER: Is our concern only to repeat Heraclitus?

FINK: Our concern is a conscious confrontation with Heraclitus.

HEIDEGGER: But we find this with Hegel. He also stood under a challenge by the Greeks. Only he can be challenged who himself . . .

FINK: . . . has a readiness to think.

HEIDEGGER: In what regard are the Greeks a challenge for Hegel?

FINK: Hegel had the possibility to gather up, sublate, and change the tradition in his language of concepts.

HEIDEGGER: What does his language of concepts mean? Hegel's thought is the thought of the Absolute. From out of this thought, from the fundamental tendency of mediation, the Greeks appear for him . . .

FINK: . . . as giants, but as precursors . . .

HEIDEGGER: . . . as the immediate and still not mediated. All immediacy depends on mediation. Immediacy is always seen already from mediation. Here lies a problem for phenomenology. The problem is whether a mediation is also behind what is called the immediate phenomenon. In an earlier session we have said that need is a fundamental rubric in Hegel. For Hegel's thinking—which now is meant not in the personal but in the historical sense—need consisted in the fulfillment of what is thought, whereby fulfillment is to be understood literally as the reconciliation of the immediate with the mediated. But how about us? Do we also have a need?

FINK: To be sure, we have a need, but not a ground as in Hegel. We do not have a conceptual world at our disposal, into which we . . .

HEIDEGGER: . . . can integrate the Greeks, . . .

FINK: . . . rather, we must put aside the impliments of this tradition.

HEIDEGGER: And then?

FINK: We must begin in a new sense.

HEIDEGGER: Where does the challenge lie for you?

FINK: In that we have come in the course of the history of thinking to an end in which a richness of tradition becomes questionable. Our question is whether, not in a new turn toward what the Greeks have thought, we can encounter the Greek world with our new experience of being. We must ask ourselves whether we already have an experience of being that is not stamped by metaphysics.

HEIDEGGER: Is that to be thought such that our experience of being matches up to the Greeks?

FINK: This depends on the truth of our situation, out of which we can ask and speak. We can only speak with the Greeks as nihilists.

HEIDEGGER: Do you think so?

FINK: That does not mean that a finished program lies in nihilism.

HEIDEGGER: But what if there had been something unthought in the Greeks, something which determines precisely your thinking and what is thought in the whole history?

FINK: But how do we catch sight of this? Perhaps this glimpse only results from our late situation.

HEIDEGGER: The unthought would be that which shows itself only to our view. But the question is how far we understand ourselves. I make a proposal: the unthought is ἀλήθεια. In all of Greek philosophy, there is nothing to be found concerning ἀλήθεια *as* ἀλήθεια. In paragraph 44 b of *Being and Time,* it is said regarding ἀ-λήθεια that, "Translation by the word 'truth', and above all the theoretical conceptualization of this expression, covers up the sense of that which the Greeks made 'self-evidently' basic to the terminological use of ἀλήθεια as a pre-philosophical understanding." (*Being and Time,* 7th unrevised edition, 1953, p. 262 = H 219.)

ἀλήθεια thought *as* ἀλήθεια has nothing to do with "truth"; rather, it means unconcealment. What I then said in *Being and Time* about ἀλήθεια already goes in this direction. ἀλήθεια as unconcealment had already occupied me, but in the meantime "truth" came inbetween. ἀλήθεια as unconcealment heads into the direction of that which is the clearing. How about the clearing? You said last time that the clearing does not presuppose the light, but vice versa. Do clearing and light have anything at all to do with each other? Clearly not. "Clear" implies: to clear, to weigh anchor, to clear out. That does not mean that where the clearing clears, there is brightness. What is cleared is the free, the open. At the same time, what is cleared is what conceals itself. We may not understand the clearing from out of light; rather, we must understand it from the Greeks. Light and fire can first find their place only in the clearing. In the essay, "On the Essence of Truth," where I speak of "freedom," I have the clearing in view, except that here truth always walked behind. The dark is, to be sure, without light, but cleared. Our concern is to experience unconcealment as clearing. That is what is unthought in what is thought in the whole history of thought. In Hegel, the need consisted in the satisfaction of thought. For us, on the contrary, the plight of what is unthought in what is thought reigns.

FINK: Professor Heidegger has already officially ended our seminar with his words. I believe I can also speak on behalf of all the participants when I thank Professor Heidegger in warmth and admiration. The work of thought can be like a towering mountain range in stark outline, like "the safely built Alps." But we have here experienced something of the flowing magma which, as a subterranean force, raises up the mountains of thought.

HEIDEGGER: At the close, I would like the Greeks to be honored, and I return to the seven sages. From Periander of Corinth we have the sentence he spoke in a premonition: μελέτα τὸ πᾶν. "In care, take the whole as whole." Another word that also comes from him is this: φύσεως καταγορία. "Hinting at, making nature visible."

NOTES

TRANSLATOR'S FOREWORD

1. λόγος is customarily translated into English as "reason," "speech," or "word." However, Heidegger says in the "Logos" essay that the word "names that which gathers everything present into presence, and lets it present itself." ἀλήθεια is customarily translated into English as "truth," but Heidegger specifically rejects the German equivalent, *Wahrheit,* and uses *Unverborgenheit,* which may be translated as "nonconcealment."
2. Page 73 below.
3. Page 67 below.
4. Martin Heidegger, *Kant and the Problem of Metaphysics,* tr. James S. Churchill (Bloomington: University of Indiana Press, 1962), p. 206.
5. Page 50 below.
6. Page 51 below.
7. Loc. cit.
8. Page 73 below.
9. Pages 82 f.
10. Page 96 below.

HERACLITUS

1. Comments of the seminar participants, predominantly of a philological kind, are not included for copyright reasons.
2. See Kathleen Freeman, *Ancilla to the Pre-Socratic Philosophers: A Complete Translation of the Fragments in Diels, Fragmente der Vorsokratiker* (Cambridge: Harvard University Press, 1966). Though Freeman has been consulted, Diels' renditions of the fragments are newly translated throughout the present work. (Tr.)
3. Diels translates: "Of the Logos, as is here set forth, men are always unable to understand, both before they have heard it and when they have first heard it. For though everything happens according to this Logos, men still resemble inexperienced people, even when they have experienced such words and deeds as I discuss, analyzing each thing according to its nature and explaining how it behaves. But other men remain unaware of what they do after they wake up, just as they lose awareness of what they do in sleep."
4. Diels' translation has the following wording: "If all things were to become smoke, then we would discriminate them with the nose."
5. Diels' translation runs: "and that everything happens according to dissension and obligation."
6. Diels translates: "out of everything, one; and out of one, everything."
7. Diels translates: "(For) there is one thing which the best prefer to all else: eternal glory rather than transient things."
8. "Heraclitus' Teaching on Fire," untranslated. (Tr.)
9. Diels' translation has the following word order: "The wise is one thing only, to understand the thoughts which steer everything through everything."

10. Diels translates: "Alternate change: of everything for fire and of fire for everything."

11. Diels translates: "The wise is set apart from everything."

12. See Karl Jaspers, *The Great Philosophers*, trans. Ralph Manheim (New York: Harcourt, Brace & World, Inc., 1966), Vol. II, p. 20. (Tr.)

13. See *Timaeus* 30 a ff. (Tr.)

14. From *Alcaic Poems* by Friedrich Hölderlin, translated by Elizabeth Henderson, © 1962 by Elizabeth Henderson, published by Oswald Wolff (Publishers), Ltd., London. (Tr.)

15. These are the offspring of Zeus and Themis [Law]. See Hesiod, *Theogony*, translated, with an Introduction, by Norman O. Brown (New York: Bobbs-Merrill Co., 1953), p. 78. (Tr.)

16. Regarding growth, see Aristotle, *Metaphysics* 1069^b 11; regarding wasting away, see *History of Animals* 582^b 2, and *Generation of Animals* 767^a 4; regarding genesis and ceasing to be, see *On Generation and Corruption, passim;* regarding productiveness, see *Physics* 243^a 8, and *Generation and Corruption* 319^b 32; and regarding alteration, see *Physics* 226^a 26. (Tr.)

17. "... *die Zeit bringt mit sich bzw. die Zeit wird es bringen.*" Literally, "time brings with itself, that is, time will bring it." (Tr.)

18. Parmenides, Fragment 8, line 53. The above translation is taken from G. S. Kirk and J. E. Raven, *The Presocratic Philosophers: A Critical History with a Selection of Texts* (Cambridge: Cambridge University Press, 1957), p. 278.

19. Diels translates: he "does not say and does not conceal; rather he gives a sign." (Fr. 93).

20. A search of the *Library of Congress and National Union Catalogue* and the *General Catalogue of Printed Books of the British Museum* reveals no English translation of this book. (Tr.)

21. *Wege und Formen frühgriechischen Denkens; literarische und philosophiegeschichtliche Studien.* Hrsg. von Franz Tietze, 2 erweiterte Aufl. München, Beck. 1960. The book is not translated. (Tr.)

22. See Martin Heidegger, *Zur Sache des Denkens* (Tübingen: Max Niemeyer Verlag, 1969), pp. 1–25, esp. p. 15. See also Martin Heidegger, *On Time and Being*, trans. Joan Stambaugh (New York: Harper & Row, 1972), pp. 1–24, esp. p. 14.

23. Regarding Λόγος and Ἀλήθεια in Heidegger's thinking, see "Logos (Heraklit, Fragment 50)" and "Aletheia (Heraklit, Fragment 16)" in Martin Heidegger, *Vorträge und Aufsätze* (Pfullingen: Verlag Gunther Neske, 1954). (Tr.)

24. Diels translates: "How can one hide from that which never sets?"

25. The book, published in 1955 by Deutsche Verlags-Anstalt, Stuttgart, is not translated. (Tr.)

26. This translation is from *Friedrich Hölderlin: Poems and Fragments*, translated by Michael Hamburger (Ann Arbor: The University of Michigan Press, 1966), p. 79. (Tr.)

27. This translation is taken from G. S. Kirk, *Heraclitus: The Cosmic Fragments*, edited with an introduction and commentary (Cambridge: Cambridge University Press, 1970), p. 393 ff. (Tr.)

28. Separation of the English prefix "re-" seems necessary to acknowledge

Heidegger's usage. But without qualification, it could be misleading. For the prefix "re-" carries quite different meaning from the German "*ver-*." English "re-" means "again" or "back," meanings that are carried by German "*wider-,*" but not by "*ver-*." "*Ver-*" has a range of meanings deriving from Latin and Gothic. The possibility on which Heidegger seems here to depend is that of intensifying or heightening the meaning carried by the stem *halten,* meaning to keep or hold. For more information, see C. T. Onions, *The Oxford Dictionary of English Etymology* (Oxford: Oxford University Press, 1969), and George O. Curmé, *A Grammar of the German Language* (New York: Frederick Ungar Publishing Co., 1960). (Tr.)

29. One must also hear the same about death as what is said about sleep. For each shows the departure of the soul, the one more, the other less, which it is possible to get from Heraclitus. (Tr.)

30. Diels translates: "Connections: wholes and not wholes, concord and discord, harmony and dissonance, and out of everything one and out of one everything."

GLOSSARY

The following glossary serves the basic function of any glossary, namely, to provide a partial list of the more frequently occurring important words, with some explanation of their meaning. However, some qualifications must be made.

First, the reader should understand that the meanings given to the various Greek words are sometimes an English translation of the German used by Heidegger and Fink. The English meanings are *not* necessarily those given, for instance, in Liddell and Scott, *A Greek English Lexicon.*

Second, not all of the words glossed are Greek. Because it is important, special reference is made to the German word *Da.*

Third, the glossary is highly selective. Many more words could have been included. This selectivity is partly due to the fact that the first occurrence of each Greek word in the text is accompanied by an English gloss in square brackets, provided none is given by Heidegger or Fink. The selectivity of the glossary also results from other motives.

The glossary has been constructed with the intent of helping the reader gain better access to the text. First, I have tried to include some of the more important Greek words. But the glossary may be supplemented with such other works as: G. J. Seidel, *Martin Heidegger and the Pre-Socratics* (University of Nebraska Press, 1964); Martin Heidegger, *Early Greek Thinking* (Harper & Row, 1975), and William Richardson, S. J., *Heidegger: Through Phenomenology to Thought* (Martinus Nijhoff, 1963). Second, the glossary may be used to gain some grasp of the Greek language. The English transliteration, for example, may be used in learning how to sound the various Greek words. Effort in handling the Greek will be aided by reference to such books as: Stephen Paine, *Beginning Greek* (Oxford University Press, 1961), Francis Fobes, *Philosophical Greek: An Introduction* (University of Chicago Press, 1957), and F. E. Peters *Greek Philosophical Terms: A Historical Introduction* (New York University Press, 1967). Using an inductive method, the reader can gradually extend understanding to include words and phrases not treated in the present glossary.

| 1. ἀλήθεια | *aletheia* | **nonconcealment.** See the Translator's Foreword, especially the first footnote. |
| 2. ἄριστοι | *aristoi* | **the best.** Heraclitus was traditionally said to have been born into a patrician family. This bestowed upon him certain political and religious privileges which he nevertheless rejected. Hence, when he refers to "the best" among humans, it may not be di- |

rectly concluded that he was an "elitist" in the sense often criticized by modern (especially leftist) political and social critics. The counterconcept is *polloi*, the many. See entry twenty-six below.

3. ἀρχή — *arche* — **ultimate principle.** Though variously characterized, Heraclitus seems to hold that the ultimate principle in the changing *kosmos* is *logos*. See entries fifteen and seventeen below.

4. γένεσις — *genesis* — **genesis.**

5. γνῶσις — *gnosis* — **inquiry.** See entry seven below.

6. Da — This German word means, literally, "here" or "there." However, in Chapter 11 of the present book Heidegger interprets *Da* in terms of *Lichtung,* which may be translated by "clearing." The point is that a "here" or a "there" can be manifest to us only within a "clearing" which is primordial to the particular "here" or "there." Interpretation of *Da* as "clearing" is helpful in understanding the word *Dasein. Dasein* is the word Heidegger uses to indicate the kind of being (*sein*) unique to humans.

7. διάγνωσις — *diagnosis* — This is the same as entry five, except for addition of the prefix "*dia.*" As is pointed out early in Chapter 1, this prefix means "throughout," or perhaps "thoroughly." Thorough inquiry leads to a diagnosis.

8. εἶναι — *einai* — **to be.** As Heidegger has said, the central question of his thinking is the question of the meaning of being. No single work of Heidegger's exhausts

		this question. The translator has found the *Introduction to Metaphysics* helpful.
9. ἕν	*hen*	**the one.** The counter-concept, with which *hen* is always associated in Heraclitus, is *panta,* the many. See entry twenty-two below. See also the Translator's Foreword.
10. Ἥλιος	*Helios*	**the Sun.** Along with lightning, fire, and other images, the Sun is a visible analogue of *hen.* By providing an illuminating clearing, the Sun brings the many things of the universe (*panta*) together for a unified (*hen*) perception.
11. θάνατος	*thanatos*	**death.**
12. ἰδέα	*idea*	**idea.**
13. κεραυνός	*keraunos*	**lightning.** See entry ten above.
14. κίνησις	*kinesis*	**motion.**
15. κόσμος	*kosmos*	**cosmos.** The word carries the sense of a beautiful, ordered whole.
16. λήθη	*lethe*	**forgetfulness.** In mythology, Lethe is the river of forgetfulness which separates the underworld from the world of the living. In the present book, *lethe* indicates concealment. Note the relation to *aletheia,* nonconcealment. See entry 1 above.
17. λόγος	*logos*	**reason, speech, word.** For more on *logos,* see the works referred to in the Translator's Foreword.
18. μεταβολή	*metabole*	**change.**
19. μέτρα	*metra*	**measures.** See entry twenty-nine below.
20. νόμος	*nomos*	**custom or law.**
21. ὄντα	*onta*	**things which are.** The Western tradition derives its word "ontology" from this Greek word. Heidegger builds on the Greek word as well as the Western tradition when he

distinguishes the "ontic" from the "ontological" in *Being and Time*. See entries thirty and thirty-two below.

22. πάντα — *panta* — **all things, the universe.** See entry nine above for the counterconcept, *hen.*

23. ποίησις — *poiesis* — **production.**

24. πόλεμος — *polemos* — **war.**

25. πόλις — *polis* — **city.**

26. πολλοί — *polloi* — **the many.** The counterconcept is "the best," *aristoi.* See entry two above. An interesting essay is yet to be written comparing Heraclitus' expression *polloi* with Heidegger's analysis of *das Man*, "the they," in *Being and Time.*

27. πῦρ — *pur* — **fire.** See items ten and thirteen above.

28. σοφόν — *sophon* — **wisdom.**

29. τέρματα — *termata* — **boundaries.** See entry nineteen above.

30. τέχνη ὄντα — *techne onta* — **products of human technics.** See entry twenty-one above. The counterconcept is listed in entry thirty-two below.

31. τροπαί — *tropai* — **transformations, changes.**

32. φύσει ὄντα — *physei onta* — **things which are from nature.** See entries twenty-one and thirty above.

33. φύσις — *physis* — **nature.**

34. χρόνος — *chronos* — **time.** Note that time is crucial to Heidegger from *Being and Time* to the essay "Time and Being."

35. ψυχή — *psyche* — **soul.**

PAGE GUIDE

The following may help the reader to find passages of particular interest in the German original.

English	German
10	20
20	36
30	52
40	67
50	83
60	99
70	115
80	131
90	147
100	161
110	176
120	192
130	208
140	224
150	241
160	256